# Near Eastern Cities from Alexander to the Successors of Muhammad

*Near Eastern Cities from Alexander to the Successors of Muhammad* compares the evolution of several cities in the Near East from the time of Alexander the Great until the beginning of the Islamic 'Abbasid Dynasty.

This volume examines both the archaeological remains and literary sources to explain the diversity of imperial, cultural, and religious influences on urban life. It offers several case studies chosen from different regions of the Roman Near East, demonstrating that Greco-Roman and Islamic culture spread unevenly through these various cities, and that it is impossible to make broad generalizations. It argues that there were different patterns of urbanism that demonstrate a continued vitality of civic life up to the 'Abbasid Revolution.

*Near Eastern Cities from Alexander to the Successors of Muhammad* will be of particular interest to students of this period in the Ancient Near East, as well as those studying ancient cities and everyday life.

**Walter D. Ward** received his Ph.D. at the University of California, Los Angeles, USA, in 2008, with a concentration on Roman and late antique history. He is currently an Associate Professor at the University of Alabama at Birmingham, USA. He is the author of *Mirage of the Saracen: Christians and Nomads in the Sinai Peninsula in Late Antiquity* (2014) and editor of two books, *The Socio-economic history and material culture of the Roman and Byzantine Near East: Essays in Honor of S. Thomas Parker* (2017) and *Sources of World Societies* (with D. Gainty, 2009 and 2011).

## Studies in the History of the Ancient Near East
*Series Editor*
Greg Fisher, Carleton University, Canada

*Advisory Board of Associate Editors*
Ra'anan Boustan, University of California, Los Angeles, USA; Zeba Crook, Carleton University, Canada; Elizabeth DePalma Digeser, University of California at Santa Barbara, USA; Matthew Gibbs, University of Winnipeg, Canada; John Lee, University of California at Santa Barbara, USA; Harry Munt, University of York, UK; Richard Payne, Oriental Institute, University of Chicago, USA; Lucy Wadeson, Université Libre de Bruxelles, Belgium; Philip Wood, Aga Khan University, London, UK; Alan Lenzi, University of the Pacific, USA.

*Studies in the History of the Ancient Near East* provides a global forum for works addressing the history and culture of the Ancient Near East, spanning a broad period from the foundation of civilization in the region until the end of the Abbasid period. The series includes research monographs, edited works, collections developed from conferences and workshops, and volumes suitable for the university classroom.

**Discovering Babylon**
*Rannfrid Thelle*

**On the Edge of Empires**
North Mesopotamia During the Roman Period (2nd – 4th c. CE)
*Rocco Palermo*

**Children in the Bible and the Ancient World**
Comparative and Historical Methods in Reading Ancient Children
*Edited by Shawn W. Flynn*

**Near Eastern Cities from Alexander to the Successors of Muhammad**
*Walter D. Ward*

**Geography, Religion, and Sainthood in the Eastern Mediterranean**
*Erica Ferg*

For more information about this series, please visit: https://www.routledge.com/classicalstudies/series/HISTANE

# Near Eastern Cities from Alexander to the Successors of Muhammad

Walter D. Ward

LONDON AND NEW YORK

First published 2020 by Routledge

2 Park Square, Milton Park, Abingdon, Oxon OX14 4RN
605 Third Avenue, New York, NY 10017

*Routledge is an imprint of the Taylor & Francis Group, an informa business*

First issued in paperback 2021

Copyright © 2020 Walter D. Ward

The right of Walter D. Ward to be identified as author of this work has been asserted by him in accordance with sections 77 and 78 of the Copyright, Designs and Patents Act 1988.

All rights reserved. No part of this book may be reprinted or reproduced or utilised in any form or by any electronic, mechanical, or other means, now known or hereafter invented, including photocopying and recording, or in any information storage or retrieval system, without permission in writing from the publishers.

Notice:
Product or corporate names may be trademarks or registered trademarks, and are used only for identification and explanation without intent to infringe.

Publisher's Note

The publisher has gone to great lengths to ensure the quality of this reprint but points out that some imperfections in the original copies may be apparent.

*British Library Cataloguing-in-Publication Data*
A catalogue record for this book is available from the British Library

*Library of Congress Cataloging-in-Publication Data*
A catalog record has been requested for this book

ISBN: 978-1-138-18570-8 (hbk)
ISBN: 978-1-03-217774-8 (pbk)
DOI:10.4324/ 9781315644295

Typeset in Times New Roman
by codeMantra

**Shay,** *tibi multo amore*

# Contents

*List of figures* viii
*Preface and acknowledgements* xvi

1  Introduction  1
2  Urban planning and structures in the Near East  22
3  The Tetrapolis (Antioch and Apamea)  55
4  The Decapolis (Gerasa and Scythopolis)  93
5  Judea and Palestine (Jerusalem and Caesarea)  136
6  The desert fringe (Petra and Palmyra)  178
7  Conclusion  226
   Glossary  233
   *Index*  237

# Figures

| | | |
|---|---|---|
| P.1 | The Mediterranean Sea with cities mentioned in the text (Map by Amy Woods) | xix |
| P.2 | Cities of the Near East (Focus cities in bold, Map by Amy Woods) | xx |
| 1.1 | Photos taken by ISIS depicting the destruction of the Temple of Bel at Palmyra (Courtesy of the Directorate-General for Antiquities and Museums of Syria) | 2 |
| 1.2 | The Temple of Bel in 2005 (Photo by Ian Plumb, CC attribution license) | 2 |
| 1.3 | The Temple of Baalshamin (Photo by Greg Fisher) | 3 |
| 1.4 | The destruction of the Temple of Baalshamin (Courtesy of the Directorate-General for Antiquities and Museums of Syria) | 3 |
| 2.1 | The evolution of the Temple of Zeus from shrine to monumental temple (Courtesy of Jacques Seigne) | 23 |
| 2.2 | View of the cardo of Apamea to the north (Photo by Greg Fisher) | 25 |
| 2.3 | Plan of a typical cardo (Burns, R. *Origins of the Colonnaded Streets in the Cities of the Roman East.* [Oxford 2017], Figure 4.03) | 26 |
| 2.4 | Photo of a manhole cover in the Gerasa South Decumanus (Photo by author) | 27 |
| 2.5 | Artist's reconstruction of a shop along the cardo at Petra (Drawing by Chrysanthos Kanellopoulos, courtesy of Chrysanthos Kanellopoulos and ASOR. Originally published in Kanellopoulos, C. "The Architecture of the Shops and Colonnaded Street in Petra." *Bulletin of the American Schools of Oriental Research*, no. 324, 2001, p. 12. The entire article can be found at www.jstor.org/stable/1357629) | 29 |
| 2.6 | Hadrian's Arch at Gerasa (Photo by author) | 30 |
| 2.7 | The Arch of Constantine in Rome (Photo by author) | 31 |
| 2.8 | Trajan's gate at Petra looking towards the Qasr al-Bint, visible through the central arch (Photo by Carole Raddato) | 31 |
| 2.9 | The North Tetrapylon (a quadrifons) at Gerasa (Photo by author) | 32 |

2.10 Artist's recreation of the South Tetrapylon (a tetrakionion) and plaza at Gerasa (Kraemer, C. *Gerasa: City of the Decapolis* [ASOR 1938], Plan XV) 33
2.11 The nymphaeum at Gerasa (Photo by author) 33
2.12 The Trevi Fountain in Rome (Photo by author) 34
2.13 The macellum at Gerasa (Photo by author) 35
2.14 The Oval Plaza at Gerasa as seen from the Temple of Zeus (Photo by author) 36
2.15 The Parthenon at Athens (Photo by author) 37
2.16 The Pantheon in Rome (Photo by author) 37
2.17 The exterior wall of the temenos of the Temple of Bel (Photo by Greg Fisher) 38
2.18 Plan of the Temple of Bel (Map by Klaus Schnädelbach, originally published as Schnädelbach, K. *Topographia Palmyrena, 1 Topography*. Documents d'archéologique Syrienne XVIII. [Damascus 2010]. On commission by Dr. Rudolf Habelt GmbH, Bonn) 39
2.19 Propylaeum along the cardo of the Temple of Artemis in Gerasa (Photo by author) 40
2.20 The Qasr al-Bint temple in Petra with the remains of the altar in the bottom left corner (Photo by author) 40
2.21 Artist's depiction of the Temple of Zeus at Gerasa (Courtesy of Jacques Seigne) 41
2.22 The Temple of Artemis at Gerasa (Photo by author) 42
2.23 A portion of a mosaic in the Church of Saint Stephen in Umm er-Rasas (ancient Kastron Mephaa) built in 785 (Photo by author) 43
2.24 Basilica plan of the Cathedral at Gerasa (Kraemer, C. *Gerasa: City of the Decapolis* [ASOR 1938], Plan XXXI) 44
2.25 Example of the mosaics in the Petra Church (Photo by author) 44
2.26 The cruciform church dedicated to St Babylas at Kaoussie at Antioch (Antioch Expedition Archives, Department of Art and Archaeology, Princeton University, Photo 2421) 45
2.27 Mosque (left) and Basilica of St Sergius (right) at Resafa (Photo by Greg Fisher) 46
2.28 View of the scaenae frons and orchestra of the South Theater at Gerasa (Photo by author) 47
2.29 The theater at Petra (Photo by Carole Raddato) 48
2.30 Plan of the theater of Apamea with architectural features labeled (Map by Scott Ure, courtesy of the BYU American Expedition to Apamea) 48
2.31 The North Theater or odeum at Gerasa (Photo by author) 49
2.32 The hippodrome at Caesarea (Photo by Carole Raddato) 50
2.33 The *carcares* (starting gates) at Gerasa (Photo by author) 50
2.34 Interior of the Coliseum in Rome (Photo by author) 51

x  *Figures*

2.35 Plan of the "Roman Bath" at Antioch (Antioch Expedition Archives, Department of Art and Archaeology, Princeton University, Photo 1582)    52

3.1 A nine-meter-deep trench from the excavation of Antioch in 1936 in the cavea of the Hellenistic Theater (Antioch Expedition Archives, Department of Art and Archaeology, Princeton University, Photo 2647)    56

3.2 Photograph of the House of the Buffet Supper, an example of the mosaics discovered in Antioch and Daphne (Antioch Expedition Archives, Department of Art and Archaeology, Princeton University, Photo 3146)    57

3.3 Plan of Antioch (Burns, R. *Origins of the Colonnaded Streets in the Cities of the Roman East*. [Oxford 2017], Figure 6.06)    58

3.4 Plan of Apamea (Burns, R. *Origins of the Colonnaded Streets in the Cities of the Roman East*. [Oxford 2017], Figure 9.01)    60

3.5 The lake of Apamea in the distance, with the House of the Consoles in the foreground (Photo by Greg Fisher)    61

3.6 Evolution of the Cardo at Antioch (Burns, R. *Origins of the Colonnaded Streets in the Cities of the Roman East*. [Oxford 2017], Figure 6.07)    67

3.7 The cardo at Apamea, with a votive column (Photo by Greg Fisher)    71

3.8 Remains of the shops behind the colonnaded street (Photo by Greg Fisher)    72

3.9 A possible plan of the Forum of Valens according to literary evidence. The 1930s excavation revealed little of the Forum, but recent excavations (which are in the process of being published) may provide more information (Antioch Expedition Archives, Department of Art and Archaeology, Princeton University, Plan 3675)    76

3.10 Arch over the Parmenius excavated in the 1930s (Antioch Expedition Archives, Department of Art and Archaeology, Princeton University, Photo 3929)    77

3.11 Plan of the Villa at Yakto where the Megalopsychia mosaic was discovered (Antioch Expedition Archives, Department of Art and Archaeology, Princeton University, Photo 5659)    79

3.12 Representation of the Olympic stadium in the Megalopsychia mosaic from the Villa at Yakto (Antioch Expedition Archives, Department of Art and Archaeology, Princeton University, Photo 1331)    80

3.13 Photo of the cardo after Justinian's restoration of the city (Antioch Expedition Archives, Department of Art and Archaeology, Princeton University, Photo 1721)    82

3.14 The Iron Gate constructed by Justinian (Antioch Expedition Archives, Department of Art and Archaeology, Princeton University, Photo 1592)    83

Figures    xi

3.15 Plan of a lime kiln discovered at Antioch (Antioch Expedition Archives, Department of Art and Archaeology, Princeton University, Drawing 39)    83
3.16 Photo of the entrance to the House of the Consoles (Photo by Greg Fisher)    88
3.17 Photo of the peristyle courtyard of the House of the Consoles (Photo by Greg Fisher)    88
3.18 Map of the Dead Cities (Ball, W. *Rome in the East*. [Routledge 2016, 2nd edition], Figure 5.1)    90
3.19 The "andron" building at Serjilla (Photo by Greg Fisher)    91
4.1 Map of the Decapolis (Ball, W. *Rome in the East*. [Routledge 2016, 2nd edition], Figure 4.11)    94
4.2 Plan of Gerasa (Burns, R. *Origins of the Colonnaded Streets in the Cities of the Roman East*. [Oxford 2017], Figure 7.02)    96
4.3 General plan of Scythopolis (Plan by Benjamin Y. Arubas, courtesy of Benjamin Y. Arubas)    97
4.4 View of the Tell with the Scythopolis civic center in the foreground (Photo by Jennifer Ramsay)    98
4.5 Frescos from the Hellenistic Temple of Zeus displayed in the vaults under the surviving platform of the naos of the Temple of Zeus (Photo by author)    102
4.6 North gate of Gerasa at the left, the northern part of the cardo in the center, and the North Tetrapylon on the right. The agora is below the gate and cardo (Photo by author)    103
4.7 The Temple of Zeus (Photo by author)    104
4.8 View of the cardo at Gerasa looking south. Note the higher columns which mark the nymphaeum (Photo of author)    104
4.9 Remains of the Eastern Baths (Photo by author)    106
4.10 Plan of the civic center of Scythopolis (Plan by Benjamin Y. Arubas, courtesy of Benjamin Y. Arubas)    108
4.11 View of the city center from the Tell. Palladius Street runs straight towards the theater and the modern town. The Eastern Street is on the left. The remains of the basilica and the Byzantine Agora are between these two streets (Photo by Jennifer Ramsay)    109
4.12 View of Silvanus Street from the Tell. From right to left is the nymphaeum, the central monument, and finally the Roman period reflecting pool and Umayyad shops (Photo by Jennifer Ramsay)    109
4.13 Remains of the hippodrome at Scythopolis (Photo by Carole Raddato)    110
4.14 The theater at Scythopolis (Photo by Carole Raddato)    111
4.15 The propylon to the Tell (Photo by Carole Raddato)    112
4.16 Map of Gerasa created with remote sensing data. This evidence shows the changes in the late antique street system (Stott, D., S. Kristiansen, A. Lichtenberger, and R. Raja.

xii  *Figures*

"Mapping an ancient city with a century of remotely sensed data." *Proceedings of the National Academy of Sciences of the United States,* vol. 115, no. 24, figure 5. Copyright and courtesy of the Danish-German Jerash Northwest Quarter Project) 115

4.17 Map of excavations in northwest Gerasa with a plan of the synagogue church (Copyright and courtesy of the Danish-German Jerash Northwest Quarter Project) 118

4.18 Map of the early Islamic civic center of Gerasa showing the remodeled shops around the South Tetrapylon, mosque, and houses north of the South Decumanus (Map by Rune Rattenborg) 120

4.19 Palladius Street facing north towards the Tell (Photo by Carole Raddato) 123

4.20 The mosaic sidewalk of Palladius Street (Photo by Jennifer Ramsay) 124

4.21 The Sigma (Photo by Carole Raddato) 125

4.22 Plan of the Monastery of the Lady Mary at Scythopolis (Fitzgerald, G. *A sixth century monastery at Beth-Shan (Scythopolis)* (University of Pennsylvania 1939), Plate 2. Courtesy of the University of Pennsylvania Museum Archives) 126

4.23 Plan of the Round Church on Tell Beth-Shean (Fitzgerald, G. *Beth-Shan Excavations 1921–1923: The Arab and Byzantine Levels* [University of Pennsylvania 1931], plan between pp. 18 and 19. Courtesy of the University of Pennsylvania Museum Archives) 127

4.24 Plan of the Tell showing the Byzantine and early Islamic levels (Fitzgerald, G. *Beth-Shan Excavations 1921–1923: The Arab and Byzantine Levels* [University of Pennsylvania 1931], end plate. Courtesy of the University of Pennsylvania Museum Archives) 129

4.25 Example of earthquake damage at Scythopolis (Photo by Carole Raddato) 130

5.1 The Temple of Rome and Augustus at Caesarea (Drawing by Anna Iamin. Courtesy of Kenneth Holum and Marsha Rozenblit) 137

5.2 The Dome of the Rock and Dome of the Chain (Photo by Young Shanahan, CC attribution license) 138

5.3 Photo of Jerusalem taken from the Mount of Olives. The Dome of the Rock is in the center and the Ottoman period city wall can be see surrounding the Old City (Photo by Jennifer Ramsay) 139

5.4 The Kingdom of Judea at its greatest extent (Ball, W. *Rome in the East.* [Routledge 2016, 2nd edition], Figure 2.6) 142

5.5 Jerusalem in the time of Herod (Ball, W. *Rome in the East.* [Routledge 2016, 2nd edition], Figure 2.8) 144

5.6 Model of the Temple of Jerusalem built by Herod in the Holy Land Hotel, Jerusalem (Ball, W. *Rome in the East*. [Routledge 2016, 2nd edition], Plate 2.15) 146
5.7 The "Wailing" Wall, the only surviving portion of the Temple of Jerusalem from the time of Herod (Photo by Jennifer Ramsay) 146
5.8 Collapse from the time of the Roman destruction of Jerusalem (Photo by Carole Raddato) 149
5.9 Plan of Roman Jerusalem (Map by Shlomit Weksler-Bdolah, courtesy of Shlomit Weksler-Bdolah and the Israel Antiquities Authority) 150
5.10 The Ecce Homo arch marking the entrance to the eastern forum (Photo by Carole Raddato) 153
5.11 Plan of Caesarea in the early Roman period (Courtesy of Kenneth Holum and Marsha Rozenblit) 155
5.12 Example of a horrea at Caesarea (Photo by Jennifer Ramsay) 156
5.13 Remains of Herod's Palace at Caesarea (Photo by Carole Raddato) 157
5.14 Jerusalem on the Madaba Map (Photo by author) 160
5.15 Reconstruction of the western cardo from late antiquity (Photo by Carole Raddato) 161
5.16 Map of Jerusalem showing the late antique churches and early Islamic buildings on and around the Temple Mount (Map by Gideon Avni, plan courtesy of Israel Antiquities Authority and Gideon Avni) 162
5.17 Plan of late antique Caesarea (Courtesy of Kenneth Holum and Marsha Rozenblit) 168
5.18 Plan of the praetorium with Archives Building and adjoining warehouses (Courtesy of Kenneth Holum and Marsha Rozenblit) 169
5.19 Artists depiction of the Octagonal Church (Drawing by Anna Iamin. Courtesy of Kenneth Holum and Marsha Rozenblit) 171
5.20 The "Byzantine esplanade" (Photo by Carole Raddato) 172
5.21 The bath in the praetorium (Photo by Jennifer Ramsay) 173
6.1 The Petra Siq (Photo by author) 179
6.2 The Treasury (Al-Khazneh) in Petra (Photo by author) 179
6.3 View of Palmyra at sunset (Photo by Greg Fisher) 180
6.4 Photograph from the 1884 Wolfe expedition showing the mudbrick houses built inside the temenos of the Temple of Bel (Photographs of Asia Minor, #4776. Division of Rare and Manuscript Collections, Cornell University Library) 181
6.5 The Temple of Bel as seen from the oasis (Photo by Greg Fisher) 181
6.6 Rockcut tombs along the path to the theater (Photo by author) 183
6.7 The Qasr al-Bint, a temple likely dedicated to the chief Nabataean god Dushares (Photo by author) 184

xiv  *Figures*

6.8 The "Royal Tombs" from left to right, the Palace Tomb, the Corinthian Tomb, and on the far right, the Urn Tomb (Photo by author) 184
6.9 Plan of the city of Palmyra and surrounding region (Map by Klaus Schnädelbach, originally published as Schnädelbach, K. *Topographia Palmyrena, 1 Topography*. Documents d'archéologique Syrienne XVIII. [Damascus 2010]. On commission by Dr. Rudolf Habelt GmbH, Bonn) 185
6.10 The Nabataean Kingdom at its greatest extent (Ball, W. *Rome in the East*. [Routledge 2016, 2nd edition], Figure 2.9) 186
6.11 Location of Hellenistic period finds in Petra (Plan by Sebastian Hoffman) 188
6.12 Plan of Hellenistic Palmyra based on geophysical survey (Map by Klaus Schnädelbach, originally published as Schnädelbach, K. *Topographia Palmyrena, 1 Topography*. Documents d'archéologique Syrienne XVIII. [Damascus 2010]. On commission by Dr. Rudolf Habelt GmbH, Bonn) 189
6.13 Map of the civic center of Petra (Map courtesy of Talal Akasheh, Hashemite University, Chrysanthos Kanellopoulos, the American Schools of Oriental Research, and American Center of Oriental Research, Amman. Originally published in Kanellopoulos, C. and T. Akasheh. "The Petra Map." *Bulletin of the American Schools of Oriental Research*, no. 324, 2001, pp. 6–7. The original article can be accessed at www.jstor.org/stable/1357628.) 192
6.14 The Treasury (Al-Khazneh). The grate at the bottom covers the earliest tombs (Photo by Carole Raddato) 194
6.15 Plan of the Qasr al-Bint, likely dedicated to Dushares (Courtesy of François Larche) 195
6.16 Plan of the Temple of the Winged Lions (Plan by Qutaiba Dasouqi, courtesy of the Temple of the Winged Lions Cultural Resource Management Initiative) 196
6.17 Photo of the Great Temple (Photo by author) 197
6.18 Digital reconstruction of the civic center of Petra south of Wadi Musa (Drawing by Chrysanthos Kanellopoulos, courtesy of Chrysanthos Kanellopoulos and ASOR. Originally published in Kanellopoulos, C. "A New Plan of Petra's City Center." *Near Eastern Archaeology*, vol. 65, no. 4, 2002, pg. 254. The original article can be found at www.jstor.org/stable/3210854) 198
6.19 Map of Palmyra (Burns, R. *Origins of the Colonnaded Streets in the Cities of the Roman East*. [Oxford 2017], Figure 10.05) 202
6.20 Plan of the Temple of Bel, with the House of Cassiopeia and the House of Achilles located to the east (Map by

Klaus Schnädelbach, originally published as Schnädelbach, K. *Topographia Palmyrena, 1 Topography*. Documents d'archéologique Syrienne XVIII. [Damascus 2010]. On commission by Dr. Rudolf Habelt GmbH, Bonn) 202
6.21 Temenos wall of the Temple of Bel (Photo by Greg Fisher) 203
6.22 Columns at the rear of the cella of the Temple of Bel (Photo by Greg Fisher) 204
6.23 Adyton of the Temple of Bel (Photo by Greg Fisher) 204
6.24 Detailed view of the civic center of Palmyra (Burns, R. *Origins of the Colonnaded Streets in the Cities of the Roman East*. [Oxford 2017], Figure 10.09) 206
6.25 Columns along the Grand Colonnade (Photo by Greg Fisher) 206
6.26 The tetrapylon (a tetrakionion) at the intersection of Sections C and B (Photo by Greg Fisher) 207
6.27 The monumental arch connecting Sections B and A as seen from the Temple of Nabu (Photo by Greg Fisher) 208
6.28 Tombs at Palmyra (Photo by Greg Fisher) 210
6.29 Collapsed columns from an earthquake at the Great Temple (Photo by author) 212
6.30 The Urn Tomb, converted into a church in 446 CE (Photo by author) 214
6.31 The three churches on the Petra North Ridge (Plan by Chrysanthos Kanellopoulos, using the map of the Hashemite University and ACOR Petra Mapping Project. Fiema, Z. et.al. *The Petra Church*. [ACOR 2001], xii. Courtesy of ACOR) 215
6.32 The ed-Deir (Monastery) (Photo by Jennifer Ramsay) 216
6.33 Plan of the Camp of Diocletian, built around the Temple of Allat (Map by Klaus Schnädelbach, originally published as Schnädelbach, K. *Topographia Palmyrena, 1 Topography*. Documents d'archéologique Syrienne XVIII. [Damascus 2010]. On commission by Dr. Rudolf Habelt GmbH, Bonn) 217
6.34 The churches in the northwest quadrant of Palmyra (Map by Klaus Schnädelbach, originally published as Schnädelbach, K. *Topographia Palmyrena, 1 Topography*. Documents d'archéologique Syrienne XVIII. [Damascus 2010]. On commission by Dr. Rudolf Habelt GmbH, Bonn) 219
6.35 Paintings of Jesus and Mary inside the cella of the Temple of Bel (Photo by Greg Fisher) 220
6.36 Plan of the Umayyad suq at Palmyra (Map by Klaus Schnädelbach, originally published as Schnädelbach, K. *Topographia Palmyrena, 1 Topography*. Documents d'archéologique Syrienne XVIII. [Damascus 2010]. On commission by Dr. Rudolf Habelt GmbH, Bonn) 222

# Preface and acknowledgements

In 2010 I taught my first graduate seminar at the University of Alabama at Birmingham, called "From Alexander to Muhammad: The Near East under Greek, Roman, and early Islamic Rule." In preparing for that course, and then teaching it, I realized that my students needed extensive knowledge of the region just to make the most accessible books on the subject understandable. My hope is that this book is understandable for a general audience like my students and at the same time makes a contribution to scholarly debates about the Near East under Greek, Roman, and early Islamic Rule.

My primary innovations in this work are three-fold. First, my focus is on the development of eight cities in the Near East. I have selected these eight cities based on geography, culture, and archaeological data. They are discussed in groups of two based on their geographic, political, and cultural contexts. The first two cities, Antioch (modern Turkey) and Apamea (modern Syria), represent cities founded early during the Greek rule of the Near East in one of the most prosperous agricultural regions of ancient and modern Syria. Their founding, expansion and monumentalization provide key insights into Greek and Roman occupations in the Near East. The next two cities, Gerasa (Jerash in modern Jordan) and Scythopolis (Beit She'an in modern Israel, called Beisan in Arabic), are examined as examples of Greek enclaves within more indigenous communities. They also provide important information about how Islamic rule transformed Near Eastern urbanism. Jerusalem and Caeserea (both in modern Israel) show the difference between a city primarily famous for its religious importance (Jerusalem to Jews, Christians, and Muslims) and a city founded by a Near Eastern king as a Greco-Roman showpiece and later used by the Romans as a provincial capital (Caesarea). The final set of cities explores the fringe of the desert and Roman control – Petra (modern Jordan) and Palmyra (modern Syria). In total, the eight cities presented here explore well-preserved archaeological sites and cover an expansive area from the Mediterranean Sea to the Euphrates River and from the Taurus mountains in Turkey to the Red Sea and Arabian Desert (Figures P.1 and P.2).

Second, I cover the Near East in terms of a vast chronological period, from the death of Alexander the Great in 323 BCE until the collapse of the first ruling Islamic dynasty, the Umayyads, circa 750 CE. This thousand-year period allows me to examine the founding and growth of these communities prior to the Roman conquest of the Near East and to survey the changes which these cities underwent over time, such as the growth of Roman power, the rise of Christianity and the Islamic conquest. No other work has attempted to survey these periods together, but I believe that only by studying this entire time period, the necessary narrative to understand urbanism and its associated cultural identities in the Near East can be accomplished.

Third, I have approached the evolution of these cities in terms of the *longue durée*, or in English, we might call it a "bird's eye view" or "big picture" study. By this I mean that I am primarily interested in examining the changes these cities underwent over periods of centuries, rather than years or decades. This means that precise dating is less important to me than getting a sense of how different (or not) the cities were under the Greek rulers versus the Romans, and so on. Thus, large changes within civic plans will be noted, but not renovations and minor changes to structures except when I believe these to be particularly insightful. This obviously impacts the resolution and scale that I am dealing with and, to some, my work may appear imprecise. I am aware of many debates regarding exact dates, but I have decided that there are people more qualified than I to debate the questions of the dating of individual monuments and artifacts. Instead, I want to get the most information I can out of these cities' evolutions, and to do it in the most user-friendly way possible. For me, this means focusing on the most important changes to the urban environment and not getting distracted by the minutiae of scholarly and archaeological debate. To make the changes to these cities more manageable, I've adopted the following scheme of periodization: The Hellenistic period runs from the death of Alexander the Great in 323 BCE until the Roman annexation of Syria in 64 BCE. The Roman period starts in 64 BCE and continues until the beginning of the reign of Diocletian in 284 CE. Late antiquity begins at that point and continues until the middle of the eighth century with the victory of the Abbasid dynasty over the Umayyad.

I have chosen not to use footnotes in this work because I wanted it to be accessible to a wide audience, and my fear was that footnotes would reduce the readability of the text in such a way to turn off all but serious scholars. I have included a list of books and articles at the end of each chapter for further reading. These are the most readable sources in English. I have generally included excavation reports only if there were no synthetic essays available or if the excavation reports themselves were particularly accessible or interesting. In no way do these sources represent the breadth of my research, which covered hundreds of books and articles. At all times I endeavored to consult the original excavation reports if published. Unfortunately, I do not read Hebrew, which meant that some of the excavation reports from Caesarea, Scythopolis, or Jerusalem were off limits to me. Luckily, those sites are extensively published in languages that I do read.

I am thankful of all the assistance I received in the development of this book from friends, family, and colleagues. Several scholars gave me access to images, figures, and unpublished materials. To give a short and incomplete list, I would like to thank: S. Thomas Parker, Susan Downey, Claudia Rapp, Ronald Mellor, Andrew Smith II, David Graf, Megan Perry, Jennifer Ramsay, Leigh-Ann Bedal, Alan Walmsley, Ina Kehrberg-Ostrasz, Zbigniew Fiema, Martha Joukowski, Jodi Magness, Ken Holum, Marsha Rozenbilt, Ross Thomas, Chris Tuttle, Barbara Porter, Glenn Corbett, Louise Blank, Rubina Raja, Kristoffer Damgaard, Jacques Seigne, Sebastian Hoffman, Michal Gawlikowski, Klaus Schnädelbach, Thomas Schneider, Christopher Rollston, François Larché, Benjamin Arubas, Marta Żuchowska, Chrysanthos Kanellopoulos, Ross Burns, Joel Kalvesmaki, Julia Gearhart, Eisha Neely, Cynthia Finlayson, Scott Ure, Rune Rattenborg, Inda Omerefendic, Jennifer Stabler, Greg Mumford, and Ulrich Weferling. Several research institutions and libraries provided figures or information, including the American Center of Oriental Research, the American Schools of Oriental Research, the Image and Historic Collections at Princeton University, the University of Pennsylvania Museum and Archives, Centre de Recherches en Archéologie et Patrimoine, the Israel Antiquities Authority, the Directorate-General for Antiquities and Museums of Syria, and the Division of Rare and Manuscript Collections at Cornell University Library. My sister, Amy Woods developed the original maps in this book. My department at UAB and the College of Arts and Sciences has proven to be very supportive of my research. I would especially like to thank Dean Robert Palazzo, chairs Colin Davis, John van Sant, and Jonathan Wiesen, and colleagues. As this work was inspired by my classes, I must thank the students who were in the two "From Alexander to Muhammad" graduate courses that I taught at the University of Alabama at Birmingham in Fall 2010 and Fall 2014. I apologize for anyone I have missed. All mistakes are of course my own.

I wrote this book while a number of changes were occurring in my family life. I want to especially thank my family and loved ones for their support during this time: Shay, Agatha, Nico, Ansel, Elowen, Ruby, Amy, Don, and my mother.

Thanks very much to Greg Fisher for supporting and encouraging this work, even when it took longer to complete than expected. Greg's encouragement and support (and tireless effort to make sure my writing made sense) were instrumental in completing in this project, and thanks to Elizabeth Risch and the staff at Routledge for their support throughout this process.

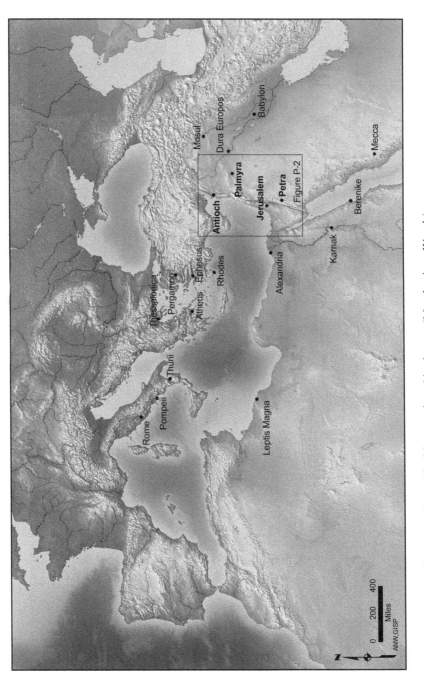

*Figure P.1* The Mediterranean Sea with cities mentioned in the text (Map by Amy Woods).

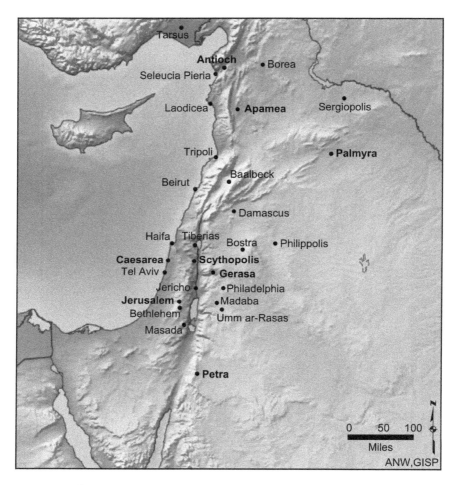

*Figure P.2* Cities of the Near East (Focus cities in bold, Map by Amy Woods).

# 1 Introduction

The men drove into the newly captured town on a mission. Dressed in a makeshift mix of combat fatigues and civilian clothes, they stopped, climbed out of their trucks, and began unloading several large blue barrels. The barrels were heavy, requiring several men to carry them with improvised litters. Some of them, likely fearing the dangerous chemicals within, wore medical masks over their faces. They carried these explosives into the middle of one of the most well-known and celebrated monuments in the Near East – the Temple of Bel in Palmyra. Who knows if they looked around at the ancient temple, much of it dating back to the first century CE, and thought about the history those blocks had witnessed. The main building of the temple, called a *naos* in Greek or *cella* in Latin, was originally built to honor a triad of gods of Palmyrene people (Bel, Yarhibol, and Aglibol), but over the years, it had also been used as a Christian church and an Islamic mosque (Figures 1.1 and 1.2).

These men, militants fighting on behalf of ISIS, detonated their explosives on August 30, 2015, completely destroying the *naos* and three of the four walls of the massive *temenos*, which separated the sacred temple complex from the surrounding city. Just a few days earlier, ISIS had blown up another famous temple dedicated to the Syrian sky god Baalshamin by placing explosives on the empty niches that had held statues in antiquity (Figures 1.3 and 1.4).

ISIS fighters had captured the city of Palmyra (whose name in modern Arabic and ancient Palmyrene is Tadmor) in May 2015. At the time, Palmyra was one of the most well-preserved sites from the Roman period in the entire world, rivaled only by Gerasa (Jerash) in Jordan, Leptis Magna in Libya, Ephesus in Turkey, and Pompeii and Ostia in Italy.

In May 2015, ISIS was on a roll – it was spreading in Syria and Iraq, and in June, it even conquered the major city of Mosul. ISIS (alternately called the Islamic State, ISIL, or Daesh) was seeking to spread its particularly extreme version of Islam to the entire Middle East. Its leader, Abu Bakr al-Baghdadi, had declared himself Caliph, or "successor" to Muhammad, claiming that he had authority over all the Muslims in the region, even though at the time

*Figure 1.1* Photos taken by ISIS of the destruction of the Temple of Bel at Palmyra (Courtesy of the Directorate-General for Antiquities and Museums of Syria).

*Figure 1.2* The Temple of Bel in 2005 (Photo by Ian Plumb, CC attribution license).

*Figure 1.3* The Temple of Baalshamin (Photo by Greg Fisher).

*Figure 1.4* The destruction of the Temple of Baalshamin (Courtesy of the Directorate-General for Antiquities and Museums of Syria).

he only ruled over a small area in Iraq and Syria. While the power of ISIS has been greatly reduced since 2015 and it no longer controls much territory in Syria and Iraq, its impact on the material culture of the Near East has been quite destructive and likely permanent.

One of the goals of ISIS was to desecrate and destroy pre-Islamic artifacts, religious or not, in an attempt to efface previous religions and cultures from the area. They heavily damaged ancient Christian monasteries, the cities of the ancient Assyrians (dating back to at least the eighth century BCE), and even Islamic shrines that they considered violations of their fundamentalist interpretation of Islam. In Palmyra, in addition to the destruction of the temples of Bel and Baalshamin, ISIS fighters destroyed the Roman monumental arch, the lion statue of Allat, several tombs in the ancient necropolis, a medieval castle, and dozens of statues that were on display in the museum. They also executed Syrian archaeologist Khaled al-Asaad who had worked at the site for over forty years and killed dozens of other inhabitants of the modern city. After being pushed out of Palmyra by the Syrian army, they returned again in December 2016 and destroyed the Tetrapylon and portions of the Roman-period theater. In a very brief period of time, the spectacular ancient remains of Palmyra have been reduced to a sad shadow of their former selves.

ISIS' actions in Palmyra demonstrate the continued importance of ancient remains in the Middle East. While ISIS finds the evidence of the past as an insult to their fundamentalist beliefs, many countries and peoples there have based portions of their identity on the ancient inhabitants and their surviving monuments. Israel, for example, has embraced the Masada story from the First Jewish Revolt against Rome as a demonstration of their determination to resist oppressive outside influences on their country. The Jordanians have used their ancient Nabataean heritage, especially the city of Petra, as a nationalist focal point. The ancient remains in the Middle East, therefore, are not just interesting curiosities but important pieces in constructing modern identities.

In the ancient world, cities, in particular, became the focal point of identity formation. Palmyra is a good example of this process, in which tribal identity slowly transformed into civic pride. Individuals from Palmyra could be found throughout the Roman Empire and beyond, and they proudly proclaimed their identity as citizens of Palmyra. As first Greek, and then Roman, civic ideals and expressions fashioned the culture of the Near East, citizens of every city of the Near East came to identify themselves with their home city. While the classical Greek city-states of the fifth and fourth centuries BCE competed with each other militarily, the wealthy citizens of the Roman Near East during the *pax romana* (the "Roman peace," roughly the first two centuries CE) competed to embellish their cities with monuments or by seeking distinctive titles for their cities from the Roman authorities, such as metropolis (mother city) or colonia (Roman colony).

## Introducing urbanism and culture in the Near East

Greek-style ideals of citizenship and civic structure in the Near East resulted from the conquests of Alexander the Great (356–323 BCE), who in 333 and 332 BCE conquered the eastern shore of the Mediterranean Sea on his way to Egypt. Although Alexander is credited in the ancient sources as founding at least 70 cities, it was his successors who truly brought Greek civic ideas to the Near East. After a generation of warfare and shifting alliances upon the death of Alexander in 323 BCE, three major powers consolidated their rule over Alexander's empire – the Ptolemies in Egypt, the Antigonids in Macedon, and the Seleucids in the Near and Middle East. Each of these ruling families promoted the growth of cities under their control. For example, Cassander of Macedon (though not an Antigonid) founded Thessalonica in 315 BCE. Ptolemy I either founded or greatly expanded Alexandria, which eventually became the largest and most important city in the Mediterranean during this Hellenistic period. Under the Seleucids, Greek-style cities spread widely throughout the Near and Middle East, from Laodicea on the Mediterranean in the west to Ai Khanoum in modern-day Afghanistan in the east.

The Seleucids had several reasons for promoting Greek-style urbanism throughout their territories. First off, these cities were founded with the settlement of veteran soldiers, many of whom originally fought with Alexander the Great or in the wars of succession after his death. As these Greek and Macedonian soldiers were given land and a superior position over the indigenous peoples where they settled, this retirement benefit provided a future source of income and local power for the settlers. These communities in turn attracted Greeks and Macedonians from the Aegean world, who brought varied skill sets to these new communities. As the communities grew by exploiting the local labor and agricultural production, trade and other forms of exchange expanded.

Second, the Seleucids would have found it incredibly difficult to rule over the vast territories that they controlled so they founded cities (or supported those cities founded by Alexander) as bulwarks against resistance to their rule. These cities could then serve as sources of military support during periods of emergency, much as Roman colonies did during the middle Republic period. They also served as economic outposts as well, directing resources from the hinterlands farmed by indigenous peoples into the Greek cities, which could then be funneled to the ruling dynasty through taxation and tribute.

Third, during the second century BCE after the Seleucids began to lose some of their power and territories, they used cities to promote Greek culture (also known as Hellenism) among the indigenous peoples. For example, Antiochus IV (r. 175–164 BCE) attempted to restore Seleucid power in the eastern Mediterranean and he believed that by promoting Greek culture, he could establish a stronger grip on power. It is hard to trace how successful this process was under the Seleucids, but it utterly failed in the one location where we have written sources – Judea. There, many members of the Jewish elite, including the high priest of the Temple of Jerusalem, sought greater adoption of Greek culture and customs, which sparked the famous Maccabean revolt, now commemorated during Hanukkah. This revolt led to a further weakening of the power of the Seleucid state, despite the fact that the long-term trend in Judea and throughout the Near East was towards greater acceptance of Greek culture.

For the Seleucids, then, the expansion and growth of Greek cities served many functions. Unfortunately, we do not know how or if the cities were incorporated into the rule of the Seleucid state, or what institutions may have existed in the cities. Almost all of our evidence for Near Eastern cities and their governance come from the Roman period, which used cities as the basic building blocks of administration in the provinces. While it is tempting to retroject evidence from the Roman period into the Hellenistic period, it is unwise to do so. It seems that the Seleucid state was quite underdeveloped in comparison with the hierarchy imposed by the Roman Empire which then evolved over several centuries. That the Seleucid state had largely collapsed by the time the Romans arrived in 64 BCE lends further credence to this assertion.

Under the Romans, the cities of the Near East became instrumental in controlling the region. As they became integrated into the imperial bureaucracy and local elites began to be rewarded for their cooperation with honors and benefits such as Roman citizenship, the cities became the focal point for the spread of Greco-Roman culture in the region. As the cities controlled their hinterlands, the Near East could be controlled by a minimum number of Roman officials as long as they had the cooperation of the local cities and their elites. As mentioned above, the Romans developed a hierarchy of cities as denoted by honorific titles, such as metropolis and colonia, which enabled the cities to compete amongst themselves for Rome's favor. Elites within the cities also competed against each other for honor, leading to a massive monumentalization of the Near Eastern cities, largely in the second century CE. In the third century CE, when Roman power was threatened in the Near East by the Persians, the civic development slowed, and one city, Palmyra, even attempted to establish itself as the nascent center of empire.

Christianization of the Roman Empire saw the expansion of the emergent church hierarchy into areas often associated with non-religious power, and in many locations of the Near East, bishops came to wield as much or even more power than the secular authorities or the local elites, evidence of whom begins to decline after the fourth century CE. The transformation of the cities in the Near East in this period, often called late antiquity, impacted all levels of the city, from its landscape to its social and economic functions. Christians of the Near East reoriented the city around a new type of monumental structure, the church.

When the Arab armies invaded in the early seventh century CE, the Near East had just been liberated by the Emperor Heraclius after nearly twenty years of Sasanian Persian rule. Within a decade, Arab armies led by the Caliphs (successors of Muhammad) had conquered the entire Near East. The Roman Empire, which in this period is often called the Byzantine Empire, could not reclaim these lands. The impact of the Persian and Arab conquests on the cities of the Near East remains an open question that this work will try to answer. Some have argued that the cities were already in "decline" in the sixth century, well before the Persian or Arab invasions. Clearly the cities were being transformed, as the mosque became a center of political control in addition to its religious importance.

The impact of Christianity and early Islamic rule on the classical city is a topic that has been increasingly studied in the past thirty years, as has the nature of Roman rule in in the Near East. Scholars, discussed in more detail below, have debated the nature of culture in the Near East under Roman rule. Some have argued that Greco-Roman culture was a "thin veneer" that obscured a prevalent indigenous culture. Others have suggested that most cultural influence was Greek and/or Roman, at least until late antiquity. More recent work has argued that locals used Greco-Roman culture as a way to express their own unique identities. Most often, the written sources, whether inscriptions or literary works, have been used to understand the dichotomy of Greco-Roman versus indigenous (Syrian) influences. This book, instead, uses the cities' the civic plans, structures, and role in imperial administration to approach this problem.

## Current debates

In this book, I have selected eight cities of the Near East – Antioch, Apamea, Caeserea, Jerusalem, Gerasa, Scythopolis, Petra, and Palmyra – to use as evidence for understanding three major debates within modern scholarship about culture and urbanism in the Near East from Alexander the Great to the mid-eighth century CE. First, previous scholarship has tended to stress diametrically opposed cultural systems (Hellenic and indigenous) at work in the Near East, especially during the Hellenistic and Roman periods. For example, Millar's *Roman Near East* (Harvard 1995) argues that cultural expression in the Near East during the Greco-Roman period was almost entirely Greek [Hellenic]. This was challenged by several books and articles – including Ball's *Rome in the East* (Routledge 2001, second edition 2016), Butcher's *Roman Syria and the Near* East (Getty 2004), and Sartre's *The Middle East Under Rome* (Harvard 2007). New scholarship argues that Hellenism and Roman culture did not replace indigenous culture; rather, it provided an outlet for indigenous culture to express itself.

The second major debate that this book focuses on is the changing uses of the city by imperial powers (Hellenistic dynasts, Roman Emperors, and Caliphs) to project the dominance of their own culture. Such uses of the cities appear to have begun under the Seleucid monarch Antiochus IV as a way to consolidate the rule of the Seleucids in the face of increasing threats. Roman rulers appear to have taken a very "hand-off" approach to the urban plans and structures of cities, as the emperors are not mentioned often in the inscriptions of the first through third centuries CE. Rather, it appears that local elites themselves were responsible for the constructions in their cities. After the legalization of Christianity, church leaders and imperial officials became more influential in the building process.

The third debate concerns the expansion, decline, and transformation of Near Eastern cities in the period known as late antiquity, from roughly the late third century CE to the mid-eighth century CE. Scholarship before the late 1970s and 1980s tended to view the transformation of cities in the Near East as resulting from the Islamic conquests of the early seventh century and a mistaken belief that the classical culture of these cities was decimated by the Muslims. Hugh Kennedy's article, "From Polis to Madina: Urban Change in late antique and early Islamic Syria," profoundly changed scholarly views on the subject and suggested that changes to the city began much earlier than the Islamic conquest, probably by sixth century. More recent scholarship, exemplified by Gideon Avni's book *The Byzantine-Islamic Transition in Palestine*, argues that there was more continuity in civic developments from the fifth until the tenth centuries than previously detected.

### Hellenism and indigenous culture

Fergus Millar's *The Roman Near East (31 BC–AD 337)* is responsible for developing the geographical and chronological parameters under which scholars have debated cultural identity in the Roman Near East. His scope was more limited than this book, as he began with the coming of the Romans and ended with the death of Constantine. Millar argues that all of the cities in the Near East were organized on a Greek model imported into Syria by the Greeks (and later supported by the Romans) and that Greek was the primary language of cultural expression. In his view, Greco-Roman culture was dominant, with evidence of indigenous cultures relegated to the peripheral zones of settlement, such as the regions controlled by the Nabataean Kingdom or the city of Palmyra. Even noting the rise of an indigenous language (Syriac) in the second century CE, Millar claims

> that we should see both the pagan and the Christian culture of this area, as expressed in Syriac, as derivatives of Greek culture, and not as a source of influence on the culture of Syria proper ... the notion that there was a 'Syrian' culture ... goes beyond our evidence.
>
> (Millar 493)

Millar's work concentrated on written sources, primarily inscriptions, which in the first through fourth centuries CE were almost entirely in the

Greek language (Palmyra and Nabataea excluded). This suggested to him that "the Greek language, Greek social structures and Greek frameworks for the construction and worship of deities penetrated to the most remote of rural contexts" and therefore dominated the cultural life of the urban and rural elements of the Roman Near East (Millar 523).

While many scholars adopted the framework that Millar constructed, Warwick Ball drew a diametrically opposite conclusion and argued that Greek culture was a thin "veneer" hiding a dominate Semitic, Near Eastern society. Ball's primary evidence for this assertion was the archaeological remains of the cities, countryside, and individual monuments. One of Ball's chief arguments is that Greeks did not physically found new cities in the Near East. Instead, he argues that they used the claims of civic foundation as a way to appropriate previously existing communities for themselves. He suggests that as most of these "Greek" communities reverted to using the Semitic name for their cities after the Islamic conquest, this fact proves that these communities were predominately Semitic and not Greek.

Using surviving archaeological monuments, Ball concludes that the function of many structures was largely non-Greek even though they were designed with Greek elements. For example, he suggests that the colonnaded streets found throughout the Near East, at Apamea or Palmyra for example, were intended as processional ways or as Near Eastern markets (a *suq* or *bazaar*). Therefore, even though colonnaded streets appear to be Greco-Roman in design, they were in fact used for typically Near Eastern purposes.

Ball also argues that the temples in the Near East were used for Near Eastern rituals even though they appear "western" in style. Some features that Ball concludes are Near Eastern, rather than Greco-Roman, include high places for sacrifice, as seen at the Temple of Jupiter at Baalbeck and Temple of Bel in Palmyra, circumabulatories inside temples (most often in the Nabataean realm), and large *temenos* squares with decorated *propylae* (entrances). He concludes,

> [t]here are resemblances [to Roman architecture], admittedly, and it would be folly to overlook them. But the resemblances are superficial. In terms of function, liturgy, antecedents and overall concept, these massive temple enclosures with their elaborate entrances have no counterpart in Roman architecture of the West.
>
> (Ball 383–384)

Butcher's *Roman Syria and the Near East* and Sartre's *The Middle East Under Rome* emphasize more complex relationships between identity, culture, and artifacts than the more polarized views of Millar and Ball. Butcher argues that Greek education and culture allowed an individual access to imperial and cultural power, and that individuals who chose to adopt of Hellenic culture obtained significant advantages, such as access to the power of the emperor, local autonomy, positions in the imperial bureaucracy, and, above all, entrance into a unified elite that spanned the entire empire.

Butcher argued that "Hellenism can hardly be regarded as a superficial 'veneer' disguising a native substratum" (274). He believed that cultural activities in the Near East until the fourth century were influenced or conducted using Greek thoughts and idioms. Only the conversion of Christianity provided an alternate source of cultural power that allowed cultural non-Greeks to obtain positions of power, which is apparent with the spread of the Syriac language. The fact that Greek names were replaced by Semitic ones after the Muslim conquest does not represent a "thin veneer" but the end of usefulness (98–100). Greek culture brought benefits because it allowed access to power in the Roman period, but once Roman power was no longer accessible in the Near East, Hellenic culture did not provide the same tangible benefits.

In the religious sphere, he argued that Syrian cults appear in both a Greco-Roman style and in the styles of various indigenous peoples. Some of these cults originated before the Hellenistic period. Syrian gods were often "equated" with Greco-Roman gods, thus assimilating them into Hellenic culture. Butcher suggests that this is another syncretistic movement which shows the fluidity of identities in the Near East. Like Ball, he also analyzes temple forms, beginning with the non-classical, Near Eastern temples of Dura Europos on the Euphrates River. Throughout Syria, Butcher notes the non-classical elements of the temples, but unlike Ball, gives equal weight to the classical and non-classical elements. He stresses that the temples which stray the most from classical forms lie in the steppe or desert region on the edge of settlement, and that the majority of temples in the more fertile regions are composed mainly of classical elements. He argues that it is difficult to detect the indigenous cultures of the Near East in this period, largely because almost all forms of cultural expression – such as literary texts, inscriptions, architecture, and art are heavily influenced by Greco-Roman ideals. According to Butcher,

> if Greek became the common language of inscriptions in the villages and at rural religious sites, does this imply a fuller and deep Hellenization of the rural populations, and the successful imposition of a dominant cultural identity at the expense of others? It is very difficult to answer such important questions given the current limited state of the evidence.
>
> (Butcher 277–278)

Nevertheless, Butcher suggests that Near Eastern ideas were combined with Greco-Roman ideals to form a mixed culture through syncretism (281–283). As an example, he presents the Temple of Bel at Palmyra, which contains many Greek features, such as Corinthian columns, triangular pediments, and a symmetrical form, but it includes Near Eastern features such as tower staircases, an entrance in the widest section of the temple, and a flat roof. These were features that lead Ball to believe that this temple was entirely Near Eastern in substance, disguised in a veneer of Greco-Roman features, but as Butcher notes,

> [t]he classical form concedes the other forms, but is not negated by them. Indeed, the use of the 'Graeco-Roman' form implies profound respect for whatever symbolism it evoked... The combination is not a random hodgepodge of disparate elements, but a deliberate scheme, and with this in mind we should perhaps exercise caution before considering the classical forms to be a 'veneer', masking native forms and intentions. 'Veneer' implies something superficial and deceptive about the outward form, and something authentic and more meaningful in that which is hidden.
> (Butcher 283)

Butcher sees three zones of Hellenization in the Near East based on material culture. The first, close to the Mediterranean, appears to be highly influenced by Greco-Roman culture. Further inland, indigenous styles appear more forcefully. Finally, along the steppe and desert, farthest from the Mediterranean, many Greco-Roman features are present, but these are combined with much more intensive contact with Middle Eastern genres and styles from beyond the Empire (272).

Although Hellenism represented only one cultural identity, it could allow the expression of many different elements of many cultures, and did not necessarily mean the "obliteration of other identities" (Butcher 332–333). In summary, "[w]e are often left with impure genres of overlapping identities, deployed in situations that we cannot determine for reasons that are lost to us" (Butcher 334).

Sartre's *The Middle East Under Rome* makes a strong case that "Greek" and "Indigenous" are artificial terms and do not reflect life in Rome's Near Eastern provinces. Instead, he argues that these two cultures interacted to form a third culture which was a hybrid of both. He believes that the inhabitants were not averse to living in many different cultural worlds, but over time Greek became the *lingua franca* to express those identities. Sartre examines the production of Greek literature in Syria and concludes that almost every city in Syria had a thriving Greek intellectual environment; nevertheless, indigenous cultures remained strong, and most names in the countryside and villages retained their Semitic roots. Semitic languages may have flourished amongst the people, but only with Syriac and later Arabic were these languages expressed in literature or inscriptions. Sartre concludes, "[t]his persistence of local languages helps explain the rapid disappearance of the veneer of Greek culture when new masters whose language was no longer Greek but Arabic took control of the country" (295).

In terms of religious belief and architecture, Sartre argues that Near Eastern and Roman gods assimilated to such an extent that "it is not always possibly to identify them with certainty" (297). He describes how Near Eastern gods were often portrayed as Greek ones, for example Allat as Athena, and Greek ideas influenced Nabataean and Jewish religion. Sartre also argues that although almost all of the temples in the Near East were built in a Greco-Roman style, the actual cultic rituals performed in the temples were indigenous. He provides examples of the Temple of Bel in Palmyra, the huge altar in the courtyard in the Temple of Jupiter at Baalbek, and open-air sanctuaries in Petra, the Sinai, and northern Syria. He concludes,

> [t]his 'Greek' style of temple decoration contributed to the assimilation between 'Hellenism' and 'paganism' that took place over time following the triumph of Christianity ... Hellenism seems to have penetrated sufficiently for us to view all pagan cults as 'Greek'.
>
> (Sartre 318)

In summary, Sartre expressed his overall view as, "the inhabitants of Greco-Roman Syria shared what the Greeks called a *mixobarbaros* culture, at heart barbarian even though cloaked in forms that looked Greek" (366).

Peter Richardson's book, *City and Sanctuary: Religion and Architecture in the Roman Near East*, focuses largely on the archaeological ruins and urban plan of cities of the Near East – in this case, Jerusalem, Caeserea, Gerasa (Jerash), Petra, and Palmyra. Richardson is chiefly concerned, though not exclusively, on the Roman period, and on what the temples and their integration into the civic plan suggests about religious experience in the Near East. His conclusion is that Romanization was broadly supported by the imperial government, that elites in many communities adopted many Greek and Roman cultural ideas, and that religious identities retained Near Eastern elements. He sees the focus of urban design in the Near East on temples as one major indication of the importance of indigenous religions, especially in Petra, Palmyra, and Jerusalem, as alternative sources of cultural organization and identity. Richardson seems to indicate that continuance of indigenous religion was an act of resistance against the Roman order.

More recently, Nathanel Andrade's *Syrian Identity in the Greco-Roman World* examines the development of Syrian expressions of "Greekness." He argues that Syrians, writing in Greek and engaging in debates about the nature of Greek culture, influenced the development of Greek identity in ways that have previously gone unnoticed. He sees Greek and Syrian cultural expressions as overlapping sets utilizing polyvalent symbols (symbols with multiple meaning) which interacted in complex ways. In short, to define the Near East as either Greek (and Roman) or indigenous or a mixture simplifies the complex intertwining of people's identities. Andrade's evidence is primarily literary, for example, he argues on the basis of Lucian's *On the Syrian Goddess*, that Syrians both consumed and created Greek culture for their own purposes. Therefore, we should see Syrians as co-opting Greco-Roman culture to advance themselves within the Greco-Roman system. Andrade, however, also examines Antioch, Apamea, and Jerash as examples of Near Eastern cities to argue that Greek and Syrian were categories that overlapped each other, both sharing and creating polyvalent meanings in relation to each other.

## Cities and their role in imperial administration

Andrade argues convincingly that in the Seleucid realm until the reign of Antiochus IV, "Greekness" was largely limited to the ethnic Greek descendants who had moved to the Near East. Under Antiochus IV, indigenous communities, such as the Jewish community in Jerusalem, were invited to participate in Greek-style civic communities. As the Maccabean revolt demonstrates, such attempts could be unsuccessful and led to the fragmentation of the Near East until the Roman organization of Syria under Pompey in 64–63 BCE.

Local dynasts, such as Antiochus I of Commagene (died in 38 BCE), were able to cooperate with Roman officials to preserve security in the region, while also creating new cultural identities. Like other near Eastern rulers such as Herod, Antiochus I was able to "domesticate" Greek and Roman expressions for a Near Eastern context, eventually making local dynasts irrelevant for governance (92). The Romans were then able to support the development of these cultural expressions and rule based on Greek civic communities, largely inhabited by an acculturated Syrian population. Unlike the Seleucids and Parthians, the Romans were able to unite the Syrian and Greek elements into a common governance structure composed of peer cities, which enabled the consolidation of Roman rule in the region.

Sartre and Butcher stress the importance of a civic council (*boule*), municipal offices (such as city councilors – called *bouleutes* in the east and *curiales* in the west), competition between powerful individuals and families for honors, competition against other cities, and the spread of Roman citizenship as indicators of a substantial culture of urban life. They argue that the cities during the Roman period were constantly trying to prove themselves to be "superior" than other cities in terms of social importance (or at least equal to the others) through public buildings and constructions, such as theaters, baths, aqueducts, colonnaded streets, and fountains, and the use of prestigious titles, such as *autonomia* (living under their own laws) or *metropolis* (mother city) or *colonia* (Roman colony). One cannot help but wonder if this worked as an ingenious system of social control which allowed the Roman authorities to exert a minimum amount of effort to obtain a maximum amount of compliance. By allowing the municipal elites to compete with the elites in other cities for prestige and imperial favor, the Romans diverted energy which could be turned against Roman dominance.

In late antiquity, as will be demonstrated in the following chapters, local involvement in building construction transformed. The city councilors (*bouleutes*) appear to be less and less involved in performing the liturgies in the city, such as sponsoring constructions and religious festivals. Instead, construction was financed by two organizations – the imperial government, including the emperors themselves and local officials such as provincial governors, and the Christian church.

Some have argued that this transformation in city construction reflects a real decline in the civic life of the cities or a collapse of the economy which destroyed the class of civic councilors. However, most recent evidence suggests that the decline of the civic councilor class in the cities of the Near East was caused by several factors, including religious and social change, and are not representative of a collapse of urbanism in the Near East in late antiquity.

The religious changes in late antiquity were exceedingly complex. The most important change was the adoption of Christianity by large numbers of people and by the imperial government. Beginning with Constantine, the imperial authorities patronized Christian worship and constructions in cities throughout the empire. As locals converted, Christians began to donate to the churches in their communities. This was especially true for the *bouleutes* class who had the resources to make extravagant gifts to the church. Some of these donations were in objects (elaborate textiles or silver plates for the liturgy for example) but much was in hard cash. The church used this money both to finance its expansive welfare programs but also to build and enhance churches. Church holidays based around feast days came to replace the games, theater performances, and pagan festivals. The imperial authorities reinforced this behavior with their active promotion of Orthodox creeds against other forms of Christian belief, the occasional suppression of pagan (to use the most commonly used term) sacrifices and the closing of temples in the late fourth century, and the forced conversion of Jews especially in the sixth century CE and later.

However, not all of the religious changes that impacted the cities were tied to Christianity. Paganism prior to the sixth century CE was quite diverse. People not only worshipped the famous gods and goddesses of Greek and Roman mythology, but also a plethora of local and community oriented deities. These civic cults often involved athletic competitions, large public festivals and animal sacrifices at the pagan temples. By the turn of the first century BCE/CE, the importance of other types of cults, called "mystery religions" by scholars, can be clearly detected. Most of these cults originated in the eastern Mediterranean during the Hellenistic period, but the expansion of Roman power provided easy access to travel and allowed for the rapid spread of beliefs. Other pagans were more interested in philosophy or actively ignored the gods altogether. The third century witnessed a number of changes in pagan belief and worship. Pagans in the third century seem to have gravitated towards a kind of pagan monotheism, often oriented around a sun god, such as Sol Invictus (the unconquered sun). Most importantly, enthusiasm for public sacrifices seems to have waned in many parts of the empire, though whether this was impacted more by changing beliefs or by economic change (such as increased taxation) is unknown. The last pagan Emperor, Julian (361–363), attempted to restore the civic cults with limited success suggesting that there was little enthusiasm for the traditional ways of pagan worship. This is not to say that pagan beliefs or other practices did not survive. Civic festivals, such as the infamous Maiuma in Antioch and Gerasa, continued despite the condemnations of Christian leaders, who complained that Christians should not partake in such debaucheries. Yet they obviously continued to do so!

One imperial policy that shaped the decline of the civic councilor class was the creation of a Senate and imperial bureaucracy centered at Constantinople during the fourth century. The tax burden also seems to have substantially increased since the height of the *pax romana*, and the responsibility for making sure that the cities met their obligations fell to the *bouleutes* class. Entrance into imperial service at the *perfectissimi* (equestrian) level and above exempted a person from having to perform the local liturgies, and so many *bouleutes* did everything in their power to obtain those positions. At the same time, imperial authorities, such as the provincial governors and higher, came to take on larger roles in regulating the cities and their expenses. For the *bouleutes* then, their role in the cities decreased in terms of the honor they received and power they held, while at the same time they had to take on more unwanted responsibilities.

If the *bouleutes* as a class began to lose power, the cities themselves still required local leadership, which came to be in the hands of a fewer number of people (Butcher uses the term "grandees") who exercised power in private. These might be imperial officials, local wealthy landowners, phylarchs (leaders) of local allied peoples (especially along the desert frontier), and most often bishops or other church officials. Because power operated behind closed doors, there was less of a requirement to maintain public buildings, other than churches.

### *Cities in late antiquity*

The cities of late antiquity have often been thought of as representing "decline" from the high point of the second century, as shown by the monumentalization of the cities in that time. This has often been linked to an economic or demographic crisis which threatened the very nature of Greco-Roman civilization, especially in the Near East.

In the early twentieth century, the belief that the Greco-Roman cities of the Pax Romana collapsed as a result of the Muslim conquests were pervasive. These beliefs were held both by historians such as Henri Pirenne (who wrote the famous book *Mohammed and Charlemagne*) and by archaeologists such as Carl Kraeling (who published the excavations of Gerasa). Under this paradigm, the Muslim conquest swept aside the trappings of Greco-Roman civilization from the Near East. They believed that the cities began a catastrophic decline, with whatever inhabitants remained classified as a "squatter" occupation. They believed that Christians were in general oppressed and prevented from building churches and worshipping without restrictions. They argued that the "Islamic" city was marked by a lack of town-planning, with the long, wide, straight streets of the classical period replaced with narrow, winding, alleys. Private space encroached on public space whenever possible, creating the appearance of chaos. Merchant activity moved into indoor, or at the very least, crowded and cramped outdoor *suqs* or *bazaars* which lacked a formal division of commercial space. Monumental and public building largely disappeared. Within several hundred years, the city was virtually unrecognizable compared to Greco-Roman models.

The growth of well-stratified archaeological excavations, especially at Antioch, Apamea, Gerasa, and Damascus, led Hugh Kennedy to argue that the cities lost many features of the classical period, but they did so much earlier than the Islamic conquest. He argues that unlike in the western Mediterranean, where there is generally a sharp break in the importance of urban culture, in the eastern Mediterranean the wealthy lived and exercised power in the cities throughout late antiquity. He argued that the process of transformation began sometime in the sixth century and continued after the Islamic conquest by tracing the fate of bath complexes, theaters, and colonnaded streets. He believed these changes resulted from five developments, First, he believed that there was demographic decline as a result of plagues, famines, and invasions, beginning in the mid-sixth century. The second cause was the changing nature of later Roman imperial taxation and civic burdens (as discussed above) which took away revenues that could have been used on constructing and maintaining buildings. Third, he thought that the change from Roman to Islamic law meant that there for fewer legal protections for public space, resulting in the changes to city streets. Fourth, he argued that commercial and industrial activities were more accepted in Islamic cities than in their classical antecedents. Finally, he argued that modes of transportation changed, with wheeled vehicles replaced with pack animals such as camels, making the wide straight classical streets unnecessary. According to Kennedy, then, cultural, social, and economic developments were more important than the Islamic conquest in transforming the nature of the city in late antiquity.

Much of the archaeological information that Kennedy drew on was published in only a preliminary form, and now our dating of artifacts from this period is much more precise than when he wrote in the mid-1980s. It is now possible to test his conclusions against dozens of well-excavated and published cities throughout the Near East, as are the focus of the following chapters of this book. Gideon Avni's approach in *The Byzantine-Islamic Transition in Palestine* is to emphasize "the role of internal processes and regional variability in the metamorphosis of urban settlement" (17). Avni cites evidence from Caesarea, Scythopolis, Gerasa, Tiberias, Jerusalem, Ramla, and the countryside to demonstrate that there was a long continuity of urbanism from the fifth until the tenth centuries throughout the Near East. His argument is that urbanism transformed more quickly in some places than in others, with new urban centers replacing ones that had declined or were abandoned. He believes that significant decline in urban populations throughout the Near East is clear only in the eleventh century CE. Avni does not see evidence of demographic decline that Kennedy postulated for the sixth century. He argues that there is little archaeological data that plagues, famine, or invasion decreased population numbers of the region (though individual cities may have been impacted by one or more of these events). In dating the changes which occurred in these cities, it is clear that in some it started as early as the fourth century, in others the fifth, in others in the sixth, and so on. From this new archaeological evidence, it seems clear that the processes described by Kennedy and Avni took several centuries and were profoundly uneven in their extent and impact.

## Geography

In this book, I define the term "Near East" as a convenient shorthand to refer to the region of the Middle East from the Taurus Mountains in Turkey to the northern border of Saudi Arabia and from the Mediterranean Sea to the Euphrates River. This area roughly corresponds to the ancient idea of greater Syria, which the Muslims called Bilad al-Sham. In the Roman period, much of the northern part of the Near East was located in the province of Syria. This area roughly corresponds to the western half of the Fertile Crescent and excludes Mesopotamia. For convenience, I will use the word "Syrians" to describe the people who lived in this area, whether culturally Greek, Roman, or indigenous. The ancient Near East and Bilad al-Sham does not include Egypt, which was very different culturally and politically from the Near East.

Despite the popular view that the Near East is largely a desert, in reality, this region of the world encompasses many different types of climate and geological zones. The most basic geography of the region consists of a coastal plain that ranges from a few kilometers wide in what is today southern Syria and Lebanon to several dozen at the Cilician plain in south-eastern Turkey. Moving away from the Mediterranean, the coastal plain ends with a series of highlands and mountains divided by a rift valley that created, from north to south, the Beqaa valley, the Jordan River, Dead Sea, and the Wadi Araba. Beyond the mountains and the rift valley is a wide steppe that in the north runs down to the Euphrates River and in the south slowly becomes the Arabian Desert.

Beginning in the northwest of this region, in what is now southern Turkey, there lies a coastal plain, which was very productive for agriculture. The largest city in this region was Tarsus; it became famous as it was the birthplace of the thirteenth Christian Apostle, Paul. This region was known in antiquity as Cilicia and was separated from greater Syria by the Amanus

18  *Introduction*

mountain range. At the bend of the Mediterranean as the coastline turns south, was the narrow plain of Issus where Alexander the Great defeated Darius III for the first time. Passing through the "Syrian Gates" leads to the inland plain of ancient Antioch and modern Aleppo.

The northern half of the coastal plain, stretching down to about modern Beirut, possesses a very narrow coastal plain, with mountains stretching down almost to the sea in many places. The coastal mountains are occasionally broken up by rivers, such as the Orontes River in the north, on which Antioch was located. The Orontes River connected Antioch to its port, Seleucia Pieria. Further south is the Homs Gap between the Ansariyeh and Lebanon mountain ranges. This provides inland access from the narrow Akkar plain to the upper Orontes valley along the ancient Eleutherus River.

The Orontes travels north from the Beqaa Valley through a vibrant area known as the Ghab, which was very fertile, and included the city of Apamea. Beyond the mountains and the Orontes River, the land becomes a dry steppe and more arid as one travels to the south and east. Portions of this steppe land include excellent agricultural zones such as around the modern city of Aleppo (ancient Borea). Several rivers, many of them seasonal (*wadis* in Arabic), flow from highland areas into the steppe. Some reach the Euphrates River in the east, but many terminate in the steppe or at an oasis. Thus, portions of this region supported agriculture, whereas large amounts of it were used by pastoralists.

Returning to the coast, from Tripoli down to Haifa was the core of ancient Phoenicia filled with famous cities such as Beirut, Byblus, Tyre, and Sidon. The northern end of this region was largely cut-off (perhaps protected would be a better term at some points of history) from the interior of Syria by the high Lebanon Mountains. Though there are a few mountain passes, they could be impassable in the winter. In the southern zone of this region as one approaches modern Haifa, one enters into more-traversable hills, separated by valleys which provided access from the sea to the rift valley. This was the land of Galilee, which was separated from Samaria by the Jezreel valley, which connected Scythopolis to Caesarea.

Just to the east of Beirut lies the Lebanon Mountains which even today are snowcapped in the winter months. These mountains run for approximately 250 km from the Homs gap in the north down to the Golan Heights and the rift valley. In the northern zone are mountains which average over 2,000 m in height, while the southern mountains are slightly lower. As mentioned above, there are passes through the mountains, but the mountains remained an effective impediment to travel.

The Beqaa valley runs between the Lebanon and the Anti-Lebanon Mountains. This valley is approximately 25 km long and over 100 km long from north to south. As noted above, the mountains are high and difficult to cross, meaning that most traffic flows north-south through the valley. The valley itself has many incredibly complex ecological niches, which include arid zones and swamps and fertile zones. Portions of the valley obtain ample rainfall for agriculture, especially in the southern end. Today only one-third of the valley is cultivated, mostly in the south. The southern Beqaa is drained by the Litanti River which empties into the Mediterranean between Tyre and Sidon. Rainfall in the northern half flows into the Orontes River before passing into the Lake of Homs and continuing to Antioch.

East of the Anti-Lebanon mountains lies the city of Damascus and an increasingly arid zone divided by mountain ranges such as the Jebel Rawaq and Jebel Abu Rijmen. The oasis city of Palmyra lay approximately halfway between Damascus and the Euphrates River on the route between these two highland zones. South-east of the mountain ranges is open desert.

The final coastal region of the Near East runs from Haifa down to the modern border between Israel, the Gaza Strip, and Egypt. This long stretch of approximately 200 km lacks good locations for harbors. This necessitated the creation of an artificial harbor for the city of Caesarea, which eventually became the Roman capital of this region. The Israeli coastal plain begins as the Galilee levels out into very narrow strip of land, running south between the Judaean highlands and the coast, and becoming wider as it approaches the more arid region known as the Negev Desert. This region was and remains very fertile. Between the coastal plain and the Jordan River and the Dead Sea is the region known as the Judean highlands, much of it now under the control of the Palestinian Authority. Jerusalem lies in this area, contested by the modern Israeli and Palestinian peoples.

A rift valley lies directly behind the southern part of Phoenicia and Galilea, Samaria, and the Judaean highlands. The River Jordan begins at the southern end of the Lebanon Mountains near Mount Herman, and runs south through the sea of Galilee before continuing on to the Dead Sea. The Jordan Valley is several degrees warmer than surrounding regions, but has ample water supplies and excellent soil. This combination led to the city of Scythopolis becoming one of the most prosperous and most populated cities in the southern Near East. The Dead Sea, the lowest location on the earth, is highly saline and does not support aquatic life fit for human consumption nor is the water suitable for irrigation. However, the land just south of the Dead Sea supported large date plantations in antiquity and much agriculture today. Running from the Dead Sea down to the Gulf of Aqaba is the Wadi Araba, an arid zone which today serves as the border between Jordan and Israel. The Wadi Araba separates the highland areas of the Negev desert to the west and the Sharra mountain range which received little rainfall. Petra was the most important community south of the Dead Sea.

The area to the east of the rift valley is composed of highlands, becoming increasingly arid as one travels from north to south. Southern Syria is marked by the remains of volcanic activity in the region known as the Hauran and around the Jebel Druze. Today the highlands of southern Syria and northern Jordan support the highest populations east of the Jordan. Temperatures are temperate, and rainfall is sufficient for agriculture. Gerasa was one of the major cities in this highland zone. Rivers, such as the Wadis

20  *Introduction*

Yarmuk, Zerqa, Mujib, and Hasa, bisect the highlands and flow down to the River Jordan or the Dead Sea. In some regions, for example around the Kerak Plateau just east of the Dead Sea, the rivers cut deep gorges which made travel more difficult. The cultivated zone is narrower in the south at the Kerak Plataeu, but everywhere to the east is a desert. There are still some oases, such as at Azraq, but in general, only nomadic populations could survive in this zone. South-east of Azraq and about 150 km east of the Kerak Plataeu lies the Wadi Sirhan, a chief route into the interior of the Arabian peninsula which runs from the northwest to southeast.

**Plan of the book**

Chapter 2, "Urban planning and structures in the Near East," examines the physical space of cities. It begins with a discussion of urban planning and how and why the cities developed as they did. It examines the various structures of cities, such as colonnaded streets, temples, churches, marketplaces, theaters, bathhouses, and other civic monuments.

The next four chapters explore the case studies of individual cities in their regional context. Chapter 3, "The Tetrapolis (Antioch and Apamea)," examines the development of the cities founded by the Seleucid dynasty as a means to control their Near Eastern territories. Antioch later became an imperial capital of the Roman Empire and an important ecclesiastic center. Apamea'sruins have been extensively excavated, in ways that Antioch, as a continually inhabited city, could not have been. Chapter 4, "The Decapolis (Gerasa and Scythopolis)," examples the "virtual island" of Hellenic cities located in northern Jordan, Israel, and southern Syria. I used the excavated cities of Gerasa (Jerash) and Scythopolis as examples. New research is showing that both cities remained important into the Islamic period. Chapter 5, "Judea and Palestine (Jerusalem and Caesarea)," studies the transformation of Jerusalem from Jewish city, to Roman colony, to imperially supported Christian holy land, and its continued importance under the Ummayads, as demonstrated by the Dome of the Rock. Caesarea stands out as a non-Jewish Romanized city, which eventually became an important administrative city. It later served as a base for Byzantine resistance against the Islamic conquests, and consequently, it lost most of its importance in the Islamic period. Chapter 6, "The desert fringe (Petra and Palmyra)," examines two cities, Petra and Palmyra, that were founded by indigenous peoples who spoke Aramaic. These cities were initially constructed independent of outside control, but both came to be ruled by the Roman Empire. This chapter examines how these cities developed with Greco-Roman style buildings and civic layouts as expressions of local culture. New excavations at Petra reveal the continuing importance of the city until the late sixth century, whereas Palmyra remained important in the new Islamic Caliphate. Chapter 7, "Conclusion," examines how we can use the evidence from Chapters 3–6 to understand the trajectory of urbanism in the Near East from Alexander the

Great until c. 750 CE. I will, furthermore, use the evidence from these eight cities to enter into the three debates mentioned in this chapter.

## Suggestions for further reading

American Schools of Oriental Research reporting on the destruction of archaeological sites in Syria and Iraq: www.asor-syrianheritage.org/.
Andrade, N. *Syrian Identity in the Greco-Roman World* (Cambridge 2014).
Avni, G. *The Byzantine-Islamic Transition in Palestine* (Oxford 2014).
Ball, W. *Rome in the East* (Routledge 2001, second edition 2016).
Butcher, K. *Roman Syria and the Near East* (Getty 2004).
Kennedy, H. From Polis to Madina: Urban Change in Late Antique and Early Islamic Syria. *Past and Present* 106: 3–27.
Millar, F. *Roman Near East 31 BC – AD 337* (Harvard 1995).
Richardson, P. *City and Sanctuary: Religion and Architecture in the Roman Near East* (SCM Press 2002).
Sartre, M. *The Middle East under Rome* (Harvard 2007).
Segal, A. *From Function to Monument: Urban Landscapes of Roman Palestine, Syria, and Provincia Arabia* (Oxbow 1997).

# 2 Urban planning and structures in the Near East

The damage to the archaeological sites of Syria from the civil war and ISIS has been extensive, and not just in Palmyra. This damage is real and permanent; however, the cities will be reconstructed as much as they can and tourists will return when the conflict ends. Even during the recent conflicts in the Middle East, tourists remained a frequent sight in the archaeological parks in Israel and Jordan. When I have visited the archaeological remains of the cities such as Petra and Gerasa, there is virtually no sign of the vibrant life of the living ancient city. As Ross Burns points out,

> [t]oday's experience is vastly different from how these cities appeared to the visitor 1,800 years ago – a visual field animated by crowds, chaotic activity, the hazards of traffic, and the sense that this ever-changing vista was encompassed within a world where an overarching order prevailed.
>
> (Burns 5)

In the time that Burns is referencing here, circa 200 CE, the overarching order was that of the Pax Romana, the Roman peace, that united the Mediterranean and Near Eastern worlds and which created the conditions for the blossoming of trade, culture, and economic expansion.

The exposed remains of these cities, as will be shown in the following chapters, proudly display the monumentalization characteristic of the cities of the Pax Romana, to the detriment of other periods. The Pax Romana represents the period when the street plans of these cities were developed, when colonnaded streets were first installed, when the cities were beautified with grand temples and street monuments such as fountains and large arches, and when entertainment facilities such as theaters, baths, and hippodromes (stadiums for chariot racing) made their mark on the urban landscape.

There are several reasons why other periods are less well-represented than the Roman one. The remains of the earlier, Hellenistic cities, lay under these Roman levels. Modern governments want to monetize and preserve their cultural heritage, so it is unlikely that any government or archaeologist would remove large, standing, extant remains to see what lies beneath, except in a few small or exceptional cases. For example, sacred space in the Near East was often quite conservative, so temples to the same (or syncretized) gods and goddesses were often built on top of the remains of earlier temples. Thus, the Roman period temples largely obscure the remains of the earlier, less monumental ones. Limited excavations at, for example, Gerasa have revealed the differences between the Hellenistic and the later Temple of Zeus on the site, but this is exceptionally rare (Figure 2.1).

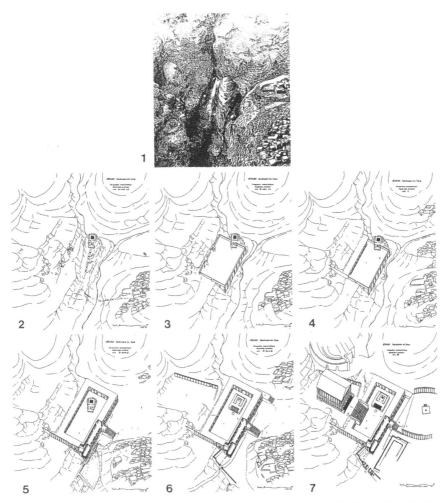

Fig. 1 — Schémas évolutifs du sanctuaire : - 1 : La zone du sanctuaire avant toute construction. Hypothèse (Dessin : J.-P. Lange). - 2 : État supposé du sanctuaire vers 80/100 av. J.-C. (Dessin : J. Seigne). - 3 : État supposé du sanctuaire vers 60 av. J.-C. (Dessin : J. Seigne). - 4 : État supposé du sanctuaire vers 0 (Dessin : J. Seigne). - 5 : État supposé du sanctuaire vers 30 ap. J.-C. (Dessin : J. Seigne). - 6 : État supposé du sanctuaire vers 70 ap. J.-C. (Dessin : J. Seigne). - 7 : État supposé du sanctuaire vers 170 ap. J.-C. (Dessin : M.A.F.J.).

*Figure 2.1* The evolution of the Temple of Zeus from shrine to monumental temple (Courtesy of Jacques Seigne).

For similar reasons, it is difficult to investigate the evolution of paved streets except in some limited circumstances. So the remains of the Roman period, which were more substantial and monumental, eclipse the remains from the earlier Hellenistic city.

Later periods, especially those associated with Islamic rule are often less well represented as well, especially in cities that were excavated before the 1990s. There are several causes of this: (1) remains from late antiquity and the early Islamic periods tend to be less monumental and so less interesting for tourism and also much easier to remove, (2) late antique, especially Islamic period, remains were viewed as less important or less interesting, and therefore, they were removed to get down to the Roman layers, which were deemed more important or vital to understanding city life, and (3) there was a conscious or unconscious bias against the Islamic period remains as most of the scholars who have excavated these sites tended to be Jewish or Christian westerners. Not surprisingly, the one major exception to this pattern is that Christian churches were always deemed worthy of preservation by scholars. Not only were churches saved for religious reasons, but they were one of the few types of monumental structures built in the late antique period. They also provided ample opportunities for the study of ancient art and culture, for many churches of this period (and synagogues and large houses too) were richly decorated with mosaics depicting Christian, pagan, and naturalistic scenes.

A visitor to these sites today, then, largely sees the Roman period city with the addition of some late antique structures, mostly churches. The streets have been cleared of all non-durable, monumental structures but we have to imagine the streets teeming with stalls and other wooden structures, at least in some periods. The cities appear yellowish-white from the stone columns and street pavements, whereas in antiquity they would have been richly colored. The cities themselves are quiet, with none of the noise from economic activity or religious festivals. They smell of dust and dirt only, without the richness of cooking food, incense, animal manure, and body sweat... well, maybe it's not a total loss! For all of these reasons, a visitor cannot completely understand or appreciate what these ancient cities would have been like to live in (Figure 2.2).

Instead, visitors and scholars are left with the durable remains of these ancient cities in order to understand how they functioned and how people of the ancient period experienced them. This creates a bias in terms of period as mentioned above, but also in terms of structures, for largely only the well-built, monumental structures have been excavated and studied. It has only been in more recent decades that lower class domestic structures have been thought worthy of study, excavation, and publication!

In order to understand the archaeology of the cities of the Near East, it is important to first understand how the cities were planned and what structures were common in them. This chapter, therefore, attempts to provide the reader with a basic description of city planning in the ancient world, before

*Figure 2.2* View of the cardo of Apamea to the north (Photo by Greg Fisher).

moving on to describe the various types of buildings that existed in these cities, including religious, commercial, and entertainment structures.

## City planning

Most cities in ancient Greece and the Near East developed organically with little civic oversight, in marked contrast (for example) to the cities of the Harappan civilization in India. Our sources claim that the first city planner of the Greek world was Hippodamos, who designed the Piraeus (the port of Athens), Rhodes, and the colony of Thurii in the fourth century BCE. Thurii, as a new foundation, was laid out with a grid pattern, with streets that intersected at right angles. The city blocks are termed *"insulae"* (Latin for islands). Public buildings were located in the heart of the town and along the main streets, with residential structures radiating out from the center. From this point forward, a city designed on a grid pattern with intersecting streets can be called "Hippodamian."

Modern scholars use terminology from Roman land surveying and military camps (both of which were designed with a grid pattern) to label the streets of a city. Cardo is the Latin term used for a north-south street, and decumanus is used for those running east-west. The designation maximus indicates the most important cardo or decumanus. As a shorthand, the main street in these towns is sometimes called the cardo, even if that street ran east-west, for example at Petra. These terms were not used in antiquity for city planning.

26  Urban planning in the Near East

**Colonnaded streets**

All of the cities described in this book had a Hippodamian street plan by the late second century CE, at least as far as the topography of the city allowed. Furthermore, each and every city developed at least one colonnaded street by the end of the second century CE. These colonnaded streets, which were broad avenues lined with columns, were a form of monumental architecture reserved for the most important streets of the city (Figure 2.3).

The origin of the colonnaded streets in the Near East is unknown – they are not found in Rome or mainland Greece before the end of the first century BCE when Herod [r. 37–4 BCE], King of Judea, is said to have constructed the first example in Antioch. Three possible origins of colonnaded streets have been proposed. First, colonnaded streets may have their precursors in Greek *stoas* – roofed buildings with a row of columns in front of a long

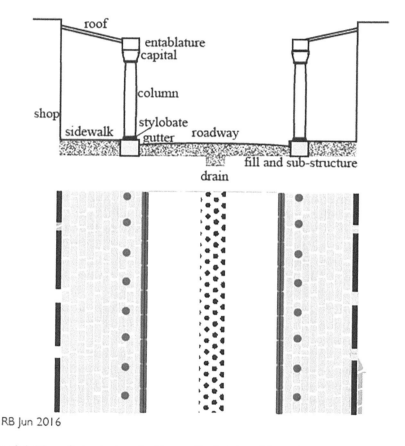

*Figure 2.3* Plan of a typical cardo (Burns, R. *Origins of the Colonnaded Streets in the Cities of the Roman East.* [Oxford 2017], Figure 4.03).

wall. These buildings provided shade and cooling breezes for political or philosophical discussions (hence the name Stoicism for a type of philosophy that became popular in Rome, after having been developed in Athens in the third century BCE). Second, the inspiration may have come from the colonnaded, roofed structures (porticos) often used as the entrance to a temples. A third possibility is that they were derived from earlier Near Eastern architecture from the Persian or Pharaonic periods.

As will be seen in the following chapters, most of the archaeologically attested colonnaded streets date from the second century, though there are examples from the late first century CE (as at Gerasa) and from later periods (sixth century Jerusalem, for example). The features of the colonnaded streets are several but generally conform to a similar plan: a wide, paved street that often ran over sewer lines or water pipes. The street paving stones were large square or rectangular blocks, often laid perpendicular to the sidewalk, but occasionally laid diagonally. Manhole covers are visible in many of these streets, such as at Gerasa, Jerusalem, and Caesarea (Figure 2.4).

Curb stones separated the animals and vehicular traffic from humans. Flanking the street were a series of columns, often of the Corinthian type, though Ionic columns were sometimes used. A roof normally covered a sidewalk between the columns and flanking shops. Topography sometimes played a role in this arrangement, as at Jerusalem, whose hills sometimes prevented columns or shops on both sides of the street. According to Ross Burns, colonnaded streets in the Near East in the second century CE

*Figure 2.4* Photo of a manhole cover in the Gerasa South Decumanus (Photo by author).

"became the favoured tool of urban architects seeking new visual devices and the loosening of traditional formats." He continues,

> In many cases (Apamea, Jerash [Gerasa]) the new building programmes and materials improved on – or juxtaposed – existing axes or grids. Other cities would feel that they had to acquire the axial perspective even at the expense of the heart of their existing urban centers (Palmyra)... [c]ities outbid each other in razzle-dazzle effects, and with the new phases of 'monumentalization' that came with the Antonines and Severans few cities could afford to be left behind in the prestige stakes.
>
> (Burns 7)

In other words, the colonnaded street came to be seen as the most important element of design in Near Eastern cities, and the cities of the Roman period competed amongst themselves for the grandest or longest stretch of colonnaded street.

The importance of the axial nature of these streets cannot be emphasized enough, as they were often used as processional ways to the most important temples of the city—following in the footsteps of the processional ways of Egyptian temples, such as the Avenue of the Sphinxes between the Karnak and Luxor temples. Two good examples of processional ways are the long colonnaded streets in Petra and Palmyra, which end at the entrance to the temples of Dushares (Qasr al-Bint) in Petra and Bel in Palmyra. Both of these processional ways traveled through the main street of the city, but other cities had processional ways along other streets, such as Gerasa, where the sacred way to the Temple of Artemis was not along either of the two main east-west roads.

Over time, the colonnaded streets took on many functions. The most obvious function was that they provided a clear visual field that focused the eye in a specific direction. In addition, the colonnaded streets made it easy to mark the focal points of the city as major buildings along the road, such as temples and later churches, were visible along the street because of large gates (*propylaea*), porticos, or by higher columns. Shops were often constructed behind the colonnaded streets (Figure 2.5).

These shops may have sold services, such as haircuts, or goods, or served as restaurants. Many of them included spaces for light industrial work such as baking or weaving. The sidewalks themselves could have been occupied by vendors or people providing services. The shops and the sidewalks slowly came to replace the open-aired marketplaces, such as the *agora* or *forum*, and the other functions of these plazas such as political and philosophical discussions. The main advantage of the shops and sidewalks was that their roofs provided protection from the elements. Any traveler to the Middle East today quickly recognizes the importance of shade!

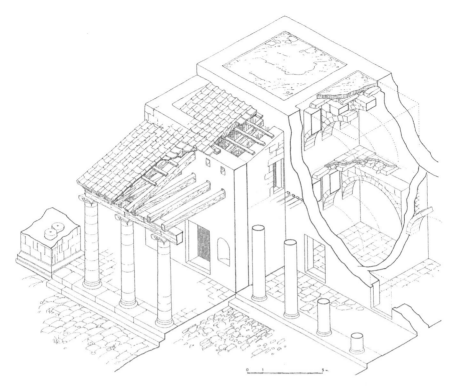

*Figure 2.5* Artist's reconstruction of a shop along the cardo at Petra (Drawing by Chrysanthos Kanellopoulos, courtesy of Chrysanthos Kanellopoulos and ASOR. Originally published in Kanellopoulos, C. "The Architecture of the Shops and Colonnaded Street in Petra." *Bulletin of the American Schools of Oriental Research*, no. 324, 2001, p. 12. The entire article can be found at www.jstor.org/stable/1357629).

## Street monuments: the monumental arch, the tetrapylon, and the nymphaeum

Columns were not the only monuments that one would see along the street, even if they were the most ubiquitous. Three other ornamental features were important – monumental arches, tetrapyla, and the Nymphaeum.

Monumental arches indicate a separation of space within a city plan. They could advertise the boundary of a city such as the Arch of Hadrian at Gerasa, or they could indicate a transition in the direction of the road system as at Palmyra, or they divided public space and sacred space like at Petra, or delineated the boundary of a forum as in Roman Jerusalem (Figure 2.6).

*Figure 2.6* Hadrian's Arch at Gerasa (Photo by author).

The main difference between a monumental arch and a gate in the Roman period is that monumental arches are freestanding, whereas gates were incorporated into city walls or other structural elements. In most time periods, gates served important defensive functions, but during the Pax Romana in the Near East, gates came to take on decorative functions. The monumental arches of the Near East are nearly identical in form to Imperial triumphal arches except they lack sculptural figures (compared, for example, to the Arch of Constantine in Rome) (Figure 2.7).

The monumental arch that connects the Qasr al-Bint sanctuary with the colonnaded street at Petra is a good example of a gate that functioned to separate divine from regular space. Excavations have shown that it dates to the early second century CE, likely confirming its long attribution to the Emperor Trajan, who was responsible for adding the Nabataean Kingdom, which included Petra, to the Roman Empire in 106 CE. It consists of a three-arched entranceway with two piers in the road and two connected to buildings on each side. The eastern façade, which is the way a visitor to the temple complex would approach, is richly decorated, with four "Nabataean" columns supporting the upper attic of the arch, which is no longer extant (Figure 2.8).

Hadrian's arch at Gerasa is an example of a gate that delineates urban from rural space – despite the fact that it is freestanding! It is possible that the builders of the arch intended to extend the city walls south to Hadrian's arch (which is 460 m south of the southern gate), but there is no evidence that they attempted to do so, suggesting the arch was intended to be a lone

*Urban planning in the Near East* 31

*Figure 2.7* The Arch of Constantine in Rome (Photo by author).

*Figure 2.8* Trajan's gate at Petra looking towards the Qasr al-Bint, visible through the central arch (Photo by Carole Raddato).

monument on the main road to Gerasa. The arch is similar in form to the arch at Petra. It has one main entrance flanked by two smaller, vaulted entrances. Instead of free-standing columns, it contains four half-columns built into the structure of the arch. Above each secondary entrance is a small alcove that is a miniature gate, complete with base, columns, and pediment. The decorations on the front and back are largely similar.

A tetrapylon (plural – tetrapyla) is a decorative structure with four square or rectangular piers that was placed at street intersections, as at Gerasa and Palmyra. If the piers were connected by arches, then the structure is called a quadrifrons (literary, "four fronts") and looks similar to a small triumphal arch on each side. This structure was often covered by a dome (Figure 2.9).

If not connected and roofed, then it is called a tetrakionion ("four columns"). Both types were found at Gerasa. In general, tetrapyla provided places for social gatherings and a social hub, for they encouraged traffic to slow down and pause. Plazas were often placed around a tetrapylon to facilitate these social functions, and these plazas must have been prime commercial space (Figures 2.10 and 2.11).

The final common street monument in the Near East is the nymphaeum (plural, nymphaea), which is a monumental, public water fountain and pool placed in front of a richly decorated backdrop (*scaenae frons*, as in a theater). The Trevi Fountain in Rome is one famous example even today, though none in the Near East would have been as richly decorated (Figure 2.12).

The origins of the nymphaea appear to go back to springs sacred to nymphs, but this sacred connection appears to have been severed when the structures became street decorations. Most often they were fed by aqueducts, though local springs (like at Philadelphia) could dictate the placement of the nymphaeum in the urban plan. There is a variant of the nymphaeum which appears only in the Near East, called a Kalybe, which did not contain water but is similar in decoration and appearance.

*Figure 2.9* The North Tetrapylon (a quadrifons) at Gerasa (Photo by author).

*Figure 2.10* Artist's recreation of the South Tetrapylon (a tetrakionion) and plaza at Gerasa (Kraemer, C. *Gerasa: City of the Decapolis* [ASOR 1938], Plan XV).

*Figure 2.11* The nymphaeum at Gerasa (Photo by author).

*Figure 2.12* The Trevi Fountain in Rome (Photo by author).

The nymphaea in the Near East are generally two stories high and covered in rich decoration, which often included statuary. Corinthian columns were often employed, as were a series of semi-circular niches. They typically had a curved back wall as at Gerasa and Scythopolis, though others are known to have flat *scaenae*. The center niche could have been topped by a dome, and it was common to have a broken, or a "Syrian," pediment. They could be of varied sizes – the one at Scythopolis, for example, appears squeezed between a temple and another public building, whereas the one at Gerasa had plenty of space to stretch out. In front of the *scaenae*, there was a large rectangular pool that stretched the length of the nymphaeum and covered the area leading to the sidewalk. The street columns in front of the nymphaeum were typically taller, thus indicating the monument's location along the street. This helped create a portico that would have provided ample shade to enjoy the sights and sounds and feeling of constantly running water.

## Plazas and markets: the agora, forum, and macellum

The agora was the heart of the ancient Athenian democracy in the fifth and fourth centuries BCE, just as Roman politicians during the Republic frequented the forum. In Rome, open-aired spaces by the Middle Republic came to be specialized, with the forum being the center of political and cultic activity, and other forums (technically *fora* in Latin) being used for commercial functions, such as the Forum Boarium (cattle market). By the

*Urban planning in the Near East* 35

first century CE in the Near East, the agora and forum had become virtual synonyms for a plaza that functioned as a civic or imperial administrative center, though these could still contain shops and other commercial activities. In Latin, macellum came to be the term used to designate a constructed market.

In the Hellenistic period, an agora, or Greek-style marketplace, consisted of an open space, bounded on four sides by stoas (covered porticos). Famous examples include the agoras at Ephesus and Pergamon in Asia Minor. The best known example of an agora or forum in the southern Levant was excavated at Philippopolis in modern Syria. Constructed in the middle of the third century CE, it contained both religious structures – such as a Hexastyle temple and a mausoleum for Philip the Arab's [Roman emperor from 244 to 249 CE] family, a basilica, and a sculptural monument (a Kalybe). It was rectangular in shape and bounded by the cardo maximus and decumanus maxmimus. It was paved and surrounded by columns (Figure 2.13).

The macellum in Gerasa derives its plan from the Latin West and is one of only two examples of this type of building in the Near East (the other is a third-century building from Dura-Europos). This structure originally consisted of an octagonal courtyard paved with white limestone with a fountain in the middle. Surrounding this courtyard were 24 Corinthian columns with semicircular exedra on three corners. The eastern vestibule opened onto the Cardo, whereas the western one had two back entrances. Along the cardo, there were eight shops, several along a road, along the south wall of the macellum, and three on the north and south sides inside the macellum.

*Figure 2.13* The macellum at Gerasa (Photo by author).

*Figure 2.14* The Oval Plaza at Gerasa as seen from the Temple of Zeus (Photo by author).

In addition to the agoras, forums, and enclosed markets, cities could have decorative open-air plazas whose function within a city plan was often to provide a connection between different sections of the urban environment. They are often found in front of monumental buildings, such as churches or theaters, but could be disconnected from any structures. The most famous of decorative plazas in the region is the Oval Plaza at Gerasa, which provided a transition between three different orientations – the Temple of Zeus, the road leading to the southern gate which ran from the northwest to southeast, and the cardo maximus that ran from the southwest to the northeast (Figure 2.14).

This plaza, therefore, served disguised the three different orientations, which were determined by the cities topography, in a way that was aesthetically pleasing. It was surrounded by ionic columns and a sidewalk, with a column (that likely supported a statue of an emperor) in the center. The semi-circular plaza just inside the Damascus Gate in Jerusalem would have provided much of the same function, linking the two main cardos with the northern city gate (though note that the modern plaza lies several meters above the ancient one).

## Religious structures: temples, churches, and mosques

Three major types of religious structures were found in the cities of the Near East – temples, churches, and mosques.

Temples were the cornerstone of the ancient city. One cannot think about Athens without the Parthenon or Rome without its myriad of temples such as the Pantheon (Figures 2.15 and 2.16).

*Urban planning in the Near East* 37

*Figure 2.15* The Parthenon at Athens (Photo by author).

*Figure 2.16* The Pantheon in Rome (Photo by author).

This was, of course, true for the cities of the Near East as well; even Jerusalem had the largest temple in the entire eastern Mediterranean at the turn of the first millennium. As sites of worship of one or more gods, the temples provided a spiritual hub for the city by directing devotion through religious festivals and processions and rituals. With the Christianization of the Roman Empire in the fourth century, temples came under both verbal and sometimes physical assault. This was especially true in the late fourth century under the reign of the Emperor Theodosius [379–395] who allowed his Praetorian Prefect of the Near East, Cynegius, to stir up monks and bishops to assault pagan temples. By the early fifth century, almost all of the city temples had been closed or destroyed.

Temples in the Near East came in many shapes and sizes, from the tiny "Small Temple" in Petra to the massive temples at Baalbeck (ancient Heliopolis) in modern Lebanon. They all, however, share many common features. Most temples were housed within a sacred space, called a *temenos*, which is often a walled compound. The wall functioned to separate the sacred space from the rest of the city. It was common for porticos or stoas to run along the inside of the *temenos* walls, as at the Temple of Bel in Palmyra (Figures 2.17 and 2.18).

Since the *naos* of these sanctuaries are often so small that only tiny numbers of people could attend the rituals inside the temple, the courtyard was constructed in a monumental fashion to allow a large number of congregants to take part in the ceremonies. Entrances to the *temenos* could be plain or extravagantly decorated. The entrance to the Qasr al-Bint complex in Petra, for example, is marked only by a monumental arch (as described above), whereas the entrance to the Temple of Artemis in Gerasa consisted of two massive gates. A massive, richly decorated gate is called a *propylaeum* (plural, *propylaea*). At the Temple of Artemis, the *propylaeum* began east of the

*Figure 2.17* The exterior wall of the temenos of the Temple of Bel (Photo by Greg Fisher).

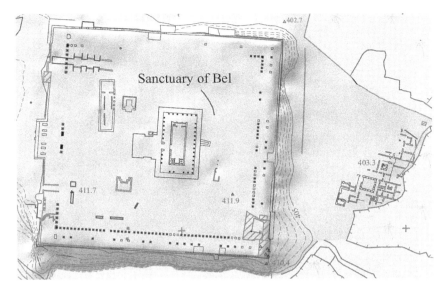

*Figure 2.18* Plan of the Temple of Bel (Map by Klaus Schnädelbach, originally published as Schnädelbach, K. *Topographia Palmyrena, 1 Topography.* Documents d'archéologique Syrienne XVIII. [Damaskus 2010]. On commission by Dr. Rudolf Habelt GmbH, Bonn).

cardo maximus with a monumental arch that led to large trapezoid exedra (a roofed space). After passing across the cardo, one then came to another massive gateway with a four-columned porch. Now, this was an extravagant entrance suitable for a goddess! (Figure 2.19).

Within the temenos, there could be several different structures. Most temples contained some sort of free-standing altar where animal sacrifices were performed. The altars are typically of moderate size, but occasionally, as at the Temple of Jupiter of Baalbeck, they could become buildings themselves. The altars were most commonly placed directly in front of the steps leading to the temple itself (Figure 2.20).

The actual temple is called the *naos* in Greek and could be either peripteral or prostyle. The peripteral style temple is characterized by columns, often Corinthian, surrounding the naos. Two examples are the Temple of Zeus at Jerash and the Temple of Jupiter at Baalbeck. Both temples are surrounded with Corinthian columns and have an arched roof in the classical style, and both are entered from the shorter end of the temple (Figure 2.21).

Most temples in the Near East were constructed in the prostyle or so-called "Roman style." This style placed the temple on a podium oriented along one main axis. Stairs were placed at the front of the axis that led to a porch, normally along the narrow side. Temples are described by the

*Figure 2.19* Propylaeum along the cardo of the Temple of Artemis in Gerasa (Photo by author).

*Figure 2.20* The Qasr al-Bint temple in Petra with the remains of the altar in the bottom left corner (Photo by author).

*Urban planning in the Near East* 41

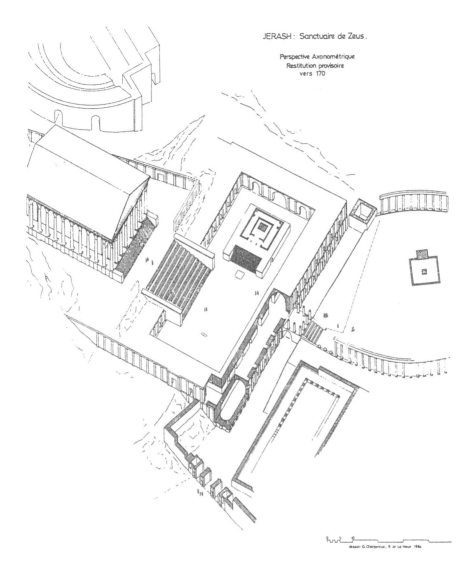

*Figure 2.21* Artist's depiction of the Temple of Zeus at Gerasa (Courtesy of Jacques Seigne).

number of freestanding columns on this porch, so a hexastyle temple indicated that there were six columns, whereas octastyle means eight. The *pronaos* (literary "in front of the temple") is the term for the inner portion of the portico, which normally would have been roofed. An entrance led into the *cella* or shrine of the temple. These could be dedicated to the worship of one or more gods or goddesses. The cult statue(s) stood within the *cella*.

*Figure 2.22* The Temple of Artemis at Gerasa (Photo by author).

The *naos* was not surrounded by columns, but they may have pilasters built into the temple walls. The Temple of Artemis at Gerasa is an excellent example (Figure 2.22).

Churches do not appear in large numbers in the Near East until the fifth century, with the sixth century representing the peak of Christian constructions. Christian bishops came to control, thereby increasing amounts of wealth in the later Roman Empire via donations, wills, and other bequests. This enabled the bishops to increase spending on social welfare and on the building of richly decorated churches, though local leaders, provincial governors, and even emperors could provide funds to build churches. Church construction continued long after the Islamic conquest of the Near East, as the churches at Umm ar-Rasas from the late-eighth century testify (Figure 2.23).

Most churches in the Near East from this period are called "basilica churches." This strange title comes from a building in Roman architecture known as a basilica (the word means "king's building"), which in the first century BCE became the prime judicial and administrative building. The form is characterized by a long open hall (called a nave) which ends in a raised platform with a semi-circular extension of the back wall (called an apse) where the Roman administrator would have sat. The sides of the nave are flanked with columns that separate side aisles (sometimes single and sometimes double) from the main hall. The roof of the nave generally rose higher than that of the side aisles, which allowed for windows to provide

*Urban planning in the Near East* 43

*Figure 2.23* A portion of a mosaic in the Church of Saint Stephen in Umm er-Rasas (ancient Kastron Mephaa) built in 785 (Photo by author).

natural light into the structure. A vestibule, called a narthex, served as an entrance and ran in front of the nave and side aisles. Famous administrative examples include the basilica at Trier and the Basilica of Maxentius and Constantine at Rome. Christians adopted this form because it was spacious and could accommodate large numbers of worshippers. It also had important associations to imperial power and authority (several of the first basilica churches were paid for by the emperor Constantine). Church floors were often richly decorated with mosaics. Donors for the church, or bishops, would proudly proclaim in mosaic inscriptions their role in financing the construction of a new church (Figures 2.24 and 2.25).

Other church forms were possible, but less common in the Near East. Octagonal and round churches are known from Caesarea and Scythopolis, respectively. These churches are often connected with saints and martyrs and, because of this, they are known as "martyrium" churches. The most

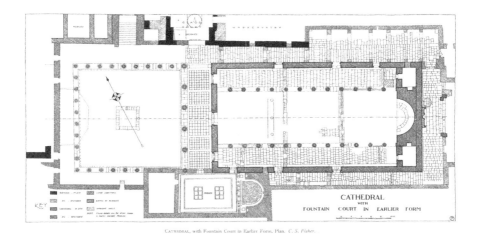

*Figure 2.24* Basilica plan of the Cathedral at Gerasa (Kraemer, C. *Gerasa: City of the Decapolis* [American Schools of Oriental Research 1938], Plan XXXI).

*Figure 2.25* Example of the mosaics in the Petra Church (Photo by author).

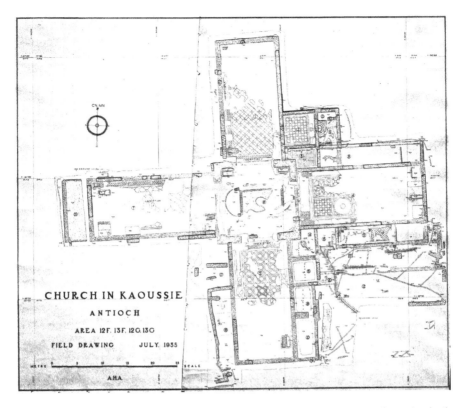

*Figure 2.26* The cruciform church dedicated to St Babylas at Kaoussie at Antioch (Antioch Expedition Archives, Department of Art and Archaeology, Princeton University, Photo 2421).

famous is the rotunda from the Church of the Holy Sepulcher in Jerusalem. Churches could also be of a cruciform (in the form of a cross) plan (Figure 2.26).

There are very few examples of mosques found in the Near East from before the middle of the eighth century, which is the end of this study. Modern mosques are oriented towards Mecca with a niche, called the mihrab, pointing to Mecca as the focal point of prayer in the mosque. Almost nothing survives of the most famous mosque, the Al-Asqa mosque in Jerusalem, from antiquity. However, an early mosque was recently discovered in the heart of Gerasa. It included an open courtyard with a portico to the north, east, and west, with a prayer hall in the southern third of building. The limited number of mosques in the Near East from before the eighth century compared to the large number of Christian churches suggests that the population remained

*Figure 2.27* Mosque (left) and Basilica of St. Sergius (right) at Resafa (Photo by Greg Fisher).

substantially Christian for several centuries after the Islamic conquest. Only a few churches are known to have been converted into mosques, or shared between Muslims and Christians such as at Sergiopolis (Rusafa) (Figure 2.27).

## Entertainment structures: theaters, amphitheaters, hippodromes, and baths

Greek culture, beginning in Athens in the fifth century BCE, had a long history of dramatic performances. Theaters have been discovered throughout the Greek colonies of the Mediterranean world and are one of the most ubiquitous buildings in the Greek cities of the Near East. The Greeks are also famously known for the celebration of games – the Olympic Games are obviously the most famous, and many of the city states of Greece and Near East had stadiums (from a Greek word indicating length – the *stadion*) for games, especially footraces. Later, these developed into horse or chariot racing centers known as hippodromes (Greek) or circuses (Latin). In addition, the two most common buildings connected with Roman influence are both entertainment facilities: large public baths and amphitheaters.

Theaters are quite common throughout the Near East, mostly in the so-called "Roman" form, which indicates a freestanding theater with rows of seats placed on man-made architectural supports, such as the South Theater at Gerasa (Figure 2.28).

*Urban planning in the Near East* 47

*Figure 2.28* View of the scaenae frons and orchestra of the South Theater at Gerasa (Photo by author).

The "Greek" style instead consists of rows of seats cut into natural hills. The best example of such a "Greek" theater is in Petra, where the rock itself was carved into seating (Figure 2.29).

The "Roman theater" in Philadelphia (modern Amman) combines elements of a "Greek" style theater as it is too built into a mountainside, but Roman elements are also clear because the hill was not ideally suited for a theater and the structure required additional structural supports.

The elements of a theater are as follows (Figure 2.30):

The backdrop is called the *scaenae frons* and was typically richly decorated with both columns and statues. The *scaenae frons* from Palmyra, for example, had a large center alcove complete with columns and a pediment flanked by twelve Corinthian columns on each side with additional alcoves. The stage was elevated above the *orchestra*, which was a semi-circular open plaza between the seats and the stage. The technical term for the seating is *cavea*.

A separate type of structure is a smaller theater called an odeum or odeon (*oideion* in Greek). Instead of seating for thousands, these theaters were often intended for audiences in the hundreds. The word itself indicates that it was intended for musical performances (an ode in Greek is a song), but these structures could have been used for any type of small gatherings. It is often thought that town councils, for example, met in these buildings. In the wider Mediterranean world, either the entire structure or sometimes

*Figure 2.29* The theater at Petra (Photo by Carole Raddato).

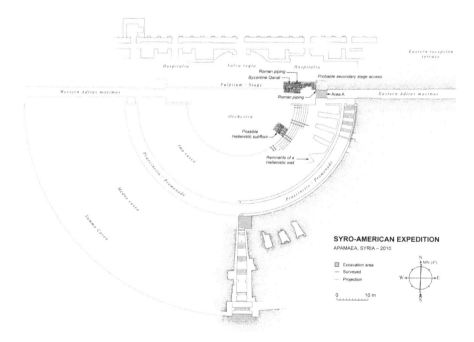

*Figure 2.30* Plan of the theater of Apamea with architectural features labeled (Map by Scott Ure, courtesy of the BYU American Expedition to Apamea).

just the stage was covered with a roof. The North Theater at Gerasa is an excellent example, which originally seated just eight hundred spectators (Figure 2.31).

In the first century BCE and first century CE, the distinction between theaters, amphitheaters, stadiums, and hippodromes was blurred. It seems that all of these types of structures could be used for interchangeable functions and that the major distinction between them appears in the late first century CE, to be codified in the second century CE. The classic example of a multi-use structure is the so-called Herodian hippodrome at Caesarea (Figure 2.32).

Josephus describes this structure, which was located on the sea shore, as a hippodrome, even though in size it lies between a Greek-style stadium (used for footraces) and the Roman-style circus (used for chariot racing). It was clearly used for the Herod's games that inaugurated the city, which included gladiator fights in addition to chariot races.

Several hippodromes have been excavated in the Near East, including the ones at Caesarea, Gerasa, and Scythopolis. It was common for one end of the hippodrome to be semi-circular, with the other end rectangular. This rectangular end held the starting gates for the horses or chariots, which are called *carceres* (Figure 2.33).

It was typical of hippodromes to have a central spine (called a *spina*) to separate the traffic and encourage racing around the course.

In contrast to the number of theaters and hippodromes in the Near East, there are few amphitheaters, perhaps suggesting that gladiatorial fights and

*Figure 2.31* The North Theater or odeum at Gerasa (Photo by author).

*Figure 2.32* The hippodrome at Caesarea (Photo by Carole Raddato).

*Figure 2.33* The *carcares* (starting gates) at Gerasa (Photo by author).

*Figure 2.34* Interior of the Coliseum in Rome (Photo by author).

beast hunts were not very popular in the Near East, or alternatively, these games took place in multi-purpose buildings. It perhaps conveys, however, that amphitheaters are generally associated with cities with a strong Roman presence, like Caesarea. No amphitheater is as famous as the Coliseum in Rome, inaugurated in 80 CE and paid for using the loot from crushing the Jewish revolt, but it is much larger and grander than those found in the eastern Mediterranean (Figure 2.34).

It should be noted that the name, amphitheater, means "two theaters" as it was designed as two theaters that were placed back-to-back, with the stage and *scaenae frons* removed. The orchestra, thus, became the arena, which means "sand" in Greek because that was used to soak up the blood. Thus, the ancient amphitheater is quite different from the modern usage of the term, which is used for any outdoor venue.

Unlike amphitheaters, which never caught on the Near East, baths spread like wildfire. Cities like Antioch could have multiple baths that were constructed over many centuries. Some could be very large, for public use, whereas others were quite small and reserved for use by individual families or government officials. Baths were used for many different activities, from actual bathing to intellectual activities (in Rome baths often had libraries attached to them). One could acquire the services

52  *Urban planning in the Near East*

of doctors, lawyers, and prostitutes. It was common for bathers to rub themselves with olive oil and then scrape it off. Baths often also had exercise areas.

Baths did not have a standard plan, though they typically had similar types of rooms. Bathers would typically start in the *apodyterium* or changing room (Figure 2.35).

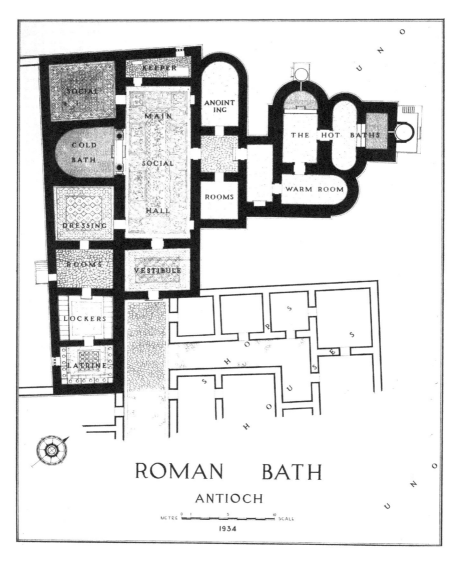

*Figure 2.35* Plan of the "Roman Bath" at Antioch (Antioch Expedition Archives, Department of Art and Archaeology, Princeton University, Photo 1582).

They often then moved into the *caldarium*, or hot room, which had a pool heated by the burning of fires. An optional room was the *tepidarium* or warm room that might or might not have a pool. Hypocaust tiles (stacks of ceramic tiles that held the pool or floor) are the most common indicator of a *caldarium* or *tepidarium*. Bathers would often finish in the *frigidarium* or cold pool.

## *Houses and palaces*

Until recently, excavations and publications focused on elite dwellings. We are well informed about elite houses from Antioch, Apamea, Petra, and Gerasa, for example. Almost all of the housing types and decoration in these cities were influenced by Greco-Roman standards. Most of the houses from Antioch were discovered in the wealthy suburb of Daphne. Because excavation concentrated on uncovering beautiful mosaics, the plans of these houses are difficult to discern. At Apamea, the houses are contained in the Hippodamian plan. There are two major types. First, the Axial plan with the example of the Maison aux consoles. It contained rooms surrounding a large Corinthian peristyle court with a possible second story. The second type is the radiating plan represented by the Maison aux pilasters, which is characterized by a large court in east of the house and a peristyle courtyard in the middle of the East-West and North-South axis. At Palmyra, elite houses are decorated with Greco-Roman motifs. Two examples are the House of Achilles with large peristyle court and smaller one for the women's quarters and the House of Cassiopeia which lacks a peristyle court. At Petra, the houses of Ez-Zantur show knowledge of Greco-Roman features such as Corinthian peristyle courtyards and are often painted in the second Pompeian style. Two palaces have been excavated from Caesarea, one which is thought to have been Herod's and another which was the home of the governor of the province in late antiquity. These correspond closely in plan and decoration to the domestic complexes at Apamea, Palmyra, and Antioch and will be examined in more detail in that chapter. Because non-elite dwellings follow no standard form, they will be covered in the cities in which they were discovered.

## Conclusion

This discussion covers just the major structures that were common in cities of the Near East, but other buildings could also be found. As with the non-elite dwellings, I have chosen to treat those structures in their urban context. In each of the following chapters, I take two cities from similar geographical or cultural environments and compare and contrast their evolution, beginning with two of the four cities of the Tetrapolis – Antioch and Apamea.

## Suggestions for further reading

Ball, W. *Rome in the East* (Routledge 2001, second edition 2016), 246–396.
Burns, R. *Origins of the Colonnaded Streets in the Cities of the Roman East* (Oxford 2017).
Butcher, K. *Roman Syria and the Near East* (Getty 2004), 237–269, 352–370.
Gates, C. *Ancient Cities* (Routledge 2011).
Retzleff, A. "Near Eastern Theatres in Late Antiquity." *Phoenix*, 57(1/2), 2003, 115–138.
Segal, A. *From Function to Monument: Urban Landscapes of Roman Palestine, Syria, and Provincia Arabia* (Oxbow 1997).
Zuiderhoek, A. *The Ancient City* (Cambridge 2016).

# 3 The Tetrapolis (Antioch and Apamea)

In early 363 CE, the emperor Julian [361–363] composed a work titled the *Misopogon* (*The Beard Haters*) and had it published on a tetrapylon outside his palace in Antioch. Julian had come to Antioch in order to prepare for an invasion of the Persian Empire, and while at Antioch, he antagonized the Christian population by favoring pagans. The people of Antioch mocked him tremendously for his shaggy beard and unkempt appearance, which was the traditional hairstyle of a pagan philosopher. In return, he attacked the people of Antioch, accused them of being impious to the traditional gods, and described them as lazy, effeminate drunkards too enamored with entertainments to be productive. He claimed that the reason for their behavior was that the city was tainted by the actions of their founder, Antiochus I, who (in)famously married his stepmother and fathered five children with her. As we will see below, the city was not in fact founded by Antiochus, but it does indicate that the city and outsiders were aware of its historical connection with the Seleucid dynasty.

Julian, unlike his immediate predecessors and all subsequent emperors, was pagan and vehemently anti-Christian and hence his later nickname "the Apostate." During his reign, he attempted to restore the vitality of the older, pagan traditions of the empire, and to limit the growth of Christianity. For example, he passed laws to forbid Christian teachers from using classical texts for education. As these classical texts were the root of ancient rhetorical practice, this action would have cost Christian teachers most of their students. It was also known at the time that he did not punish pagan mobs who attacked Christians in Alexandria and that he wanted to rebuild the Jewish temple in Jerusalem as a general snub to Christians. As one can imagine, he was a ruler hated incredibly by his Christian subjects and has remained a controversial figure in modern scholarship.

A large portion of the population of Antioch in the mid- to late fourth century was Christian (as we read in the speeches of John Chrysostom), but there was still a very large and vibrant pagan community. Its most well-known member was the rhetorician Libanius [d. 393/4], who wrote dozens of speeches and hundreds of letters that still exist today. Most importantly, he composed an entire speech dedicated to how great the city of Antioch was (*Oration* 11). Through Libanius, we can see both the built environment of the city and its changing nature in the late fourth century. He complains about increased imperial control over civic functions previously controlled by upper-class citizens like himself, and in his speech *on temples*, he describes how Christians were responsible for damaging the livability of the city by destroying pagan buildings.

From Julian, John Chrysostom, and Libanius, we get a picture of fourth century Antioch that we are denied elsewhere because of a lack of good sources. We don't have to accept Julian's characterization of the people of Antioch as effeminate, drunken hordes who were only interested in watching low-brow comedies, provocative dances, and chariot races (though Christian writers would echo his condemnations), but these sources provide at least a couple of ways to interpret the life of the city. In addition to these works, Antioch was the focus of the sixth century writer John Malalas, whose work includes information about the buildings of the city. These literary sources are important, because Antioch, unlike many of the other cities discussed in this book, has proven difficult to excavate because the modern city of Antakaya and dozens of feet of silt and debris cover the ancient ruins. Large scale excavations occurred from 1932 to 1939 at sites in Antioch proper and the suburb of Daphne where richly decorated mosaic floors were discovered in large numbers. Because of World War II, the excavations were cancelled, records and artifacts were destroyed, and the publication of the archaeological reports was delayed. Scholars are now returning to the original reports and reexamining them in light of our current knowledge of archaeology in the region (Figures 3.1 and 3.2).

*Figure 3.1* A nine-meter-deep trench from the excavation of Antioch in 1936 in the cavea of the Hellenistic Theater (Antioch Expedition Archives, Department of Art and Archaeology, Princeton University, Photo 2647).

*Figure 3.2* Photograph of the House of the Buffet Supper, an example of the mosaics discovered in Antioch and Daphne (Antioch Expedition Archives, Department of Art and Archaeology, Princeton University, Photo 3146).

Early modern visitors to Antakaya were dismayed by the poor quality of the contemporary city and lack of visible ancient remains, for Antioch had been the most important city in the Near East for centuries. Founded by one of Alexander's successors, the general Seleucus, at the turn of the third century BCE, it was the capital of the powerful Seleucid empire before becoming the main administrative center in the Near East under the Romans. Emperors and their families routinely visited and lived at Antioch. Many, like Julian, used Antioch as a base to prepare invasions or defensive actions against the empires of the east – first the Parthians, and then later the Persians under the Sassanid dynasty.

The city was also important for religious history. Antioch was the city were the word "Christian" was coined and home of one of the four original Patriarchs in the church hierarchy. One of the most important early churches, Constantine's octagonal "Golden House" was there, as was the tomb of one of the most famous early Christian monks – Symeon the Stylite, so named for the thirty years that he stood on a pillar outside of Antioch. Yet, it also experienced its share of disasters, such as floods, earthquakes, plagues, and conquests, which heavily damaged the city in the late sixth century (Figure 3.3).

Antioch is located about 15 km up the Orontes River from the Mediterranean coast (hence, the name Antioch-on-the-Orontes to distinguish it from

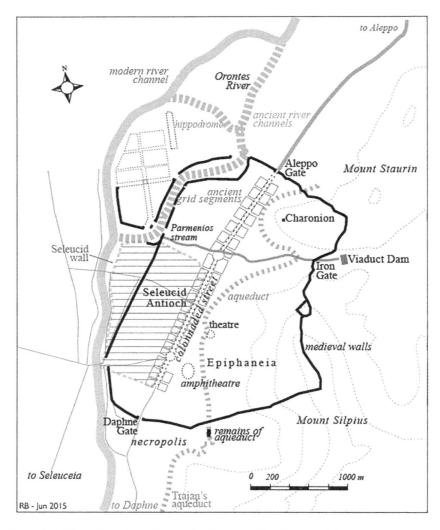

*Figure 3.3* Plan of Antioch (Burns, R. *Origins of the Colonnaded Streets in the Cities of the Roman East*. [Oxford 2017], Figure 6.06).

other cities named Antioch). The Orontes was navigable up to Antioch from the sea, where Seleucus founded a port city (Seleucia Pieria). Seleucus placed Antioch on a small plain wedged between the eastern bank of the Orontes and two mountain ridges – Mount Silpius and Mount Staurin. After a slight incline, the mountain ranges become steep on the Orontes side, limiting the growth of the city to the lower slopes. The other side of the mountains was relatively gentle, posing a defensive problem for the city, which the Persians exploited in the third and sixth centuries CE. A wadi, named the Parmenios, runs between these two mountain ranges and through the center of Roman Antioch down to the Orontes River. In the Seleucid period, it was covered with arches that supported the later Roman Forum of Valens. Despite this, it periodically flooded, eventually leading to the construction of a dam called the "Iron Gate" in the sixth century. In antiquity, the Orontes River split to form an island just north of the city of Seleucus which became the administrative and monumental heart of the city in the Roman period.

A few kilometers south of the city was the famous suburb called Daphne, which lies on a plateau at higher elevation than Antioch. Daphne was a beautiful location with several flowing springs, copses of trees, a view of the Orontes River, and cooling breezes. It was famous for its temple to Apollo for it took its name from the myth of Daphne who was turned into a laurel tree to save her from Apollo. Local legends argued that Daphne was also the site of the Judgment of Paris. Land there was limited so it became the haunting grounds of the rich and famous of Antioch. Antioch was occasionally called "Antioch near Daphne" or "Antioch by Daphne" attesting to the overshadowing of Antioch in the minds of the rich and famous. The large houses and beautiful mosaics found in the archaeological excavations confirm the wealth of the suburb.

The other city in this chapter, Apamea, did not share Antioch's illustrative history. It too was founded by Seleucus on the Orontes River. But, unlike Antioch, no modern city lies on top of the ruins of Apamea. It has been extensively excavated; the city plan, streets, and many of the major public buildings from the Roman period have been painstakingly revealed and reconstructed, providing much evidence of the evolution of the city that is lacking from Antioch. Only the earliest settlement, which was likely on the acropolis, is unknown, as it is covered by a Crusader period fortress called Qalaat al-Mundiq (Figure 3.4).

Apamea was the most important city for the defense of Syria under the Seleucids. The acropolis provided a high position to watch over the city and countryside. Apamea was placed on the plateau overlooking the main north-south route in Beqaa valley. The Orontes was located to the west of the city, where the ground was largely marshland (the Ghab valley) in the winter and spring. There was a crossing of the Orontes River just to the south of Apamea that led down to the Mediterranean through the Eleutheros gap. Directly to the east of the city was a large lake that provided ample water and fish. Agriculture is possible to the south of the city and along the Orontes River. Farther to the east of Apamea, however, the plateau rises gently in elevation and rainfall decreases. This terrain transitions to steppe land with ample pasturage. The pasturage was so good, in fact, that Seleucus made it his war-elephant and horse farm! The city was, therefore, strategically placed along several trade routes and was also an

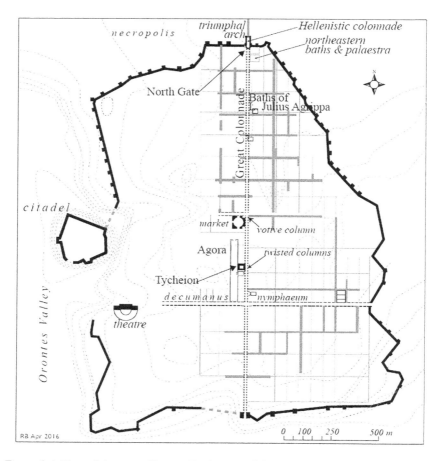

*Figure 3.4* Plan of Apamea (Burns, R. *Origins of the Colonnaded Streets in the Cities of the Roman East*. [Oxford 2017], Figure 9.01).

excellent location for mediating commerce between nomadic peoples and the Seleucids (Figure 3.5).

In antiquity, Antioch and Apamea were considered cities of the Tetrapolis ("four cities" in Greek). We have already encountered the first of these – Seleucia Pieria – which was located at the mouth of the Orontes on the coast of the Mediterranean. The fourth was Laodicea ad Mare (Laodicea on the Sea, modern Latakia in Syria), a major rival to Antioch, especially in the third century CE. Each city was named after a member of Seleucus' family – Seleucia after himself, Antioch after his son (or possibly father), Laodicea after his mother, and Apamea after his Bactrian wife. Although Seleucia Pieria was probably intended to be the main royal residence, Antioch became the preferred residence after the first century of Seleucid rule. Antioch,

*Figure 3.5* The lake of Apamea in the distance, with the House of the Consoles in the foreground (Photo by Greg Fisher).

though not a port or military base, was strategically placed along the routes that led to all parts of the Seleucid realm. It was, therefore, important for transferring troops and supplies, which could be stored at Antioch and then moved to where they were needed. Apamea's military role has already been described.

The cities of the Tetrapolis were intended to act as colonies of Greco-Macedonians to dominate the northwestern Syrian countryside, and each of them served as the center of administration for the four original satrapies (provinces) of northern Syria. These colonies included two sea ports and two inland cities and were settled by veterans and mercenaries, including Macedonians and Greeks from the Aegean and local Syrians. Survey archaeology has revealed a tremendous growth of small settlements in this period, and it is believed that these represent the settlement of veterans on small plots of land. Intended as showpieces of Hellenistic culture, these sister-cities provided a Greek foundation for the Seleucid monarchy. In this way, they functioned much like the cities of the Decapolis in southern Syria, as described in Chapter 5.

## The Hellenistic period

Little is known about the archaeology of Antioch and Apamea for the first three centuries of their existence. Antioch is mentioned in dozens of sources and Apamea in only a few. The destruction and rebuilding of Apamea in the second century CE means that few Hellenistic period remains were discovered.

## *Antioch*

Seleucus founded Antioch as his capital after testing out two other sites in the area (one of which was Seleucia Pieria). According to the sixth century CE author Malalas, there were several Greek settlements in the immediate area of Antioch before Seleucus founded the city. One was a small town named Bottia and another was dedicated to Io. According to Libanius (late fourth century CE), Alexander the Great built a temple to Zeus at Bottia and a fortress on the top of Mount Silpius, and he intended to build a city there. Whether one can trust these traditions is unknown; by the late fourth century CE, Alexander had long become a mythological figure and many cities attempted to connect their founding to him (see for example, Gerasa in Chapter 5). One of Seleucus's rivals, Antigonus, had founded a capital city, Antigoneia, less than 10 km up the Orontes from the future site of Antioch (no remains survive, so this is an educated guess). The majority of the inhabitants of Antigoneia came from Athens, making the earliest population of Antioch largely Athenian in origin. The Tyche of the Antigoneia was moved to Antioch, probably in an attempt to make them feel at home in the new city. There were Greek settlements in the wider region before Alexander—for example, al-Mina-Sabouni at the mouth of the Orontes River. As archaeology has shown that the site was abandoned around 300 BCE, it seems likely that the population of these cities were also transferred to either Seleucia Pieria or Antioch.

Antioch was laid out on a Hippodamian plan that can still be seen in the modern city. The cardo of the ancient city is now the main street running north-south through Antakaya. This route does not run parallel to the river; rather, the street plan took into account the breeze which blew from the south and designed to maximize the shade in the summer and the sun in winter. It used Alexandria as its model, and the architect is recorded to have been a Greek named Xenarius. Seleucus was also credited with building the temple of Apollo at Daphne. It held a famous statue of Apollo, which was of similar size and quality to the statue of Zeus in Olympia, one of the Seven Wonders of the world.

The size of this original community appears small, likely less than a square mile. It seems to have covered the area between the Orontes to the southern part of the Roman-period *cardo*. There were two quarters, one for the Greco-Macedonians and another for the local Syrians, which included a large number of Jews. Both quarters were walled. The *agora* was likely located on the river shore, like the Forum Boarium at Rome, which would have allowed for the easy unloading of imports from the Mediterranean coast.

The city of Antioch grew in size and population as the Hellenistic period continued, despite the difficulties of the Seleucid rulers. They were forced out of their eastern provinces by the Parthians, lost Seleucia Pieria for decades and Antioch from 246 to 244 to the Ptolemies, gave up large portions of Anatolia, and were crushed by the Romans in 190 BCE. Yet, the city continued to grow and the rulers continued to build there. By the reign of Antiochus III [223–187 BCE], there was a library in Antioch modeled on the famous libraries in Pergamum and Alexandria. It was likely under Antiochus III that the island was settled, with the palace of the Seleucid rulers being the most important building there. By 195 BCE, there was a stadium at Daphne where games to Olympian Zeus were celebrated. In his reign also, the high priest of Jerusalem, Onias III, constructed a synagogue in Daphne.

In the time of Antiochus IV Epiphanes [175–164 BCE], the settlement expanded to the east to form a new neighborhood named Epiphaneia, which doubled the size of the city. A new *agora* was added, bringing Antioch up to the standards of Miletus and Pergamum that already had two *agoras*. In this *agora*, Antiochus IV built a council chamber (*bouleuterion*) and a Temple to Jupiter Capitolinus (he had been a hostage at Rome, possibly explaining why he would build a temple to the chief Roman god). An aqueduct from the Parmenius was constructed to carry floodwaters down to cisterns for the new neighborhood. A theater built into the slope of Mount Silpius might date from this period, but it is first mentioned in literary sources in the time of Julius Caesar. Excavations under the House of the Calendar on the slope of Mount Staurin revealed large amounts of Hellenistic pottery and masonry, perhaps confirming the growth of the city to the slopes in this period. The road that previously marked the eastern boundary of the settlement became the main central city road and later was the monumental cardo in the Roman period. At this time, however, the road was unpaved, but gutters were added and shops built out of stone were constructed on both sides.

During the reign of Antiochus IV, the kingdom of Judea gained their independence. This began an even steeper decline in power. From 149 to 147 BCE, Antioch and Seleucia Pieria were independent of the Seleucid realm. Earthquakes hit the city in 148, 130, and 115 BCE. The power of the monarchy continued to decline, so that between 96 and 84 BCE, there were six different kings. Into this power vacuum stepped Tigranes of Armenia, who controlled the area from 83 to 69 BCE. The Romans defeated Tigranes (who was supporting "the poison king," Mithridates of Pontus) and then attempted to prop up the remnants of the Seleucid family as client kings, but this failed. In 64 BCE, the Roman general Pompey entered the city, ending Syria's independence and beginning the period of Roman direct rule over the Near East.

Little is known about the city and its population during these tumultuous times. A Museum with library was built in the *agora* at Epiphaneia sometime between 114 and 92 BCE (it burned down in 23/4 CE). In 67 BCE, the Roman governor of Cilicia built a palace and hippodrome (Hippodrome A) on the island to support the client king Philip II [67–65 BCE]. But, overall, the sources suggest that the city was in need of extensive renovation and repair at the end of the Hellenistic period.

## *Apamea*

When Seleucus founded Apamea, the region already was called "Pella" after the capital of the Macedonian Kingdom. This part of Syria must have reminded the Macedonians of their homeland because of the mountainous backdrop and wide meadows. Prior to Greek settlement, the area had been settled in the Persian and Egyptian periods. Another name for the site, "Pharnake," might suggest that the acropolis of Apamea was settled by Macedonian soldiers prior to Seleucus's foundation of Apamea. Alexander may have been responsible for the first Greco-Macedonian settlement at the site, but no remains of this community exist.

Apamea was the fourth city of the Tetrapolis to be founded by Seleucus. As it was in charge of the satrapy named Apamene and the satrapy was founded around 300 BCE, there is enough evidence to believe that the literary sources are correct that Apamea was founded by Seleucus around 300 BCE, even though the name Pella was sometimes used for a few decades after that.

The acropolis lies to the west of the planned town. This seems to have been a pattern in the Seleucid realm (other examples include Seleucia Pieria and Kyrrhos), where the acropolis is situated near the city, but not within the city (as in ancient Athens). This suggests that the acropolis was intended as a primarily military stronghold to watch over the city. Unfortunately, because the acropolis is covered with the Crusader fortress, that assumption cannot be tested. Some scholars have argued that the original settlement was on the acropolis, and that the city below was not inhabited until a hundred years later. Some confirmation of this idea may come from the fact that excavation of the northern city wall dated to the end of the second century BCE or beginning of the first century BCE.

Apamea's role as a military town declined substantially when Antiochus III [222–187 BCE] conquered Phoenicia and Palestine from the Ptolemaic Kingdom in 198 BCE. The frontier shifted so significantly southward at this time that a military base at Apamea made no strategic sense, though the horse and elephant farms likely continued. It is thought that the city may have declined in population once the military headquarters and troops were moved, as the support personnel and anyone who provided services to the soldiers (like cooks and prostitutes) would have followed them to their bases in the south.

From this point, Apamea is only occasionally mentioned in the historical records which record the various civil wars during the collapse of Seleucid power. Apamea is recorded as supporting both kings and pretenders during this time. In this chaos, a former village dependent on Apamea, Larissa, broke away and even fought a war against Apamea, likely in the 140s BCE. At the beginning of the first century BCE, Antiochus VIII Grypos [125–96 BCE] built a fortress at Apamea, probably on the acropolis. The fortress lasted until Pompey's conquest of Syria when one of his generals destroyed it. This fortress marked some revival of Apamea as it was restored to a strategic military site in the wars versus usurpers, local tyrants, and the independent Hasmonean kingdom.

Some limited archaeological evidence of the Hellenistic period has been discovered just north of the north gate. Archaeologists discovered an 80 m long forecourt attached to a stoa. As this was aligned with the later colonnaded street, it was suggested that it could be evidence of a very early colonnaded street at Apamea. There is a problem with this theory because excavations across the street did not discover a corresponding set of columns or stoa. However, this could possibly be explained by a sixth century earthquake and subsequent rebuilding.

During the 2008–2010 excavations of the Roman Theater, archaeologists discovered evidence that suggests that there was a theater in the Hellenistic period on the same site. Excavation under the paved orchestra revealed that there had been a previous use of the site. The excavators suggest that evidence of drains indicates a Hellenistic-period theater.

It was also discovered that the expansion of the Roman-period theater to the south was constructed on top of a Hellenistic residential area. Although the excavated area was limited, this evidence suggests that the city of Apamea had roughly the same footprint as the second-century monumental Roman-period city, for both excavations in the northern and southern parts of the city indicate Hellenistic occupation, and limited excavation of the city wall indicated a Hellenistic date. All evidence suggests that the later Roman city followed the city plan from the Hellenistic period.

## The Roman period

Having defeated Mithridates of Pontus, the Roman general Pompey turned his attention to Syria. In 64 BCE, he entered Antioch, removed Antiochus XIII from power, and granted Antioch and other Syrian cities *libertas*. This was not freedom from Roman control but instead autonomy to manage civic affairs through a town council. Antioch became the residence of the governor of the province of Syria, who was also responsible for administering the cities of the Decapolis (discussed in the next chapter) and guarding the frontier with Parthia.

The invasion of the Parthians in 51 BCE following the disastrous invasion by Marcus Licinius Crassus in 54 BCE and the capture of Antioch by the Parthians in 41 BCE caused major disruption in Syria that wasn't corrected until after the conclusion of the civil war between Mark Antony, Cleopatra, and Octavian. After this, the entire Near East benefited from over 200 years of relative peace during the *Pax Romana*. Population levels rose, more land came under cultivation, cities competed amongst themselves for honor and prestige, and trade flourished. An earthquake in the early second century destroyed both Antioch and Apamea, but subsequent rebuilding created the model for monumental cities in the Near East. Both cities prospered until the mid-third century when the problems of the "Third Century Crisis" heavily impacted Syria.

## *Antioch*

The final decades of Seleucid rule over Antioch, earthquakes, and the conflicts between Seleucids, Romans, Armenians, and Parthians suggest that Antioch was in sad shape after Octavian united the Mediterranean world. This was despite the efforts of the Romans to improve the city when they could. Julius Caesar, for example, visited Antioch in 47 BCE while heading north to attack Pharnaces, king of Pontus (this was his famous *veni, vidi, vici* campaign). Caesar's most famous building in Antioch was the first basilica in the east called the Kaisarion, which was built opposite a temple to Ares close to the Wadi Parmenius. Caesar was also credited with rebuilding a Pantheon (temple to all the gods), an amphitheater, an aqueduct, and a public bathhouse. As mentioned above, the theater built into Mount Silpius is credited to Julius Caesar, but it may be dated earlier. The theater was enlarged during the reigns of Tiberius and Trajan, suggesting a large appetite for theatrical performances in the city. The amphitheater is likely the oldest in the Near East.

The real work of improving the city came after Octavian's defeat of Mark Antony and Cleopatra in 31 BCE. Augustus (as he was known after 27 BCE), his general Agrippa, and the client king of Judea, Herod, all visited Antioch and were responsible for new constructions in the city. Agrippa built two new baths in the city, added new seats to a theater, and renovated the hippodrome, which had been built in 67 BCE. A new suburb of the city was named after him. Augustus inaugurated games, which under Claudius became known as Olympic Games, and which were held every five years.

According to Josephus, at this time, the main street (cardo) at Antioch turned to mud during rainstorms. Apparently, water swept down the mountains and turned the street into a rushing torrent that left behind large amounts of silt and debris (this continued to happen after antiquity, which caused the deep layers of sediment found during the excavations). Josephus credits Herod with both paving the cardo with polished marble and placing columns on each side of the street to create stoas (*Jewish War* 1.21.11; *Antiquities* 16.5.3). The paving improved the road's drainage and helped prevent the accumulation of silt. Malalas, on the other hand, says that Herod was only responsible for the paving, whereas the colonnade was built by the emperor Tiberius [14–37 CE] (9.15, 10.23). Very soon after the initial construction, an earthquake knocked down portions of the colonnade, which were rebuilt during the reign of the emperor Claudius. Burns argues that the literary and archaeological evidence (described below) indicates that the first colonnaded street evolved over the course of decades and that Herod was not solely responsible for its invention. For the purpose of this study,

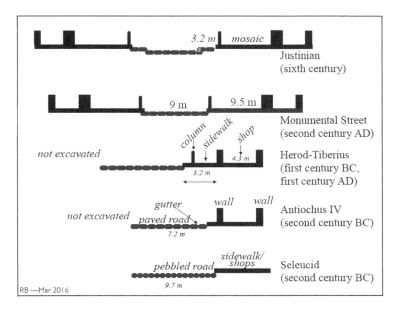

*Figure 3.6* Evolution of the Cardo at Antioch (Burns, R. *Origins of the Colonnaded Streets in the Cities of the Roman East*. [Oxford 2017], Figure 6.07).

the important factor is that this was the first colonnaded street in the Mediterranean world (Figure 3.6).

In addition to the first colonnades along the cardo, Tiberius is credited with several other public works. It is said that he had tetrapylons built at the intersection of the cardo and other streets, showing his interest in beautifying the street plan. He built a gate decorated with the she-wolf and Romulus and Remus and another public bath. According to Malalas, the people of Antioch celebrated Tiberius with the erection of a statue on a column in a plaza in the center of town, possibly at the point where the road bends slightly. A similar plaza can be seen today at Gerasa. During his reign, a fire burned the agora in Epiphaneia, destroying the *bouleuterion* and Museum.

At the end of the Jewish War, there was another fire in Antioch, which is said to have destroyed the "tetragonal agora" which contained record offices and a basilica. Presumably, these structures were rebuilt, but their location is unknown. At this same time, Titus constructed a theater at Daphne which was paid for by plunder from the Jewish War.

While Trajan was at Antioch in 115 CE, he fled the imperial palace to take shelter in the nearby hippodrome during an earthquake. Much of the city was heavily damaged. For example, the debris from this earthquake resulted in a three-meter increase between the earlier Herodian-Tiberian street level and the new second-century one. Because of this damage, the earthquake of 115 gave Trajan and Hadrian, governor of Syria and successor to the throne in 117, the unprecedented opportunity to rebuild the city of Antioch in a new and grandiose style. One of the first tasks was to rebuild the streets and colonnades with a uniform, monumental vision. The remains of this second-century street largely obscured the earlier ones, making it virtually impossible to ascertain the exact date or configuration of the Herodian-Tiberian cardo. The paving, colonnade, and shops were all completely built anew, and gutters were added under the roofed colonnade. In this phase, the street was widened to approximately 9 m with the sidewalks on both sides being 9.5 m. Greyish and pink granite from Egypt was imported for the project. The project was executed with imperial funds, possibly over a twenty-year period and required approximately 1,400 columns to complete. Even though the earlier cardo was colonnaded and some other cities had developed colonnaded streets (for example, at Gerasa), this was the first true "monumental" colonnaded axis in the Near East. According to Burns, "the new colonnaded axis [at Antioch] became the benchmark against which all other street regeneration projects in the future were to be measured" (212). The work carried out by Trajan and Hadrian on the colonnaded street was intended to survive earthquakes, with massive stone blocks and heavy-duty columns. This seems to have worked because this colonnade survived until the sixth century largely intact.

In addition to the work done to recreate the colonnaded street, much reconstruction work is recorded from this time period in the literary sources, including the Middle Gate, a monumental arch near the Kaisarion, the restoration of a theater, and a temple to Artemis at Daphne. Trajan and/or Hadrian added another aqueduct. Hadrian also had a nymphaeum built at Daphne with an attached temple to the Nymphs.

Little is known about the island during the Roman period. Presumably, the Roman governors and visiting imperial family members continued to use the Seleucid royal palace (like Trajan). A hippodrome was nearby, probably Hippodrome A. The island may have attracted wealthy landowners because the famous Atrium House was discovered there dated to the second century. This house became world famous for its mosaics, including the Judgment of Paris on display at the Louvre and the Drinking Contest of Hercules.

In the late second century, Antioch backed two losers in civil wars. In 175 CE, Antioch supported the claim of Avidius Cassius against Marcus Aurelius. In punishment, the Olympic Games were banned. The people of Antioch later begged Commodus to restore the games, which he did, and new facilities were constructed for these games, including one called the Xystos, which was a covered racetrack near the Kaisarion. Nearby, Commodus constructed a Temple to Olympian Zeus, a public bath (the Commodion), and restored a temple to Athena. In 193, a building was added for wrestling tournaments called the Plethrion. This building appears to have consisted of a square orchestra with rows of seating on the four sides (originally two rows in stone) that limited attendance to the wealthy.

Then, in 192, Antioch supported Pescennius Niger against Septimius Severus. Antioch's rival, Laodicea, supported Severus. When Septimius Severus won, he punished Antioch by naming it a "village" under the control of Laodicea, which he made the capital of Syria and moved the Olympic Games to Issus. These punishments didn't last long, because within a decade, Septimius Severus and his family stayed at Antioch and built two new public baths, and his son Caracalla restored Antioch to city status, improving it with the title *colonia* and allowing the Olympic Games to return.

Antioch was tremendously impacted by the Third Century Crisis of the Roman Empire. In 253, the first ruler Sassanid of the Persian Empire, Shapur [240–270], conquered Antioch and deported hundreds (perhaps thousands) of captives to Persia, where he put them to work constructing Greek-style monuments in his honor. The Roman Emperor Valerian quickly recaptured the city and began the construction of a fortress on the island, which later became the basis of Diocletian's palace there. In 260, the Persians recaptured Antioch, deporting more people of Antioch and settling them in a new city named "Shapur's Better-than-Antioch!" Antioch then came under control of the Palmyrenes who, at first, cooperated with the Roman Emperor Gallienus [260–268] but later decided to break away from the empire. When the new Roman Emperor Aurelian [270–275] marched into Asia Minor to attack the Palmyrenes, who were now under the control of Zenobia, she based her army at Antioch. Aurelian won a spectacular victory, and the city surrendered quickly and was not looted.

These details are gleamed from literary sources, which suggest that the city suffered much throughout the third century. The actual impact of these disasters on the city itself is unknown, but the city plan appears to have changed little this period.

## *Apamea*

Tigranes of Armenia granted the city of Apamea the title *asylos* and maintained the fortress there. In contrast, Pompey granted the city autonomy and destroyed the fortress. This seems to have guaranteed the freedom of the city, for no longer could a leader occupy the acropolis and threaten the city. During the Roman civil wars, the city supported Q. Caecilius Bassus against Julius Caesar. It is unknown to what extent the chaos of that period impacted the city, but it remained a peaceful member of the province of Syria after Octavian's unification of the Mediterranean world.

According to an inscription of a Roman census in 6 CE, Apamea had 117,000 *homines civium* (literally, "male citizens"). What this means is unclear. Is this total population or literally just male citizens? Based on this number, figures ranging from 117,000 to 500,000 people have been suggested for the population of the city. Half a million is clearly too high, but by how much? Even 117,000 appears to be too high for just the city itself, so this number must include the population of dependent villages and country dwellers. As one can see, even when we get precise numbers from ancient sources, there can still be difficulties in interpretation.

The Romans adopted Apamea as a military arsenal, especially for the training of cavalry troops. They recognized, as the Seleucids earlier, that the access to water and wide pasturage allowed for the raising of large number of horses and provided ample space for military exercises. Approximately, ten legions and several cavalry divisions are known to have trained at Apamea in the second and third centuries CE. Apamea was also well positioned as a military reserve for the Euphrates frontier, where the Romans faced the Parthians and later the Sassanid Persians. It lays only three to five days' march from the Mediterranean and only a couple of weeks' march to the Euphrates. Troops could, therefore, easily be brought to the Near East, allowed to rest with ample food and comfort, and then quickly marched to the Euphrates to deal with Persian invasions or for offensive actions as occurred in the reigns of Trajan, Septimius Severus, and Valerian. The importance of the military to the city and the size of the forces serving there created an increased demand for agricultural and commercial products and entertainment.

Agriculture, fishing, and providing services to the Roman military were not the only reasons for the growth of Apamea during the Roman period. In addition to these features, we would consider Apamea a "university town." It was renowned for the teachers of philosophy who frequented the city, including Numenius [late second century CE] and Iamblichus [d. 325], who were instrumental in founding the philosophical school of Neoplatonism. The Emperor Julian famously believed that Iamblichus was only slightly inferior to Plato. The Temple of Zeus with its oracle also provided inspiration for these Neoplatonists. Teachers of Stocism and Epicuranism also competed for students there. Christians in the area took classes with these teachers. A mosaic from the fourth century that was discovered under the eastern Cathedral depicted Socrates with his students, perhaps in recognition of the importance of the philosophical schools in the city.

Understanding the city plan of Apamea before the second century CE is impossible, because, like Antioch, Apamea was devastated by the 115 CE earthquake. And, also like Antioch, this catastrophe was seen as an opportunity to radically monumentalize the city. The newly rebuilt streets of Apamea obscure the prior city plan, but excavation of part of the *decumanus maximus* suggests that it follows a previous street. This first-century CE street may have been paved with blocks with gutters and a sidewalk for foot traffic. No evidence was found of colonnades nor of an earlier Hellenistic street. Recent excavations revealed an expansion of the Hellenistic-period theater that occurred around the beginning of the first century CE. This altered the entrances to the theater and converted it into a Roman-style one. It was heavily damaged in the 115 CE earthquake.

While the imperial government poured resources into the rebuilding of Antioch, the renovations at Apamea were built largely through the involvement of local elites. An example of this is the bathhouse built by Lucius Julius Agrippa in 116 CE about 400 m south of the north gate. An inscription attests that he personally paid for the land, the construction costs of the baths, an internal basilica, and a frontal portico (another inscription mentions he built an aqueduct to supply water to the baths).

Despite the local involvement in the repairs, Antioch provided the model for the monumentalization of the city. The best example of this influence is the cardo, which was built on an even grander scale than at Antioch. It was the longest (nearly 2 km) and widest (35 m) in the entire Near East (Figures 3.7 and 3.8).

There is ample evidence of the shops which were constructed behind the sidewalks, some of which survive up to two stories in height. The walls of the shops revealed extensive fresco decorations in very bright colors. Some of these decorations had crosses on them, indicating that those sections were painted later. It is likely that some of the frescos would have dated to the time of the second-century street, and they would have been periodically updated or restored when repairs happened to the walls or when they had faded. The sidewalks under the porticos were paved with mosaics. Topography was not a problem at the site, which was laid out on a relatively level plain. The axis itself is almost perfectly straight and barely deviates from true north-south.

*Figure 3.7* The cardo at Apamea, with a votive column (Photo by Greg Fisher).

*Figure 3.8* Remains of the shops behind the colonnaded street (Photo by Greg Fisher).

Inscriptions attest that the northern colonnade was completed during the reign of Hadrian. The central section of the street (which runs in front of the *agora*) was completed in the middle of the second century. The most southern portion of the street was completed by the end of the second century CE, and at the same time, the theater, the largest in Syria, was finished. A small nymphaeum was located right inside the northern gate and a larger one near the center of the town.

Even a cursory glance of the city plan of Apamea reveals that it was laid out with virtual unflinching dedication to a Hippodamian city plan. There is almost no deviation in the path of streets. Insulae are almost completely uniform in size with single and double insulae used throughout the city plan. The plan conforms to the ideal in that the center of the city is occupied by an open public courtyard. This agora (dated to 139 CE by an inscription) is bounded on the east side by the cardo maximus and the south side by the decumanus maximus. It is unique in the Near East in that it is much longer from north to south (300 m) than east-west (45 m). Access to the *agora* was through two stoas. Just to the north of these stoas, there was a temple dedicated to the goddess Tyche called the Tycheion. The temple was erected on a Roman-style podium so it would have overlooked the agora. It consists of a hall with three naves that would have been covered with an arched roof. Several spiral-fluted columns along the cardo marked the location of the Tycheion. Three spiral-fluted columns stood in front of the east entrance to the agora. Dated to 166 CE, they supported bronze statues of Antoninus Pius, Marcus Aurelius, and Lucius Verus. Two local citizens paid for these columns.

Opposite the southern end of the agora stood a small nymphaeum on the eastern side of the Cardo Maximus just 50 km north of the most important intersection in the city. It too was constructed towards the end of the second century CE. The nymphaeum differs from many in the Near East because it is horseshoe in shape – it is deeper than it is wide. The structure was two stories high, covered with a semi-dome made of concrete. There were dozens of niches, each with a statue of a god or goddess including representations of Hygeia, Asclepius, Athena, and Heracles. A latrine was discovered just behind the nymphaeum. A ramp provided access to the latrine from the nymphaeum. This arrangement allowed one canal to supply water to both installations.

There was a famous Temple to Zeus Belos at Apamea located directly in the center of the town just north of the *agora*. This was an oracular temple, which was consulted by Cleopatra and at least three emperors in the second and third centuries CE (Hadrian, Septimius Severus, and Macrinus) and was visited by people from as far away as Gaul. According to the account of its destruction in 386 CE, the temple had a portico along the entire circumference of temple, which supported a second story (Theodoret, *History of the Church*, 5.21). The temple was so thoroughly destroyed that so far no remains of it have been discovered. It is possible that one of the extant churches was built on its location, but which one is unknown.

The theater was located on the western end of the main decumanus. It is extremely large and estimated to have been able to hold over 20,000 spectators. It is possible that the large numbers of soldiers who served or trained at Apamea meant that such a large theater was necessary. The theater is unique in the Near East, not only for its size but also for its plan, which is also unique and different from other Roman-period theaters of the Near East. See Figure 2.30.

While only portions of the theater have been excavated, it is clear that the theater could have been flooded for naval battles or religious festivals, such as the infamous Maiumas festival, celebrated at Daphne near Antioch and Gerasa. The orchestra was covered in cement and terracotta tiles, which were known by the Romans to be nearly waterproof. The back central entrance to the theater is very large compared with other theaters in the Near East. An access corridor through the *cavea* connects to a monumental street entrance on the south side. When the orchestra was flooded, it would have been impossible to use the regular entrances and exits between the *cavea* and the stage. This rear entrance was clearly added after the second-century construction and has been dated to the mid- to late third century when Apamea became much more important for the defense of the eastern frontier during the third-century crisis (that saw Antioch sacked by the Persians). Sections of the theater were paved with an orange-yellow marble flecked with a black and white serpentine matrix which was imported from Anatolia.

In addition, the theater seems to have been built on top of several large cisterns. As a part of the theater was built over a wadi that drained to the Orontes valley, these cisterns would collect the natural water flows from winter rains and snow melt that are still a problem at the site today (water erosion has heavily damaged the remains exposed during the 1930s excavation of the theater).

Two houses were discovered about 200 m west of the cardo at the second intersection from the northern gate. This suggests that the city conformed to the "ideal" with the public buildings located near the center of town and along the main streets and domestic complexes outside this public area. The House with the Bilobed Columns (Maison aux colonnes bilobées) had a beautiful geometric mosaic triclinium. It is dated to the second-half of the third century. The other house, House with the Trilobed columns (Maison aux colonnes trilobées) has a peristyle courtyard and triclinium paved in opus sectile.

Like Antioch, Apamea was also taken in 252 or 253 by Shapur. There is little information about the impact on the city at this time, but as a major headquarters and staging site for the Roman military, it would have been a strategic target prior to advancing on Antioch. It is unknown if large numbers of people from Apamea were deported as happened at Antioch, or if there was major damage to the city. The ramparts were repaired in several places using spolia from nearby buildings in the middle of the third century. But did this happen before or after the city was captured?

## Late antiquity

Although the emperor Aurelian gets credit for restoring Roman rule in the Near East, his assassination in 275 meant that his rule was too short for a real consolidation of power that occurred during the reign of Diocletian [284–305] and then Constantine [312–337], who both ruled long enough to stabilize imperial administration in the Near East. The fourth, fifth, and most of the sixth century saw increasing prosperity throughout Syria. New lands were placed under cultivation and the population exploded. This is evident from the founding and expansion of new communities located between Antioch, Apamea, and Aleppo, which are now known by the name "the Dead Cities." Christianity flourished in both the cities and the countryside. The mid-sixth century, however, brought increasing difficulties to Syria. Plague, earthquakes, and invasions heavily damaged both Antioch and Apamea. While there is very limited evidence from Antioch from the early Islamic period, archaeological excavations suggest that Apamea still had a large population into the tenth century.

### *Antioch*

Although it is impossible to know the extent of the damage to Antioch from the crises of the mid-third century, the evidence presented above suggests that the population of the city would have declined, wealth decreased, and the city's buildings damaged and neglected. Reconstruction began quickly after the eastern frontier was secured. Diocletian visited Antioch several times and was responsible for extensive construction in the city. His most famous building was the palace built on the island. Nothing has been excavated of this palace, but descriptions in sources like Libanius suggest that it was built in the style of a Roman military camp and served as the prototype for Diocletian's palace at Split. It was located near the hippodrome just south of the Orontes, and it was so large that it occupied almost a quarter of the island. The southern wall contained a second storey portico, so that the emperor could look out over the city. He also built two weapons factories, granaries, a mint, and five public baths. In Daphne, Diocletian restored the stadium. Either Diocletian or Constantine may be responsible for the restoration of Hippodrome A.

Just as Constantine built the first major churches in Rome and Jerusalem, he is credited with the ordering the construction of the Golden Church in 325, which was completed in 341. The remains of this church were not found, but it was described as octagonal with two-storey side aisles. The most impressive feature was a hemispherical dome gilded in gold, hence the name of the church. It was likely built near the imperial palace on the island and built on top of an abandoned bath complex, but some scholars have suggested that it was located inside the palace itself. The mosaic of the Megalopsychia suggests that the church stood in a plaza that was surrounded by a colonnade. Other sources mention that it was surrounded on four sides by *triclinia*.

In addition to the palace on the island, there were other administrative centers located throughout the city. The *comes Orientis* or Count of the East was an imperial official in charge of supervising the vicars of the Near East. The first *comes Orientis*, Rufinus, was given the Temple of the Muses in the agora in Epiphaneia for his headquarters. This suggests that the temple was no longer being used for religious rituals, a pattern seen elsewhere in the empire as old sacred structures could be repurposed for new functions. As the temples were often the most ornately decorated buildings in the city, repurposing them helped beautify the city and kept them from falling into disrepair. Located near the Temple of the Muses was a basilica called "of Rufinus" that Constantine also ordered to be constructed on the ruins of a shrine to Hermes. Later sources (mentioned below) describe that the area had another basilica ("of Zenodotus"), the bath of Olbia, and two tetrapyla.

Building continued throughout the fourth century, especially as emperors such as Constantius [337–361], Julian, and Valens [364–378] resided there. Constantius was praised by Julian (*Oration* 1, 40d–41a) for constructing so many stoas, fountains, and other buildings (he is not more specific) that the citizens of Antioch voted to change the name of their city to Constantia (the name did not last). Julian and the people of Antioch did not like each other (which is clear from the *Misopogon*), though Julian seems to have worked hard to alleviate a famine and economic problems in the city. The city experienced a conflict between Christians and pagans during his visit, and the Temple of Apollo was burned to the ground. Julian did create a library in the Temple to Trajan, but this was burned soon after his death.

The emperor Valens completely transformed the center of the city where the cardo and main decumanus intersected (Figures 3.9 and 3.10).

This was the location of the Temple of Ares and the Kaisarion. To obtain space for his new forum, Valens removed part of the Kaisarion (but not the vaulted apse) and had the Parmenius vaults covered with marble paving. The forum was bounded by four porticos and shops built with marble imported from modern Croatia. Valens reworked the forum in such a way that it was surrounded by important buildings from the past – the Plethrion stood on one side, with the apse of the Kaisarion on the other. On another side stood the Bath of Commodus, which became the *praetorium* of the governor of Syria, and the Xystos, whereas on the opposite side, Valens constructed a new basilica. The Temple of Ares behind the Kaisarion was demolished and replaced with a *macellum*. Valens also altered an amphitheater to make it

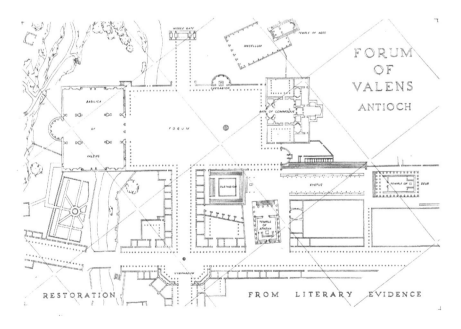

*Figure 3.9* A possible plan of the Forum of Valens according to literary evidence. The 1930s excavation revealed little of the Forum, but recent excavations (which are in the process of being published) may provide more information (Antioch Expedition Archives, Department of Art and Archaeology, Princeton University, Plan 3675).

*Figure 3.10* Arch over the Parmenius excavated in the 1930s (Antioch Expedition Archives, Department of Art and Archaeology, Princeton University, Photo 3929).

more conducive to beast hunts. Libanius demonstrates that the Plethrion was expanded by a Roman senator (and by one of his uncles) and complains about how the rabble is now able to attend (*Oration* 10)!

The city of the late-fourth century is particularly well known because of the description provided by Libanius in his encomium of the city. He described how a visitor would enter the city through the north gate and then follow the long colonnaded street with its shops and public buildings visible along the way. The colonnades were two stories high and interrupted occasionally with staircases that led to the second floor of galleries.

In one of the rare finds of a public building from the Princeton excavations, the shrine of St. Babylas was discovered across the Orontes River from the city (see Figure 2.26). This was a cruciform church and a stone sarcophagus was discovered at the transept. The church may have existed by the time of Julian, but the relics were moved there permanently during the reign of Theodosius. The Megalopsychia mosaic from the Yakto villa shows that there was a workshop nearby that produced souvenirs for pilgrims. Over 25 churches and monasteries are mentioned in the literary sources as being located in or near Antioch. Only the shrine of St. Babylas and a small church in Daphne were discovered.

During the reign of Theodosius II, imperial benefactions added several buildings to the city. In 438, the Empress Eudocia traveled through Antioch on her pilgrimage to Jerusalem, and while there, she donated the money to restore the baths of Valens. Her visit also coincided with her husband, Theodosius II, ordering the construction of an additional city wall which ran a mile south of the previous city wall. A new gate was built which was named the Golden Gate because it was gilded in gold. Theodosius also sent three officials (Memonius, Zoilus, and Callistus) to build at Antioch. One built a law court, another a basilica, and a third a stoa. Then in 439, he ordered the construction of an ornate basilica called "of Anatolius." The names of these officials became attached to the structures, but the money came from the imperial treasury. The description of these buildings is so sparse that their locations cannot be located with certainty (though they may have been built in any of the existing fora or agoras).

A major earthquake struck the city in 458. Evagrius wrote that it destroyed most of the buildings on the island. This earthquake destroyed half of the imperial palace, a bath, the tetrapylon in front of the palace, the colonnaded street that led to the palace, and the towers at the hippodrome. The core city was only slightly damaged, but the baths of Trajan, Hadrian, and Severus were harmed. A quarter of the city called Ostakine was heavily damaged, with the colonnade and nymphaeum destroyed. Evagrius reports that the Emperor Leo [457–474] undertook responsibility for restoring the damaged buildings. In 459, St. Symeon died, and a church was built to hold his relics at Antioch (Figure 3.11).

The excavations from Daphne revealed several houses from this period. One small church was excavated, but the attention of the excavators was drawn to recovering mosaic floors from wealth houses. This was partially because the mosaics were being uncovered and destroyed by the locals, but also because the sale of the mosaics allowed the excavations to continue. Thus, the excavators discovered many mosaics to the detriment of archaeological methodology. The houses are clustered on the northern side of Daphne and appear to date from the third to the fifth century. They are quite large and must have been owned by the wealthy class, as they contained the spectacular mosaics in their *triclinia* (dining rooms). The remains of the structures do not seem to conform to a planned city pattern, suggesting that Daphne grew organically in the later Roman and late antique period. While this assumption cannot be tested by the archaeological data, it appears that the houses conformed to the following pattern: the triclinium (dining room) opened to a portico and fountain. Some of the houses contained internal gardens which would have been at home in Italy or pools for the collection of water or for raising of fish. In the mid-fifth century, several houses, such as the Yakto villa, were built over the remains of previous third-century houses. These new structures were larger, often being built over a portion of the nearby road, and much more extravagant. The Yakto villa, for example, included a private bath and held a cruciform hall in addition to several public meeting places. It must have been owned by one of the most powerful individuals in Antioch or an imperial official (Figure 3.12).

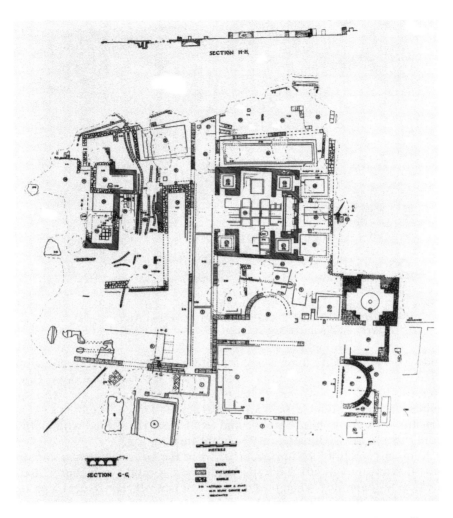

*Figure 3.11* Plan of the Villa at Yakto where the Megalopsychia mosaic was discovered (Antioch Expedition Archives, Department of Art and Archaeology, Princeton University, Photo 5659).

Chariot races were extremely important to the city, as indicated by the number of hippodromes in the city and references to the racing teams. To replace Hippodrome A, the Byzantine (or Hippodrome B) was built in the fifth century. Riots between chariot factions (named after their colors, the Greens and the Blues) and anti-Jewish pogroms during the reign of Zeno [474–491] damaged several buildings, including the Xystos, portions of Valens' colonnade, two synagogues, and several nearby buildings. This violence is an indication of how Christianity became a divisive force in some cities in the fifth

*Figure 3.12* Representation of the Olympic stadium in the Megalopsychia mosaic from the Villa at Yakto (Antioch Expedition Archives, Department of Art and Archaeology, Princeton University, Photo 1331).

and sixth centuries. In these cases, the Greens supported the Monophysite Creed, whereas the Blues supported the official imperial Orthodoxy. However, it is also during the time that a private citizen, Mammianus, who was senator in Constantinople, paid for several new buildings, including a public structure of some kind in Daphne and two colonnades paved with marble from Proconnesus, with a tetrapylon at the intersection.

Another round of violence occurred when the Greens attacked another Jewish synagogue in 507. This site became the location of a church dedicated to St. Leontius. When the emperor sent new officials to deal with the violence, the Blues allied with the Roman officials. There were fighting in the streets and the Greens won. They burned the Basilica of Rufinus and the Basilica of Zenodotus, two tetrapyla, and the office of the *comes Orientis*. When order was restored, the emperor Anastasius [491–518] paid to restore the damaged buildings. Violence continued between the factions, leading the emperor Justin [518–527] to ban the Olympic Games and later shows at the theater.

The sixth century was a period of general disaster for the city, with fires and earthquakes in the mid- and late sixth century causing a large amount of damage to the city. For example, a fire in 525 burned down a Church of St. Stephen and the headquarters (*praetorium*) of the Master of Soldiers (*magister militum*), which was near the Forum of Valens. The earthquake of 526 and subsequent fires are said to have killed 250,000 people (the Patriarch

Euphrasius was killed) and destroyed all the buildings of the city except those on the slope of Mount Silpius (though both the number of dead and destroyed buildings might be exaggerated). The Golden Church was destroyed in the earthquake of 526, rebuilt, and then destroyed again in 588. Other churches, such as the Church of the Archangel Michael, Church of the Virgin Mary, the Church of the Holy Prophets, and the Church of St. Zacharias, were destroyed by earthquake or fire. Some damage and buildings were repaired, but another earthquake struck in 528. The walls of the city and all remaining standing buildings were said to have collapsed. Destructive though these were, they were not the only disasters. In 528, Arabs in the service of Persia led by the leader al-Mundhir raided Syria all the way to Antioch. And then, in 540, the Persians captured and sacked Antioch. The walls hadn't been completely restored yet from the earthquake damage, and the Roman officials were afraid to work on them for fear of revealing to the Persians the weak spots in the defenses. As in 260, the Persians assaulted the fortifications on Mount Silpius. Once these were taken, the Persians commanded the high ground and easily overcame the defenders. Much of the population that had not fled was enslaved, and the city and suburbs were burned, though the Golden Church and some other churches were left alone. The only section of the city that survived the fire was called "Kerateion" and is thought to have been the Jewish section of the city. It survived because the decrease in population of the city meant that there was an abandoned section between it and the central city. Daphne was largely left alone, except for the church of the Archangel Michael, which was burned.

The sixth-century historian Procopius describes Justinian's efforts to rebuild the city (*On Buildings*, 2.10.2–25). Procopius began with an account of the complete devastation of the city, which included the destruction of public stoas, marketplaces, and colonnaded streets. The debris was carted away, and Justinian ordered the restoration of the urban plan, complete with new roads, stoas, marketplaces, streets, baths, and churches. This account is partially confirmed by the archaeological excavations of the main cardo that was renovated for the first time since the second century (Figure 3.13).

The road was reduced in size to create a raised walkway in front of the colonnades. The sidewalk was paved in mosaics, and shops were moved back, increasing the width of the sidewalks. Procopius claims that the city was even more beautiful than before the Persian invasion, which may have been true, but it was a much reduced city.

Procopius notes that the city walls of Justinian enclosed a much smaller area than previously, and he describes Justinian's efforts to make the city more defensible by changing the channel of the Orontes and flattening topographical features near the walls. Evidence from Procopius and the excavations on the island suggest that the buildings on the island were largely being used as a quarry to rebuild other parts of the city. Large portions of Hippodrome B were dismantled so the blocks could be used in the refortification of the city. Justinian also built the Iron Gate to contain the

*Figure 3.13* Photo of the cardo after Justinian's restoration of the city (Antioch Expedition Archives, Department of Art and Archaeology, Princeton University, Photo 1721).

Parmenius from flooding the city. A drain from Justinian's period suggests that the Parmenius was diverted from its previous bed. Large kilns were discovered in the excavations of Hippodrome B and in the remains of bathhouses, suggesting people were producing lime (to make plaster) from the marble of the abandoned buildings. These likely date from the time of Justinian into the early Islamic period (Figures 3.14 and 3.15).

Although the city was rebuilt, in 542 plague struck the city, killing perhaps 20% of the residents. Earthquakes struck again in 551, 557, 577, and 588. Large sections of the city were devastated again, two public baths were destroyed, and several churches (including the Golden Church) and the towers of the city wall collapsed. Furthermore, the Persians raided the area in 573, burning the suburbs again, but leaving the city unharmed. In 606 and 607, following the coup by Phocas over the Emperor Maurice, the Persians attacked Antioch. In 611, Antioch and Apamea were captured by the Persians, and they decided to occupy Syria instead of simply raiding it. Nothing is known of the city under Persian occupation. Antioch once again was controlled by the Romans in 628 with the collapse of the Persian government under Chosroes II, and Heraclius used Antioch as his base in the campaigns against the initial Muslim invasions in 634. Antioch surrendered quickly after the battle of the Yarmuk River in 636, and the Muslims posted a garrison at the city.

Many people today would be surprised that the Muslim conquest of the Near East happened relatively peacefully. There were a couple of battles,

*Figure 3.14* The Iron Gate constructed by Justinian (Antioch Expedition Archives, Department of Art and Archaeology, Princeton University, Photo 1592).

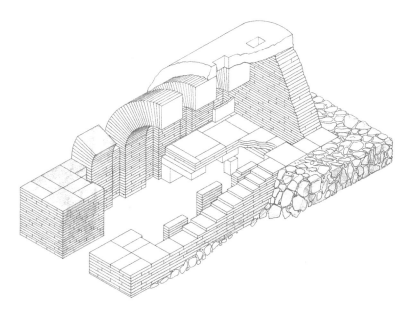

*Figure 3.15* Plan of a lime kiln discovered at Antioch (Antioch Expedition Archives, Department of Art and Archaeology, Princeton University, Drawing 39).

and a few sieges, but in general, most cities surrendered quickly without a fight, and on good terms. Muslim standard practice was to grant communities, especially religious ones, relative autonomy in exchange for a special tax paid by non-Muslims. In return, the Muslims offered security. The Muslim rulers did not care about the Christological controversies that had so inflamed religious tensions in the Near East (between the Orthodox Christians and the Monophysites, for example) and did not seek converts amongst the Christians until at least the eighth century. At first, there were few restrictions on Christians, but those increased over the next few centuries (for example, Christians in later periods could not ring church bells or ride horses).

There is very little archaeological evidence regarding the fate of Antioch in the early Islamic period, but some of this is due to the fact that the Princeton excavations were not very interested in the Islamic period remains. Earlier scholars assumed that the population of Antioch quickly began to shrink, as some moved elsewhere in the Mediterranean (especially to Constantinople, southern Italy, and Milan in particular) and as the city of Antioch lost its administrative importance, replaced by Damascus and Aleppo. Literary sources are also mostly silent about the city until the ninth century, other than to record some controversies between the Orthodox and Monophysite congregations regarding the appointments of Patriarchs. However, this interpretation is challenged by close readings of Arabic texts that mention the resettlement of Antioch by Arabs, Persians, and other peoples by the Umayyad rulers, and new investigations into the archive of the Princeton excavations. A revaluation of this material suggests that there was early Islamic remains found in most of the excavated areas of the city. For example, shops were discovered that were built on top of the main cardo street paved by Justinian in the sixth century (though this date has been questioned). Excavations thought to be near the Forum of Valens uncovered ceramic kilns and other industrial applications, possibly suggesting that the open spaces of the Greco-Roman city were now being used for other purposes, as is known from other cities of the Near East.

Literary sources show that churches continued to operate including the Cathedral of St. Peter and St. Paul and the round church built by Justinian. Several other churches were built in the city after the Islamic conquest. A mosque and Persian fire temple are also known from the texts of the early Islamic period. Some of the elites of the city stayed there after the conquest, and the city was known for its scholarly community. The city remained a strategic location along the Christina-Arab border, changing hands several times. The city still seems to have been majority Christian when the Crusaders took the city in 1098.

## *Apamea*

After the restoration of Roman rule in the Near East after the third century, Apamea once again prospered, for the same reasons as before. The sources are largely silent about the city in this period, except in regard to the Christianization of the city. As mentioned above, the Temple of Zeus was destroyed in 386 CE by the Bishop Marcellus. There were other temples in the city and in the surrounding area that were also sources of conflict in the late fourth century. For example, one temple in a rural district called Aulon was attacked by the Bishop Marcellus and a band of soldiers and gladiators, but the pagans ambushed the bishop and burnt him alive (Sozomen 7.15)!

In the fifth century, Apamea regained some of the prominence that it held as an administrative center under the Seleucids when it became the capital of the new province Syria Secunda. It has been argued that the stunning House of the Triclinium was the home of the provincial governor, based on the quality and date of the mosaic of the Hunt. Although there are only limited inscriptions, it seems that imperial officials began to take a larger role in public constructions. For example, a mosaic inscription dated to 469 notes that an official named Julianos constructed a portico in the southern part of the colonnaded street.

As at Antioch, earthquakes in 526 and 528 caused major damage to the city. The excavators report finding sixth-century repairs at almost all the surviving structures. Excavations of the large houses of the city show that they were rebuilt in a similar style as before, except with bricks and cement characteristic of the sixth century. When earlier mosaics could be conserved and reused, such as at the House of the Bilobed Columns, they were. In this case, a new column was erected directly on top of the mosaic to support a new roof structure. Columns, bases, capitals, walls, and mosaics were all reused or replaced according to their structural soundness. In other areas of the city, damage was so extensive that some of the insulae were abandoned. For example, a large commercial district was located to the north of the House with the Triclinium was completely destroyed and abandoned after these two earthquakes.

As at Antioch, Justinian ordered the restoration of the colonnaded street, which was narrowed in order to add a sidewalk on both sides of the street. New pavers, rectangular instead of polygonal, were laid over a newly built drainage system. The north gate was also restored at this time. Changes were also made to the central nymphaeum as two-third of the frontal basin was filled with concrete in order to minimize the amount of water required to fill it. Changes were also made to the latrine to reduce water use. Both changes indicate that water was not as abundant compared with the earlier period. By the second half of the seventh century, a burial occurred in the basin, indicating that the nymphaeum was out of use by that time.

Four major churches have been discovered at Apamea. These include the Rotunda Church and the Eastern Cathedral both from the time of Justinian, and the Atrium Church which was rebuilt and enlarged during Justinian's reign. Interestingly, the Atrium Church was built over a late fourth-century synagogue and a fifth-century church that was associated with the relics of St. Cosmas and St. Damian, as noted by an inscription. The additions to the Atrium Church from the time of Justinian, such as the large atrium, reflect trends in church building in Constantinople. Approximately, fifty burials from the mid-seventh century to the eighth century (and maybe later), so after the Arab conquest, in and around the church indicate that it was still functioning at that time. Diagonal from the Atrium Church at the intersection of the cardo and decumanus, the Rotunda Church was discovered.

Despite condemnations by church officials, people continued to go to the theater in late antiquity.

In Apamea, this still included using the theater for water shows (perhaps for the Maiumas festival, which was also condemned by church leaders!), as repairs to the pipes from this period demonstrate. In the late sixth century, the construction of a water channel over a portion of the stage suggests that it was still used for water performances, but not for theatrical shows. Alternatively, this could be an indication that the theater was converted to an industrial use, like the North Theater in Gerasa, or was used only in the capacity of a water catchment device.

The House with the Triclinium takes up two-thirds of an insula along the south decumanus near the eastern gate. The entrance opens onto a side cardo to the east, not along the main street to the north. It consists of forty-eight rooms arranged around a large peristyle and two interior courtyards. According to an inscription at the entrance to the triclinium, the room was (re)built in the year 539. The mosaic floor, which features a hunting scene, is considered one of the most beautiful mosaics found in the Near East and is dated to the early fifth century. The room terminates on the north side with an apse, which suggests that the triclinium room also functioned as a meeting place for the peers of the house. Mosaics in other rooms in the structure depict Amazons and other mythological figures. Later building obscures the northern end of this insula.

Just to the east of the House with the Triclinium, there was a massive church constructed with a quatrefoil plan with a square interior, and an apse with an episcopal throne. Attached to it to the east was a rectangular annex with another apse. This intriguing design was probably intended for the bishop of the city. Three massive arches on the southern decumanus mark the location of this church, which was approached via a staircase and through a large narthex that was built in 533. The excavators believe that the church originally dates to the fifth century and was designed as a martyrion to hold the relics of the "True Cross", which were thought to have saved the city from Chosroes in 540. Attached to the church to the west was the episcopal palace. To the east were rooms for baptism, a banquet area for catechumens, and a funerary chapel.

The Persian ruler Chosroes visited Apamea in 540 after leaving Antioch. Instead of destroying the city and taking the piece of the "True Cross" that was housed there, he demanded large amounts of silver from the churches and held races in the hippodrome! The Christians of the city believed that a miracle saved the city. The city did not survive the next Persian assault; however, for in 573, the general Adaarmanes is said to have completely despoiled the city and enslaved almost 300,000 inhabitants. According to Evagrius, the city had fallen into disrepair and the city wall was not standing. Archaeological evidence, on the other hand, does not show the evidence of widespread destruction nor of depopulation.

The looting of the Roman Theater for stone began towards the end of the sixth century, providing the point at which the theater was definitely out of use. This quarrying reoccurred during the Crusader period to refortify the Qalaat al-Mundiq and during the Ottoman period to build a pilgrimage mosque and caravansary. Even though the theater was no longer being used, there is evidence that the cisterns and piping continued to be repaired in this late period. Until 2008, when limited new excavations began, over two-thirds of the theater remained buried under two to four meters of earthquake damage and debris, which have made excavating the site difficult.

Excavations in the northern part of the insula of the House with the Triclinium revealed dense occupation from after the Arab conquest, consisting of approximately sixty-four shops and workshops. The plan is haphazard, leading the excavators to compare it to a modern suq. Several of the shops encroach onto the colonnade street, which was clearly still in use, possibly until the twelfth century. Another similar group of shops was discovered to the northeast of the Cathedral church from after the Arab conquest. The positioning of the shops in the quarter, which did not encroach onto the church, and entrances into the church complex, suggests that the church was still in use.

The large peristyle Roman period houses from the throughout the city demonstrate that the city continued to be densely populated in the seventh and eighth centuries. For example, the houses located in the residential area across the street from the church complex and the House of the Triclinium (such as the House with the Capitals and Consoles, the House of the Consoles, and the House with Pilasters) remained occupied throughout the early Islamic period and into the tenth century. The large House with the Pilasters, for example, was divided up into several different and much smaller dwellings. A similar process happened at the House with the Capitals and Consoles, in which the peristyle courtyard was divided between two separate living spaces. It is unknown if these changes were a result of an inheritance dispute or a decline of wealth, or changing ideas of family life. The House of the Deer (Maison du Cerf) was destroyed around 600 CE, abandoned for a time, and then inhabited again. Like the other houses in the area, the original building was divided into smaller dwellings. The House with the Arabic Graffiti was so named because of the use of Arabic writing near the doorway. Pottery from the house indicated the use of the house until the ninth century. In the north-west of the city, the House with the Trilobed Columns, saw the abandonment of some sections of the house, but the continued use of others until at least the ninth century (Figures 3.16 and 3.17).

*Figure 3.16* Photo of the entrance to the House of the Consoles (Photo by Greg Fisher).

*Figure 3.17* Photo of the peristyle courtyard of the House of the Consoles (Photo by Greg Fisher).

Towards the end of Roman rule over Apamea, it is clear that the city faced several problems like Antioch, but archaeological evidence allows us to see that the city was not destroyed by the Persian or Islamic conquests nor was it depopulated. On the contrary, all evidence suggests that the city was becoming even more densely populated. While the majority of the city has not been excavated, it is clear that there were no major changes to the street plan in the late antique period. Rebuilding during the time of Justinian focused on restoring damage, but not redesigning the city. Churches replaced pagan temples, and there is no evidence that Muslim rule impacted the Christian communities, whose churches continued to function for several 100 years after the conquest.

## Conclusion

Some 700 villages have been discovered inside the triangle formed by the cities of Antioch, Apamea, and Aleppo. These villages, now called the "Dead Cities," are poignant reminders that cities and their hinterlands are not independent of each other, but change in tandem. Abandoned for almost a 1,000 years when the first western visitors saw them, the early explorers blamed the Muslim conquest for the collapse of these communities. The "Dead Cities" lie on a plateau approximately 60 km wide and 110 km long known as the Limestone Mastiff (Figures 3.18 and 3.19).

Despite the name, they are not cities. There are virtually no public buildings other than churches (excepting an "andron" at Serjilla), and there are no streets. Over 95% of the buildings are houses that conform to the same style – animals were stabled on the ground floor and people lived and slept on a second story. The remainders of the buildings are installations for the pressing of olives into olive oil. This countryside was so productive that the Apamean city council decreed that the city double the amount of public lighting because of the excess of olive oil in the fourth century CE. Older scholarship argued that these cities practiced a monoculture of olives, but more recent evidence show that grapes and other fruits, grains, and lentils were all grown, and animals were an important part of the diet.

Recent scholarship also shows that the Muslim conquest did not cause these villages to be abandoned. Rather, it appears that the early sixth century saw the height of population and economic prosperity in these villages, just as it was in Antioch and Apamea. As earthquakes, plagues, and invasions took their toll on the cities in the mid- to late sixth century, the hinterland suffered too. Not only did the people in the countryside face similar problems but also the damage to the cities reduced the demand for the agricultural products of the countryside. The "Dead Cities" were not abandoned until the eighth century, but they declined in both prosperity and population beginning in the mid-sixth century.

The archaeology of Apamea provides a useful check on the historical sources available at Antioch. At Apamea, the rebuilding of the city after the

90  *The Tetrapolis (Antioch and Apamea)*

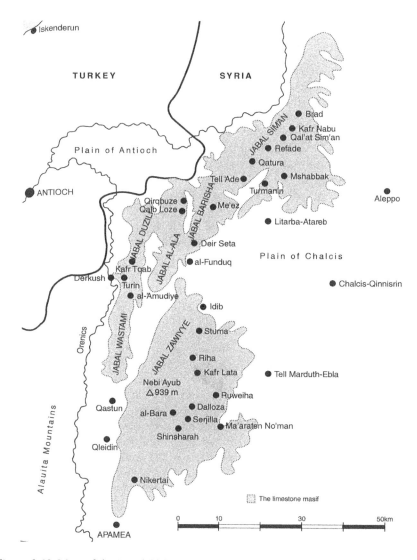

*Figure 3.18* Map of the Dead Cities (Ball, W. *Rome in the East*. [Routledge 2016, 2nd edition], Figure 5.1).

115 CE earthquake can be traced in detail. The residents there mimicked the monumentalization of the imperial city of Antioch. This is especially evident from the long colonnaded cardo flanked with sidewalks and shops. While Antioch was reconstructed through imperial involvement, Apamea appears to have relied on locals such as Lucius Julius Agrippa. Four hundred years later, Procopius described the rebuilding of sixth century

*Figure 3.19* The "andron" building at Serjilla (Photo by Greg Fisher).

Antioch, and a similar process can be seen extensively in the archaeological record at Apamea. On the other hand, the archaeology of Apamea indicates that the city was not damaged as severely by the Persian conquests as the sources indicate. Does this also mean that Antioch was not as impacted as well?

It is impossible to know what Antioch was like after the Muslim conquest, but if Apamea is a guide, then it seems possible that population levels were not much decreased from the later sixth century. The division of houses in Apamea suggests high levels of population density compared with previous centuries, but these dwellings and people were clearly less wealthy than the people who lived in the grand houses of the past. Commerce continued, as the finds of Muslim period coins in these dwellings attests, and new shopping districts appeared. They were not the ordered structures of the Roman period but grew in organic ways much like the modern suq or bazaar of the modern Middle East. Clearly some sort of changes had occurred in city planning from the Roman period, even if the street plans were not much altered. But to what extent was the city transformed? To answer this question, we need more data. In the coming chapters, we'll examine six more cities and their transformations over this vast 1,000-year period. Up next are the cities of Gerasa and Scythopolis, examples from the Decapolis. Like Antioch and Apamea, these cities were founded in the Hellenistic period as showpieces of Greek culture.

## Suggestions for further reading

Balty, J.-C. *Guide d'Apamée*. (Brussels 1981).
Balty, J.-C. "Apamea in Syria in the Second and Third Centuries A.D." *The Journal of Roman Studies*, 78, 1988, 91–104.
Downey, G. "Libanius' Oration in Praise of Antioch (Oration XI)." *Proceedings of the American Philosophical Society*, 103(5), 1959, 652–686.
Downey, G. *A History of Antioch in Syria: From Seleucus to the Arab Conquest.* (Princeton 1961).
Downey, G. *Antioch in the Age of Theodosius the Great*. (University of Oklahoma Press 1962).
Downey, G. *Ancient Antioch*. (Princeton 1963).
Eger, A. "(Re)Mapping Medieval Antioch: Urban Transformations from the (Early) Islamic to the (Middle) Byzantine Periods." *Dumbarton Oaks Papers*, 67, 2013, 95–134.
Finlayson, C. "New Excavations and a Reexamination of the Great Roman Theater at Apamea, Syria, Seasons 1–3 (2008–2010)." *American Journal of Archaeology*, 116(2), 2012, 277–319.
Grainger, J. The Cities of Seleukid Syria. (Oxford 1990).
Kondoleon, C. *Antioch: The Lost Ancient City*. (Princeton 2000).
Liebeschuetz, J. *Antioch: City and Imperial Administration in the Later Roman Empire*. (Oxford 2000 [reprint]).
Shepardson, C. *Controlling Contested Places: Late Antique Antioch and the Spatial Politics of Religious Controversy*. (University of California Press 2019).

# 4   The Decapolis (Gerasa and Scythopolis)

In a striking passage in the Gospel of Mark, Jesus confronts a demon near the city of Gerasa (5:1–20) who had possessed a man. When Jesus demanded to know the name of the demon, it responded with "Legion," the name of the Roman military units who had occupied the Near East and an indication that the man was not possessed by one but a large number of demons. After Jesus banished the demons from him, the spirits possessed a herd of pigs that happened to be in a field nearby. These demons drove the pigs insane, and they charged into the Sea of Galilee and drowned. Although the now-free man wished to follow Jesus back to Galilee, Jesus ordered him instead to spread Jesus's teaching throughout the Decapolis. In another instance in the Gospel of Mark (7:31), Jesus traveled from Tyre down to the Sea of Galilee which was "in the region of the Decapolis." The Gospel of Matthew (4:25) also mentions the Decapolis as the origin point of some of the crowd who attended the Sermon on the Mount. In all three instances, the Decapolis is mentioned as a distinctive region in the southern Levant.

And yet, while the word Decapolis means "ten cities" in Greek, no ancient author was quite sure which cities should be included. Various authors list the following cities: Damascus, Philadelphia [Amman], Raphana, Scythopolis, Gadara, Hippos, Dion, Pella, Galasa, Canatha, Gerasa [Jerash], Heliopolis, Abila, Saana, Hina, Abila, Lysanius, Capitolias, Edrei, Gadora, and Samulis – clearly more than just ten! A quick glance at Figure 4.1 will suffice to show that these cities, while clustered east of the Jordan River, cannot be considered a separate region (Scythopolis is located on the west bank). Why then were they so commonly grouped together in ancient sources?

This fact goes back to the reorganization of the East in 63 BCE by Pompey, who attached the administration of the Decapolis to the province of Syria, despite the fact that the cities of the Decapolis were not contiguous with each other or the province of Syria itself. Instead of a region, the Decapolis differentiated itself from its neighbors by their shared Greek culture. Several cities traced their origins back to Alexander the Great (whether accurately or not) or to the earliest Greek dynasts such as Antiochus or Seleucus.

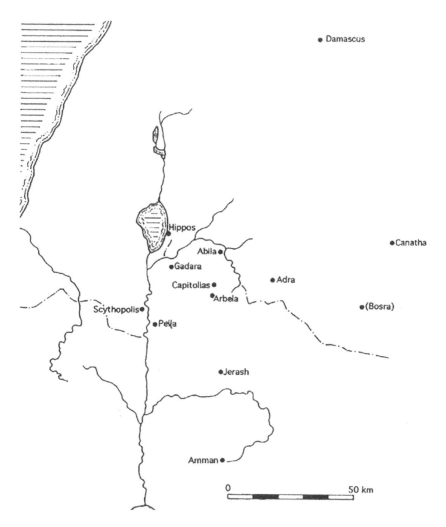

*Figure 4.1* Map of the Decapolis (Ball, W. *Rome in the East*. [Routledge 2016, 2nd edition], Figure 4.11).

Despite being grouped as a unit, these cities were not always administered by the Romans. Some (Gadara, Hippos, and Canatha) were granted to Herod of Judaea, whereas Damascus and Philadelphia were controlled by the Nabataean Kingdom for a short period of time. These cities may have celebrated religious festivals or the Roman imperial cult communally, but there isn't evidence that they worked together in any concerted way. Even when several of these cities were attacked by Jewish militias during the Jewish Revolt, they did not band together – though a massacre of Jewish inhabitants did occur in most of these cities, such as Scythopolis, but not at Gerasa where Jewish people were protected, according to Josephus. In both cities, damage from the Jewish Revolt has been credited with the vast expansion of building in the late first century CE.

This chapter concentrates on the two well-excavated cities of Gerasa (Jerash in Jordan) and Scythopolis (Beit She'an in Israel). Gerasa is located in rolling hills approximately 30 miles north of the outskirts of the capital of Jordan, Amman. The region receives a moderate amount of rainfall, and its 600 m elevation means that its climate is moderate. Agriculture can be practiced there without irrigation. However, the city owes its location to a spring (Ain Kerawan) that creates a perennial river, which ran down the middle of the city and eventually emptied into the River Jordan. This gave the city its alternate name, Antioch on the Chyrsorhoas (Antioch on the Golden River). The terrain to the east of Gerasa rapidly becomes more arid within a few kilometers and increasingly hilly and mountainous to the west, but Gerasa itself lies in an open stretch of valley. The site was, therefore, ideally situated between more hostile environments, and it attracted settlement as early as the Neolithic period. Bronze Age sites are known from the region, and some scholars have suggested that the eventual site of the Temple of Zeus in the southwest corner of the city held religious significance for these early settlers. Later inscriptions describe this sanctuary as an oracular shrine, and it is possible that this was a very ancient tradition. The present site is bisected by the river and surrounded by a second century CE city wall. The western half of the site contains the spectacular Roman and late antique remains that make modern Jerash such an exciting tourist destination. The eastern portion of the city lies almost completely buried by the modern city, though a few public buildings (the bath from the second century CE) are visible and have been excavated. Archaeologists have largely concentrated on excavating and restoring the monumental structures there, and excavations have dumped their waste into nearby areas, contaminating them and preventing excavation of non-monumental areas (Figure 4.2).

According to Pliny the Elder, Scythopolis was the most populous city of the Decapolis in the first century CE. Located in the Jezreel Valley just to the west of the Jordan River, the city was an important crossroads for travelers and a verdant agricultural site. Roads led to the coast and Caesarea, to Syria, to Pella and Gerasa, to Jerusalem, and to Tiberias on the Sea of Galilee. Like today, the Jezreel Valley was incredibly fertile, with extensive arable land and abundant water supplies, including a perennial river and associated tributaries. For these reasons, it is no wonder that the site attracted settlers in the Neolithic period and in virtually every subsequent period. Settlement is especially clear from the Egyptian period, when the Tell (fortified mound) served as the main Egyptian outpost in the region during the 18th–20th dynasties. Although the site was destroyed in the chaos at the end of the Bronze Age (12th century BCE), it was resettled

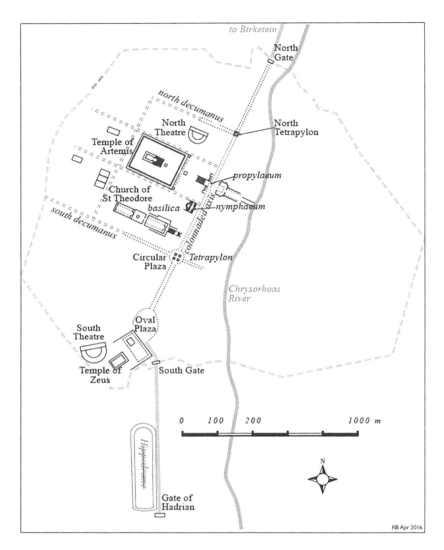

*Figure 4.2* Plan of Gerasa (Burns, R. *Origins of the Colonnaded Streets in the Cities of the Roman East*. [Oxford 2017], Figure 7.02).

by Canaanite settlers and later controlled by the Israelite Kingdom. The name for the city in these early periods was Beth Shean or Beshan. The site seems to have been abandoned from the 8th until the 3rd century BCE (Figure 4.3).

Unlike Gerasa, whose major geographic feature is a river, Scythopolis is dominated by the Tell of Beth Shean (Arabic Tell el-Hosn), which on

*The Decapolis (Gerasa and Scythopolis)* 97

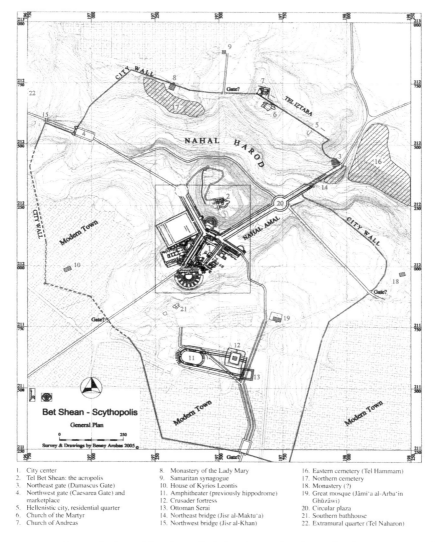

1. City center
2. Tel Bet Shean: the acropolis
3. Northeast gate (Damascus Gate)
4. Northwest gate (Caesarea Gate) and marketplace
5. Hellenistic city, residential quarter
6. Church of the Martyr
7. Church of Andreas
8. Monastery of the Lady Mary
9. Samaritan synagogue
10. House of Kyrios Leontis
11. Amphitheater (previously hippodrome)
12. Crusader fortress
13. Ottoman Serai
14. Northeast bridge (Jisr al-Maktu'a)
15. Northwest bridge (Jisr al-Khan)
16. Eastern cemetery (Tel Hammam)
17. Northern cemetery
18. Monastery (?)
19. Great mosque (Jāmi'a al-Arba'in Ghūzāwi)
20. Circular plaza
21. Southern bathhouse
22. Extramural quarter (Tel Naharon)

*Figure 4.3* General plan of Scythopolis (Plan by Benjamin Y. Arubas, courtesy of Benjamin Y. Arubas).

the north side is protected by the ravines of Rahal Harod and on the east side by the Nahal Amal. As mentioned above, the pre-Hellenistic settlement of the site concentrated on the Tell, but in the Roman and late antique periods, the plain to the south of the Tell became the main focus of the polis. Another hill, Tell Iztaba, lies just north of Rahal Harod (Figure 4.4).

*Figure 4.4* View of the Tell with the Scythopolis civic center in the foreground (Photo by Jennifer Ramsay).

## The Hellenistic period

Both Gerasa and Scythopolis were founded during the Hellenistic period likely in the context of the rivalry between the Seleucids and Ptolemies. Little remains from the Hellenistic period exist at these sites, and sources about their development are scant.

## Gerasa

The inhabitants of Gerasa liked to believe that the city was founded as a veteran colony by Alexander the Great or his general Perdiccas during the march from Egypt to Mesopotamia in 331 BCE. Unfortunately, little evidence of the city from the Hellenistic period has been recovered below the later Roman one, so the earliest civic settlement cannot be dated to this early date. Its alternative name, Antioch on the Chyrsorhoas, suggests that the city was refounded or perhaps just renamed by either Antiochus III (223–187 BCE) or Antiochus IV Epiphanes (175–164 BCE), for the city would have been under the control of the Ptolemies prior to the reign of Antiochus III. Later, when the Seleucids began to lose control of their outer territories, the city was briefly ruled by Judea after being captured in the reign of Alexander Jannaeus (103–76 BCE). The city then passed into Roman control during Pompey's expedition in the East when it, like the other cities of the Decapolis, was attached to the province of Syria.

Very little of the Hellenistic site (pre-64 BCE) has been revealed through excavation at Gerasa, but the quantities of reused material from this period in later buildings indicate that the settlement contained several well-constructed stone buildings. At present, occupation in this period has been found in the south-western portion of the site, but the evidence of *spolia* in buildings near the later Temple of Artemis suggests that occupation may have spread farther north than the current *in situ* evidence demonstrates. Perhaps the best indication of the size of the settlement in this period are the ceramic dumps and burials that cover a large area of the western periphery of the site (though it should be noted that these dumps mostly contained first century BCE and CE material, and little from the Hellenistic period). The later city walls cut through significant portions of these dumps. Like other ancient cities, burials were located on the outskirts of the settlement, as a child's tomb from the second-half of the second century BCE demonstrates, and at Gerasa, burials seem to be in the same locations as the ceramic dumps. Ceramic production in cemeteries is known from other sites, such as classical Athens and Abila of the Decapolis.

Thus, there is ample circumstantial evidence that the Hellenistic occupation could have covered roughly the southern half of the modern archaeological park, but surviving evidence of occupation is limited to the far southwestern section of the site. On the promontory where the naos of the Temple of Zeus was later located, there was a modest temple with a rock hewn altar. It is assumed that this temple was dedicated to Zeus or his local equivalent Baalshamin. To the northeast, there was a natural wadi which was covered in the first century CE with a lower platform, housing the naos for the later temple. The earliest city was probably located from this wadi, continuing to the northeast, near where the oval plaza stands and stretching to the site of the modern museum; however, the area has not been sufficiently explored down to the Hellenistic layers. This location was likely chosen because it had easy access to the river. Continued excavation of these early layers is difficult because of the mass of later Roman and late antique buildings. It has been suggested that the city was based on a Ptolemaic plan, which oriented the city along one major thoroughfare, but there is not enough evidence to support this theory at the current time.

## Scythopolis

One clue to the foundation of Scythopolis is to look at its name, which means "the city of the Scythians." The Scythians were a people who lived north of the Black Sea and were regarded by the Greeks and other sources as barbaric drunkards. They were known for being nomadic and excellent horse archers. Sources from late antiquity suggested that Scythians attacked the Near East in the seventh century BCE and that some of them decided to stay in the region and build the city of Scythopolis. Modern scholars, on the other hand, have suggested that the Hellenistic city was founded instead in the third century BCE by the Ptolemies, who used the name of the Scythians to denote either settlers from the Black Sea region (where there were numerous Greek colonies) or horse archers. So, the city may have been founded as a Greek (or mixed) military colony. Later, Greek and Roman authors were also confused by the name "Nysa", which was sometimes connected with the site. While these ancient authors thought Nysa referred to either the nurse of Dionysius or to the flight of Iphigenia and Orestes, most scholars now believe that the name refers to the daughter of Antiochus IV.

There is even less archaeological evidence of the Hellenistic period at Scythopolis than at Gerasa. Settlement in the Hellenistic period concentrated on Tell Beth Shean and Tell Iztaba. At the present, however, there is little evidence of architecture that can be linked to the Hellenistic period on Tell Beth Shean, and what has is very disturbed from late antique constructions. The excavated remains consist of domestic structures with thin walls, and ovens placed within courtyards. Pottery from the Hellenistic period was also discovered under late antique houses on the north eastern terrace, but there was no associated architecture there. If the site was developed by the Ptolemies as a garrison city, it would seem natural that a fortress would have been constructed on the Tell. Eighteen coins of Ptolemy II Philadelphus were discovered there, suggesting that the site was in fact occupied in his reign. An inscription mentions priests of Olympian Zeus at the site, suggesting that there was a temple located on the Tell to this god. The excavators in the 1920s suggested that the extant temple on the Tell dated to the 3rd century BCE, but it is now known to date to the Roman period.

Excavations on Tell Iztaba revealed a rich residential area, whose size remains unknown. It was destroyed by a massive fire at the end of the second century BCE, possibly associated with the Hasmonean conquest of the site. After this destruction, settlement on Tell Iztaba was abandoned for centuries, possibly until late antiquity. The settlement on the main Tell, however, continued, with the residential area being abandoned without destruction in the first century BCE.

The limited evidence about Scythopolis in the Hellenistic period suggests that the countryside was inhabited by the descendants of the Canaanites, with Greek speakers (including Greek speaking Egyptians) and Jews dwelling inside the city, and increasing numbers of Jews living outside the city. The Seleucids continued to control the city late into the second century BCE, when it was captured by the Hasmonean dynasty. The Hasmoneans demanded that the people of Scythopolis convert to Judaism or leave. The sources suggest that large numbers left (though this may be an exaggeration), only to return when Pompey conquered the region. This might explain why the people of Scythopolis massacred thousands of Jewish inhabitants in 66 CE during the Jewish revolt.

## The Roman period

The Pax Romana brought prosperity to the southern Levant, and this prosperity is attested in the development and growth of the civic centers of Gerasa and Scythopolis. The urban plan of both cities was laid out in this period. There may have been some damage to the cities as a result of the Jewish Revolt, possibly suggested by the building boom in both cities in the late first century CE. The second century in Gerasa was a period of extensive growth and evolution of the city, which the major temples of Zeus and Artemis being constructed in grand style. Most of the major buildings at Scythopolis also date to the second century. Unlike the cities of the Tetrapolis farther north, there seems to have been little impact of the Third Century Crisis on Gerasa and Scythopolis.

## Gerasa

Like Apamea, Caesarea, and Jerusalem, the surviving plan of the city of Gerasa dates to the Roman period. And while the late antique city, as discussed in the next section, went through several transformations, these did not include major changes to the layout of the city streets. Major temples were constructed in the first century CE and the city roads were planned. The second century CE was a period of incredible construction at Gerasa. The major temples were rebuilt in a grander style as were large sections of the city roads. The gates were constructed, and the hippodrome was built. In a move that was perhaps related to this construction boom, the Emperor Hadrian visited the site in late 129 and early 130 CE, perhaps to visit the oracular Temple of Zeus. In general, the civic plan of Gerasa west of the river accords well with the known plan of other cities of the Roman Near East. It possesses a major thoroughfare, the cardo, which runs approximately north-south, as well as a Southern Decumanus and a Northern Decumanus that run east-west and intersect the Cardo at specially designed and oriented intersections. Little is known of the plan of the city east of the river because of the modern city.

The best attested remains from the late first century BCE are those of the Temple of Zeus (called the Late Hellenistic Temple of Zeus). Excavators of the later first century CE underground vaults, which supported the later naos of the Temple of Zeus, discovered several well-decorated blocks from this earlier temple. The exact location of this earlier temple is unknown, but is presumed to be at the same site as the second century naos. These remains indicate that this Temple of Zeus was richly decorated with both stone carvings and plaster paintings (Figure 4.5).

An explosion of building activity began in the late first century CE, representing the earliest of the extant structures dating to this period. For example, the South Theater, which lies near the Temple of Zeus, was constructed in the 80s CE; however, according to inscriptions, it was not actually dedicated until the second century CE. The nearby portion of the western city wall could also have been built in this period, though most prefer a slightly later date. Since the South Theater was constructed almost directly on top of a ceramic dump, it has been argued that the ceramic kilns in this area were closed as part of a larger city plan to make room for the construction

*Figure 4.5* Frescos from the Hellenistic Temple of Zeus displayed in the vaults under the surviving platform of the naos of the Temple of Zeus (Photo by author).

of the monumentalized city. The Temple of Zeus also underwent an expansion in the late first century with the construction of the lower platform and vault. A monumental staircase was built to this lower platform from the wadi, the lowest portion of which was later covered by the Oval Plaza. The expansion of this Temple of Zeus occurred between 22/3 and 69/70 CE as attested by inscriptions honoring Zeus Olympios (see Figure 2.1). In the central part of the city, inscriptions also mention a Temple of Artemis from this period on the same site as the later one, and a temple possibly dedicated to Dionysus or Dushares (the chief god of the Nabataeans) was located under the later Cathedral. From this evidence, it seems clear that the area around the Temple of Artemis was occupied prior to the construction of the Cardo in the late first century.

The first signs of the civic plan also date to the late first century. The part of the Cardo north of the North Tetrapylon likely dates to the second-half of the first century CE (see Figure 2.9). It was given a colonnade with Ionic columns around the beginning of the second century CE. The north gate on the Cardo was constructed in 115 CE over the remains of a previous gate, which should be contemporary with the Cardo, providing a date of the late first century CE (Figure 4.6).

That the processional way of the Temple of Artemis is slightly off-center suggests that the processional way replaced an earlier road, also likely dating

*Figure 4.6* North gate of Gerasa at the left, the northern part of the cardo in the center, and the North Tetrapylon on the right. The agora is below the gate and cardo (Photo by author).

from the late first century CE. The south gate on the Cardo was built in 130 on top of the foundation of a shop from the early second century CE. It seems that shops and workshops lined the inside of the gate until they burned (from an unknown cause) in the third century. The woodworkers who owned the shops on the western side seem to have lived in apartments above their workshop (Figures 4.7 and 4.8).

The dramatic increase in construction during the second century touched almost every aspect of the city. Beginning in the south, the South Gate was constructed and the Oval Plaza was laid out with the Ionic columns along the perimeter (though the extant paving may date to the fourth century) (see Figure 2.14). The Temple of Zeus was completely rebuilt again (completed in 162/3 CE), with the surviving monumental temple on a previously unoccupied summit, and a monumental staircase was built to connect it with the lower platform and a propylon to join the whole complex with the Oval Plaza. The temple is a peripteral octastyle. The lower platform contained a naos and covered portico that marked the perimeter of the sacred complex. This new naos was built in 135 or 140 CE, and it was constructed in a smaller scale now that the main temple had been relocated higher on the ridge. This naos may be the location of the oracle. A bronze workshop was also discovered that produced basins and sculpture for the temple (see Figure 2.21).

*Figure 4.7* The Temple of Zeus (Photo by author).

*Figure 4.8* View of the cardo at Gerasa looking south. Note the higher columns which mark the nymphaeum (Photo of author).

Continuing from the Oval Plaza, the southern portion of the cardo was widened in the late second century and the Ionic columns were replaced with Corinthian ones. Sidewalks extended from the street curb to shops that ran the length of the street. Scholars continue to debate whether the street or the sidewalks were shaded, but at the very least it seems that fabric draperies could have covered the sidewalks. Entrances to public buildings along the cardo were marked by taller columns. The construction of the South Decumanus must be connected to the remodeling of the cardo because coins from the reign of Marcus Aurelius (dated 164/5) and contemporary pottery were discovered under the pavers. The South Tetrapylon in the plaza connecting the cardo with the South Decumanus likely should be dated to this period, though it was remodeled later (see Figure 2.10). The macellum was also constructed slightly earlier than the expansion of the cardo (around 130 CE) (see Figure 2.13).

Building work also monumentalized the northern portion of the city. The construction of the Temple of Artemis and corresponding processional way constitutes the most famous of these constructions, but it was not the only one (see Figure 2.22). The North Theater was built sometime in the first-half of the second century as a *bouleuterion*, but expanded into an odeon in 165/6 with additional seats and a removable velum (see Figure 2.31). The North Decamanus was built in the mid- to late second century using recycled Ionic column bases. An agora with basilica was constructed also in the early second century across the North Decumanus from the North Theater portico. To visually connect the North Decumanus and the cardo, the North Tetrapylon was built between 165 and 166, perhaps together with the construction of the North Theater (see Figure 4.6).

The construction of the Temple of Artemis in the middle of the second century (the Propylaeum dates to 150) transformed the entire central area of city. A processional way was constructed that began on the eastern bank of the city. A bridge was constructed to cross the river, which led to the Propylaeum gate just before the Cardo. Crossing the Cardo, one approached another Propylaeum, a portico, and a staircase that led up to a platform with another staircase beyond. From the staircase, one entered into the temenos of the Temple of Artemis. The temenos houses a portico along all four sides of the court. The temple appears typically Roman in design – it sits on a podium with a staircase, surrounded by Corinthian Columns with six on the front – in other words, a peripteral hexastyle temple with eleven columns on the sides (see Figure 2.19).

Just south of the Propylaeum was the nymphaeum, dedicated in 191 CE. Although smaller than others in the region (it rose to about 24 m), the first story was decorated richly in marble. Not only did it provide a water source for people in town, but was also beautifully designed with lower story statues that acted as fountains, and a public fountain topped with a half dome in between a decorated broken pediment (see Figure 2.11).

Little is known about the eastern side of the river during the Roman period (or later periods for that matter!) because of the modern town. However, it

*Figure 4.9* Remains of the Eastern Baths (Photo by author).

seems likely that the large east bath, still visible and standing several stories high, was constructed sometime in the late second century CE based on the sculptural remains of five life-size or larger statues (Figure 4.9).

Although it was long thought that the hippodrome and Arch of Hadrian were constructed near the same time, it is now clear that the hippodrome dates later, with construction beginning in the late second century, and possibly continuing into the third, when it was in use by 209–212 CE. The Arch of Hadrian would have been built during or shortly after Hadrian's visit in 129/130. It is thought that the city planners intended to build additional walls down to Hadrian's arch and to expand the city into these newly fortified areas, but these plans were never realized (see Figure 2.6).

The hippodrome remains relatively well-preserved, with some of the carceres (starting gates) in the west surviving (see Figure 2.33). It was one of the smallest hippodromes in the eastern empire, but is estimated to have been able to seat about 16,000 spectators. This may say something about the size of the population of Gerasa, but might just be a function of the limited topography suitable for the construction of such a large structure. By the end of the third century, however, the chariot races had ceased, and potters had returned to the area. They constructed kilns and simple dwellings in the cavea chambers.

The changes in the Hippodrome might suggest that the city was beginning to lose its monumental character in the third century. However, there was continued construction in the middle of the third century. For example, the building of the stoa and altar and the paving of the pronaos of the Temple of Artemis took place then. It is also possible that there were repairs in the late third of the south tetrapylon, which may have been remodeled at this time to reflect the division of the empire into the Tetrarchy (four rulers) by Diocletian.

As excavation has focused on major structures, large areas of Gerasa remain empty on the map. It is possible that these held unearthed occupation layers, but it is also possible that they were left open. This would have allowed people to erect tents or other non/semi-permanent structures or allowed the use of the open spaces for grazing animals, which can still be seen in Amman, a city of over four million people.

## Scythopolis

While it is impossible to know the extent of the Hellenistic settlement at Scythopolis, it is clear that the Roman period represented an extensive revitalization of the city. Pompey's lieutenant Gabinius, who was governor of Syria in 57–54 BCE, is especially credited with restoring the Scythopolis. As much of this earliest Roman city lies under the remains of the later periods, little of it has been extensively excavated. The city plan was designed in the first century CE with a monumentalization phase in the second. The excavated remains show an impressively built city, with basalt-paved streets lacking colonnades, a basilica, a theater, shops, temples, a bath, and domestic complexes (Figure 4.10).

As at Gerasa, the civic plan of the public city was designed in the first century CE. Examples of constructions in the first century are the basilica that lies next to the eastern street. This eastern street was lined with shops as at Gerasa. Across from the basilica to the north was an early bath that was later covered in the construction of Valley Street in the second century (the excavators are responsible for all the street names; they are not from antiquity). Another bath, called the eastern bath, dating from the first century, was later remodeled in the second. A reflecting pool and portico were built between Silvanus Street and this eastern bathhouse. The portico was supported by the bathhouse and contained Ionic capitals. On the southern end of the eastern street were several temples that backed up to the theater. The earliest phase of the theater lies near several temples at the end of the eastern street. The theater faced north so that the sun would be at the spectators' backs. A temple with the round cella stood at the intersection of Palladius Street and the Northern Street. It too was remodeled in the second century (Figure 4.11).

Also parallel to Gerasa, the surviving city plan and most of the monumental buildings from Scythopolis date to the second century. In this period, the craftsmen of Scythopolis began using limestone from the nearby Mount Gilboa that allowed them to work very large stone blocks and to

108  *The Decapolis (Gerasa and Scythopolis)*

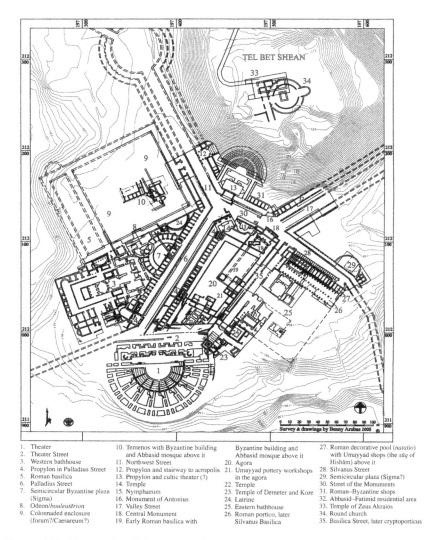

*Figure 4.10* Plan of the civic center of Scythopolis (Plan by Benjamin Y. Arubas, courtesy of Benjamin Y. Arubas).

1. Theater
2. Theater Street
3. Western bathhouse
4. Propylon in Palladius Street
5. Roman basilica
6. Palladius Street
7. Semicircular Byzantine plaza (Sigma)
8. Odeon/*bouleutērion*
9. Colonnaded enclosure (forum?/Caesareum?)
10. Temenos with Byzantine building and Abbasid mosque above it
11. Northwest Street
12. Propylon and stairway to acropolis
13. Propylon and cultic theater (?)
14. Temple
15. Nymphaeum
16. Monument of Antonius
17. Valley Street
18. Central Monument
19. Early Roman basilica with Byzantine building and Abbasid mosque above it
20. Agora
21. Umayyad pottery workshops in the agora
22. Temple
23. Temple of Demeter and Kore
24. Latrine
25. Eastern bathhouse
26. Roman portico, later Silvanus Basilica
27. Roman decorative pool (*natatio*) with Umayyad shops (the *sūq* of Hishām) above it
28. Silvanus Street
29. Semicircular plaza (Sigma?)
30. Street of the Monuments
31. Roman–Byzantine shops
32. Abbasid–Fatimid residential area
33. Temple of Zeus Akraios
34. Round church
35. Basilica Street, later cryptoporticus

embellish buildings with more sculptural detail. Contractors refurbished older buildings, such as the basilica, with this new limestone. This limestone was largely reserved for the public monuments, as it was more expensive than the local basalt, which was used for shops and residential structures.

The second century witnessed the construction of the most important surviving buildings, such as the Central Monument, nymphaeum, the odeon,

*Figure 4.11* View of the city center from the Tell. Palladius Street runs straight towards the theater and the modern town. The Eastern Street is on the left. The remains of the basilica and the Byzantine Agora are between these two streets (Photo by Jennifer Ramsay).

*Figure 4.12* View of Silvanus Street from the Tell. From right to left is the nymphaeum, the central monument, and finally the Roman period reflecting pool and Umayyad shops (Photo by Jennifer Ramsay).

and the hippodrome, and the remodeling of previously built structures, such as the basilica, a bathhouse, the temple with the round cella, and the theater. The Central Monument was constructed on top of the basilica's old northeast wall, shrinking that structure by 5 m. The nymphaeum, like at several other cities, was one of the most embellished city monuments (Figure 4.12).

It consisted of two stories of columns with a decorated entablature, which Tsafrir and Foerster called "one of the most richly decorated monuments not only in Scythopolis but also in Palestine" (1997, 96). The odeon, like the theater, faced north, and likely functioned as the *bouleuterion* like the northern theater at Gerasa. It could have held about 400 people. The hippodrome lies almost half a kilometer south of the main theater. It could not have been constructed closer to the civic center because of the slope of the Nahal Amal. It is estimated that it could hold approximately 12,000 attendees (Figure 4.13).

Although the exact date of the hippodrome is unknown, it must have been built sometime in the second century or early third century, making it largely contemporary with the one at Gerasa. A nearby gate is likely the "Gate of the Campon" mentioned in the mosaic at Rehov, a small village near Scythopolis. The temple with the round cella is the best understood temple in the city, though it is smaller than the one on the Tell and the one to the west described below. It was dedicated to an unknown god, but a statue of Marcus Aurelius stood on the lowest step for the staircase. It was a tetrastyle pronaos with a broken pediment. It was built over underground vaults, which may have been used for religious services, perhaps dedicated to Dionysius or his nurse Nysa. The theater was rebuilt, with the benches, vault, and *scaenae frons* all replaced. The *scaenae frons* was embellished with granite columns, marble and a decorated frieze (Figure 4.14).

Another major rectangular structure has not been extensively excavated, but it bounds the western side of the civic center. It appears to be a massive

*Figure 4.13* Remains of the hippodrome at Scythopolis (Photo by Carole Raddato).

*The Decapolis (Gerasa and Scythopolis)* 111

*Figure 4.14* The theater at Scythopolis (Photo by Carole Raddato).

temple enclosure, with Ionic colonnades and walls marking the complex off from the rest of the city. Its east-west dimensions are at least 100 m. It is located directly across from the propylon staircase that leads to the temple on the Tell on the northern street. So far it has not been dated, but it was clearly incorporated into the civic plan.

In the center of the city, monuments such as the Monument of Antonius and the Central Monument served to link Valley Street, Silvanus Street, and the Northern Street together, but these monuments were placed on the edge of the streets, and not at intersections such as the with the tetrapylons of Gerasa. If one approached the civic center from Valley Street, which led to the residential area, one would see the Central Monument from as far away as the northeast gate. This monument was built on the southern side of the Northern Street so that it did not restrict traffic in the street.

Although the spectacular monuments of the civic center are the most famous remains from the Roman period, it is clear that the Tell, now largely transformed into an acropolis, was an important spiritual focal point of the city. On the summit was a very large temple, measuring approximately 22 × 37 m, which had a staircase running down to a propylon at the foot of the Tell near the newly constructed town center (Figure 4.15).

It has been suggested that this gate, which appeared little used, was the via sacra for the temple. Portions of a rectangular stone podium, limestone column drums, and Corinthian capitals were discovered along with some fragmentary statues. It is possible that the entire summit functioned as the temenos for this temple, likely dedicated to Zeus Akraios, Zeus of the High Mountain. Another staircase located to the west of the propylon led up to lower portion of the Tell.

*Figure 4.15* The propylon to the Tell (Photo by Carole Raddato).

The Northern Street ran to the west gate of the city that took one to the road to Legio and then to Caesarea. Following Valley Street from the city center led to the road to Gadara and Syria after crossing over a bridge and through a gate. Both gates were constructed in the second century, with the city walls dating from a later period. They were originally freestanding, much like the Arch of Hadrian at Gerasa. It is known that Scythopolis had six gates by late antiquity, but some of these may have dated also to the Roman period.

Unlike at Gerasa, which follows an orthogonal design, the topography of Scythopolis prevented straight intersecting streets, except in the valley were the public heart of the city was located. To accomplish these, straight streets required the massive movement of earth and cutting into the Tell. There, the streets, like at Gerasa, were colonnaded with roofed porticoes functioning as sidewalks and lined with shops. There was no one cardo or decumanus inside the public center of the city. Instead, two sets of three streets intersected and surrounded the space that became the "Byzantine Agora." These streets were named by the excavators as Northern Street, which entered the center from the north-west, Valley street that led from the residential areas in the ravines of Nahal Harod and Nahal Amal, Silvanus street that entered the center from the southeast, the eastern street that ran down the eastern side of "Byzantine Agora," and finally Palladius that ran on the western side of the agora. The paving for both Silvanus Street and Palladius Street from the Byzantine period lie over Roman-period roads. As at Gerasa, the streets were lined with shops, but no forum or macellum has yet to be identified.

Few residential areas of Scythopolis have been excavated. The best guess is that residences were located on the slopes around the valleys of Nahal Harod and Nahal Amal, with the public areas located in the valley south of Tell Beth Shean. The movement of residential and public buildings to a much less protected area, compared to previous settlement on the Tell, is one indication of the enhanced security that the Pax Romana brought to the region. At this time, there hasn't been enough exploration to understand the extent of residential settlement or to determine exact periods of occupation, but it appears that the Roman period site was much smaller than the one in late antiquity. At present, there have been no findings of buildings from the Roman period on the southern plateau other than the hippodrome, on the western hill or on Tel Iztaba in the north, all of which are covered by remains from the Byzantine period. The excavators estimate that between fifteen and eighteen thousand people lived in the city by the end of the third century.

## Late antiquity

In late antiquity, the populations of Gerasa and Scythopolis continued to expand. Both cities appear to have suffered some damage from the 363 earthquake, but this damage was most heavily felt in Scythopolis. The late fourth century, then, was a time of increased building in that city to repair damage from the earthquake. Scythopolis also became capital of an imperial province around that time, which is clearly indicated by the number of buildings constructed by Roman governors there. Gerasa increasingly became a city of churches, and several of the churches occupied the space around the Temple of Artemis. There are no surviving churches from the civic center of Scythopolis, but on the Tell, a Christian church replaced the Temple of Zeus. The importance of Scythopolis for the imperial administration is perhaps shown by the continued construction of non-religious structures there, such as the Sigma. There is little evidence that the Muslim conquest substantially impacted either city, at least initially. At Gerasa, a congregational mosque was built in the heart of the civic center and was surrounded by new shops. A new commercial district was also constructed in Scythopolis during the early Islamic period, but other sections of the civic center were being abandoned.

### *Gerasa*

Gerasa continued to be a prosperous city in late antiquity, and unlike some other cities of the region, such as Scythopolis, its increasing Christian character can be easily charted through archaeological remains. At least twenty churches have been discovered in the city, most of them dated through building inscriptions. Although they are found throughout the town, including on the eastern side of the river, the majority are clustered around the

Temple of Artemis. Thus, the conversion of substantial numbers of people at Gerasa to Christianity led to a change in the focal point of the city. The plan of the cardo and North and South Decumanus remained intact, but the uses of those roads changed significantly. After the city came under control of the Muslims, they too left their mark. The churches appear to have been largely undisturbed, but a substantial mosque was built right in the heart of the city at the corner of the South Decumanus and the Cardo.

The changes to the city in late antiquity were substantial. For example, the hippodrome, which was already being used for manufacturing by the late third century, continued to be a site of industrial use, but the northern end was converted into an arena. Formerly public buildings, such as the temenoi of the Temples of Artemis and Zeus and the Northern Theater, were occupied by industrial production as well. The Temple C temenos was divided into living quarters. The building of churches also transformed previous public areas, with the Cathedral completely obscuring the remains of the Temple of Dionysus-Dushares and the Propylaeum church's construction blocked the northern bridge across the river. Almost every quarter of the city saw increased population density, but this was true especially around the South Tetrapylon, which became the focus of the city during the Islamic period.

The increasing population density meant that much of the open space that characterized the earlier Roman city disappeared. For example, the open spaces of the temple precincts were occupied with either living spaces, churches, or manufacturing. The streets seem to have become narrower as more residential structures were built that encroached on public spaces, for example in the domestic complex north and west of the Church of St. Theodore which reduced the street to an alley. Winding roads, rather than straight ones, cut through these residential complexes. The curved roads followed the topography instead of cutting through and across it, which diminished wind effects and permitted the higher population densities characteristic of this period (Figure 4.16).

The reuse of building material, called spolia, increased dramatically in the late antique period at Gerasa as the population increased and older buildings went out of use (though it must be pointed out that there is evidence of the use of spolia in the earlier period, such as for the Arch of Hadrian). For example, blocks from the Temple of Artemis were reused to create the architrave above the door of the Church of St. Theodore. Some portico columns in the Cathedral courtyard were reused from the temple of Zeus. The people of Gerasa reused a second century door in the Cathedral that was too big for the space, and the walls of the entire church were built with spolia. The Baths of Placcus in the Cathedral complex had two columns taken from the south gate and Hadrian's arch and six from the West baths. An octagonal church just north of city wall reused a large Ionic column atrium taken from the northern end of the Cardo. The Church of Bishop Isaiah reused a mix of columns and capitals including one Ionic column,

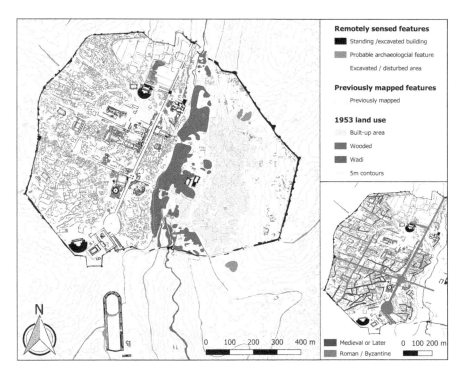

*Figure 4.16* Map of Gerasa created with remote sensing data. This evidence shows the changes in the late antique street system (Stott, D., S. Kristiansen, A. Lichtenberger, and R. Raja. "Mapping an ancient city with a century of remotely sensed data." *Proceedings of the National Academy of Sciences of the United States*, vol. 115, no. 24, figure 5. Copyright and courtesy of the Danish-German Jerash Northwest Quarter Project)

whereas the others were Corinthian. Stones bearing inscriptions, especially those to pagan gods and goddess, were used in many of the churches. It has been argued that the use of these inscriptions in churches demonstrated to Christians that the old gods had been defeated. It is not necessary a sign of "decline", as reuse was a feature of the city throughout its history – even in the Roman period.

There were many changes around the hippodrome in late antiquity. Blocks of the hippodrome were used to rebuild part of the city wall, possibly in 390, as noted in an inscription. This was perhaps related to earthquake destruction from 363, and the collapse of portions of the southern part of the cavea (seating area). This area was occupied in the fifth and sixth centuries with occupational and domestic uses until the middle of the sixth century. Once the hippodrome was out of use as an entertainment facility, industrial activities returned to the area. Pottery kilns and simple dwellings were found in the cavea chambers of the hippodrome where mass production of pottery, tiles, pipes, lamps, figurines, and Jerash bowls was located, and tanneries and lime kilns (for preparing animal skins) were also operating. These installations were abandoned at the beginning of the seventh century. In the fifth century, kilns and tanneries in the northern half closed, possibly with the resumption of some games. By the beginning of sixth, industries had returned to the cavea chambers, but the arena itself was empty without structures. There is evidence for northern use as a later entertainment facility, for example, marked seats. Over two hundred plague victims were buried on top of the abandoned workshop structures in the mid-seventh century, indicating it was no longer being used.

Just to the east of the hippodrome, the Church of Bishop Marianos was built with stones from the hippodrome in 570, and the Deacon Elias occupied part of the hippodrome as his living quarters. His house there was abandoned in first part of the seventh, and it is tempting to suggest that the Persians pushed him out in order to use the hippodrome, at which time they set up goal posts to play polo. The Church was destroyed in the earthquake of 749.

It is unknown when the Temple of Zeus went out of use, but evidence suggests that it might have continued into the early fourth century. The upper Zeus complex was covered with thick deposits, including extensive remains in the north and west temenos. The excavators are not sure how this space was being used in late antiquity, as it seems that discarded ceramics, smashed roof tiles, and other rubble were purposely laid out in the temenos court. This could be related to the closing (or destruction) of the temple and the leveling of the courtyard for industrial purposes. Blocks and columns from the Roman *naos* of the temple were removed to build the baths of Placcus in the middle of the fifth century. The area was then used by Christian monks.

Substantial changes occurred in the northern half of the city, as the Temple of Artemis went out of use by end of the fifth century as a pagan religious structure. Although the temenos of the temple was largely abandoned, the site retained some religious significance as a small sixth-century church was also built on the terrace of the temple of Artemis. In order to build the church, the Roman floor of the temenos was removed. The cella of the temple remained unoccupied from the fifth century onwards.

Christian churches surrounded the Temple of Artemis by the middle of the sixth century, and they invested the previous buildings with little regard for symmetry. They were not on the main streets, and did not follow the previous city plan. Just to the north of the temple next to the North Theater, the church of the Bishop Isiah was built in 558/9. A triad of churches built between 529 and 533 – a church to the Saints Cosmas and Damianus shared an atrium with a church dedicated to St. George and another to John the Baptist – lay directly to the southwest of the temple complex. Directly to the south of the Temple were the Cathedral church, the Church of Saint

Theodore, and the baths of Placcus. It has been suggested that the churches were built around the Temple of Artemis because those areas had open space, but this seems unlikely, especially since the Cathedral church was built over the remains of a temple. Rather, these churches were built around the Temple of Artemis because it was the heart of the public city, and the churches made a statement about the nature of the late antique community – Gerasa was now Christian.

One of the largest constructions during the late antique period was the Cathedral, built over a previous temple. The already existing city plan required elements of awkward design. For example, the Cathedral staircase cut into the street shops and was built over a previous staircase that led to the temple. This required a new, steeper staircase, which was constructed, but it led to a blank wall, with the Cathedral located on the other side! To disguise such awkwardness, a small chapel of Mary was built on the staircase landing. Any visitor to the Cathedral from the cardo was, thus, required to walk around the Cathedral to enter it.

The Cathedral complex was focused around the Fountain Court and three terraces that increased in height moving from west to east. The Cathedral itself was located to the east of the court, with the Church of St. Theodore church constructed to the west of the court in 494. The complex included the Baths of Placcus, which were built 454–455, and renovated later in 584, to the north of the Fountain Court. Although the complex is small compared to other baths in Gerasa, it does indicate the continuing desire of the Christian community to continue with some practices from the pagan past. To the west of the Church of St. Theodore is a large building around a peristyle courtyard. Many of the rooms surrounding the courtyard containing mosaic floors were perhaps the residence of the bishop or other church officials (see Figure 2.24).

In the sixth century (530/1 to be exact), the increasing Christian character of the city can be seen with the building of the synagogue church on top of a synagogue near the western wall of the city. The synagogue had likely been built in the third or fourth century. All Jewish elements in the mosaics were covered, and a new entrance to the church removed the Torah niche. And yet, the city was not yet thoroughly Christian (Figure 4.17).

An inscription from sixth-century Gerasa records the celebration of the Maiumas festival at Birketein just to the north of the city, where there is a small theater and pool complex with an associated bathhouse.

The North Theater was still in use in the late fourth or early fifth century, based on the laying down of gravel for footpaths to access the building. By the late fifth or early sixth century, the North Theater was no longing functioning, as a new structure was built in the *proscaenium*. In the early sixth century, it was being looted for building material, perhaps as a result of an earthquake that damaged the *scaenae* and collapsed portions of the seating. It was used as a dump from the mid-sixth until the eighth century when pottery production began on the site. Occupation ended in the late ninth or

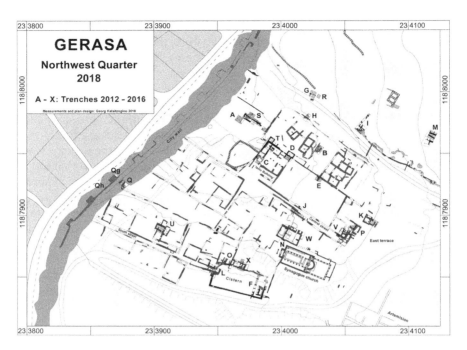

*Figure 4.17* Map of excavations in northwest Gerasa with a plan of the synagogue church (Copyright and courtesy of the Danish-German Jerash Northwest Quarter Project).

early tenth century. The areas just north of the North Theater were occupied by domestic structures in the seventh and eighth centuries.

The area around the South Tetrapylon was transformed around the turn of the third/fourth century. The South Tetrapylon itself was remodeled to display the images of the Tetrarchs. Near contemporaneously, a bathhouse was constructed at the corner later occupied by the mosque. Shops flanked an alley leading to the bathhouse along the South Decumanus, attesting to continued commercial activity in the period. A semicircular latrine was found with a water channel and evidence of seats. Other latrines include one in the baths of Placcus and one on the southeast corner of the South Tetrapylon plaza.

Evidence points to increased commercial activity in the fifth and sixth centuries in the southern half of Jerash. The macellum was expanded to the south and north, the South Tetrapylon had become a commercial center, and a commercial area opened in the eastern façade of the temple of Zeus. By the late sixth century, the macellum had been converted to industrial uses. The north and west side of the market was turned into a dye manufacturing center. Sections of the market were now used for storage and stables, possibly because animal products were used in the dye-making process. Portions of the floor were removed to create an in-ground lime kiln. For some reason, the center was abandoned and then destroyed in the early seventh century. There was some later clearing of the rubble during the Islamic period, but it is difficult to determine the extent of the use of this structure at that point.

The middle of the sixth century brought a series of transformations in the northern half of the monumental city. The entrances to shops along North Decumanus were blocked off in the early fifth century, suggesting that they had gone out of use. By 559 CE when the Bishop Isaiah constructed a church near the North Theater, it had already been abandoned as mentioned above. The north tetrapylon was also blocked around the same time, and the North Decumanus went out of use. Columns from the North Decumanus were used in building the Church of the Bishop Isaiah. The North Decumanus was filled with dirt at the end of sixth or early seventh centuries. On top of these dirt layers were occupation walls that seem to be related to kilns in North Theater.

One of the last monumental constructions in the city was the Propylaeum church, built in 565 CE inside the massive propylaea of the Temple of Artemis. One feature of this church was that it completely blocked the processional way over the northern bridge that connected the two parts of the city. The bridge had likely been heavily damaged or destroyed prior to this time, perhaps by the 551 CE earthquake that struck the region. Building this church in that location made clear that the northern bridge could not be used or repaired in the future, leaving only the southern bridge available for traffic between the two halves of the city. Here too, as with the Cathedral, construction relied on the reuse of spolia. For examples, columns for the nave were actually reused columns from the nearby street. Road curbs were used as the edges of the aisles and other boundaries of church. The continued use of the church is attested in the late sixth and early seventh centuries.

There is no evidence of a stark break between the period of Roman and early Islamic rule, instead, the growth of population that is evident in the sixth century seems to have continued unabated until the eighth century, when it seems that population reached its height in the city. Evidence of eighth century Gerasa is present in almost every excavated location around the city; however, little information of this later occupation was recorded by the earliest and most extensive excavations of the city. For example, the excavation report of the early twentieth century excavations by the Yale team described the latest occupation in the oval plaza and around the South Tetrapylon as "wretched hovels", but records from the excavation project field notes indicate very intensive settlement in that area during the early Islamic period. New excavations in the northwest sector of the city are revealing rich occupation layers from the Umayyad period, including multi-story houses that were destroyed by the earthquake of 749. The discovery of over 100,000 unused tesserae in these damaged houses demonstrate that mosaic production was continuing even in the middle of the eighth century.

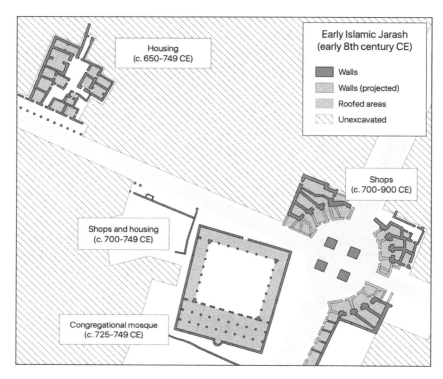

*Figure 4.18* Map of the early Islamic civic center of Gerasa showing the remodeled shops around the South Tetrapylon, mosque, and houses north of the South Decumanus (Map by Rune Rattenborg).

Archaeology of the early Islamic period in Gerasa demonstrates that settlement patterns were changing (Figure 4.18).

For example, Umayyad houses share a courtyard, such as those just north of the South Decumanus. Their plan is irregular because they used previous Roman period walls as foundations. These residences cut into the hill to the north, where a retaining wall was constructed. A staircase connected the houses with the terrace above. There was no evidence of earthquake damage from the eighth century in these houses, and occupation continued into the ninth century, when kilns were used in the courtyard. The houses opened onto the South Decumanus between two shops, indicating that commercial life on this street continued unabated.

There is ample evidence of continued industrial production throughout the city in the early Islamic period. Two pottery kilns were found across the cardo from the Temple of Artemis along with a blacksmith shop, which continued into the eighth century. Additionally, the macellum was used as a stable, tabernae, dying workshop, and ceramic production center.

There is evidence of some abandonment of churches in the early Islamic period, but many of the churches were still functioning at the time of the 749 earthquake. The Church of Saints Cosmas and Damianus was abandoned sometime in the seventh century, although the other two churches, which were connected to it by the atrium – that of St. George and of John the Baptist were still in use at the time of the earthquake of 749. At some point after the early seventh century, the Propylaeum Church went out of use, and was covered by residential structures. One of these houses had tabuns (open air ovens), and others had basins for lime to make plaster. These structures used packed earth floors to cover the pavers and mosaics of the church. The earthquake of 749 seems to have heavily damaged the area, and no later occupation was noted.

Even though many churches were still in use, the city was increasingly orientated around its mosques. The intersection of the South Decumanus and the Cardo became the focal point of the Islamic community with the construction of a large mosque in the eighth century. This mosque was framed by the South Decumanus to the north and the macellum to the south, and the cardo to the east. The mosque was remodeled at least once. For example, four doorways were later added to the plan of the mosque.

The entire area around the mosque was occupied by domestic structures. An alley runs along the west wall of the mosque, with multiple dwellings surrounding an open courtyard. This area was continuously used even after the earthquake of 749 as there is evidence of repair of earthquake damage. Umayyad and Abbasid shops were found east of the cardo across from the mosque. There was also a large building just behind them – perhaps originally Umayyad, but maybe even earlier – which was remodeled after the earthquake.

There was also a small mosque off the cardo near the processional way to the Temple of Artemis, which reused a Roman structure, and possibly destroyed the north bathhouse. It collapsed, but was later repaired with a smaller mihrab. In comparison with other cities examined in this book, there appears to be greater Islamic influence on the city of Gerasa, with the exception of Jerusalem.

## *Scythopolis*

Scythopolis achieved its largest population size in late antiquity, likely during the early to mid-sixth century. In fact, its population may have doubled to around thirty to forty thousand people, possibly making it the third largest city in the southern Levant behind Caesarea and Jerusalem. Domestic structures expanded over most of the previously uninhabited sections of the city, such as Tell Iztaba. A church and houses replaced the town acropolis and temple on main Tell. Additionally, the city wall was constructed sometime in this period, increasing intensification inside the city and suburbs were built beyond the city walls. In terms of monumental structures, the late fifth century and early sixth century (the reigns of emperors Anastasius [491–518] and Justin I [518–527]) seem to have been the period of highest construction. As Tsafrir and Foerster point out, the works in the reigns of Anastasius and Justin I transformed the civic center. These buildings emphasized the importance of the city, as it was the provincial capital of Palaestina Secunda, a province created in the late fourth century.

The city was heavily impacted by the earthquake of 363, as excavation reports describe extensive damage throughout the civic center from the mid-fourth century. Most of the structures were apparently reconstructed around 400 CE, though there is the possibility that the pagan temples were not restored, as the four or five known pagan structures were out of use by the fifth century. However, only the abandonment of one, the temple with the round cella in the civic center, can be dated with any certainty. Non-pagan monuments were repaired, for example, the nymphaeum in the civic center was restored by the governor Artemidorus at the turn of the fifth century. The nearby propylon leading from the Northern Street to the Tell was rebuilt with a slightly different plan. The portico near the eastern bathhouse was also restored with the replacement of some of the Ionic capitals. The excavators noted that the later capitals were done in a less elaborate style than those of the second century, but that the reconstruction was done with skill. At the same time, as this restoration work, mosaic sidewalks were added under the porticos that lined the streets. The theater was also damaged but later repaired, and the hippodrome may have been converted into an amphitheater at this time. The only major building that was not reconstructed was the basilica that lay in ruins for almost a hundred years before being repaired. As discussed below, this may have been because the building no longer provided important services to the city. The damage from the earthquake of 363, while extensive, does not seem to have irreparably harmed the life of the city as most structures were quickly repaired.

Evidence of population growth is quite evident outside of the monumental civic center in almost every section of the city. Tell Iztaba was inhabited for the first time since the Hellenistic period, and several churches were built on it. The Tell was completely rebuilt with large numbers of domestic structures and a circular church. Domestic structures and a bathhouse were built between the theater and the hippodrome. This marks the first time this area of the city was inhabited. Silvanus Street was lengthened in the early sixth century, connecting this new residential zone with the monumental civic center. One gets the impression that there was a rapid construction of domestic structures throughout the entire city, with the exception of the civic center, throughout the fourth through sixth centuries. It is possible that the construction of the western bathhouse, completed by the end of the fifth century, was necessitated by the rapid growth of the population.

The date of the construction of the city wall is unknown, but it was clearly built sometime during the late antique period due to the size of the enclosed space. The city wall encompassed both the northern suburb constructed on Tell Iztaba and the new southern residential area around the amphitheater. The walls were constructed with a mixture of basalt blocks and limestone ashlars from abandoned earlier Roman period structures. The walls connected the freestanding gates leading out of the city. Two inscriptions mention renovation work, likely from the first-half of the sixth century.

Extensive roadwork must be connected to the expansion of the population of the city. The civic center was repaved, beginning with Palladius Street, named after the governor Palladius who built the facing portico, which stretched from the theater to the Northern Street (Figures 4.19 and 4.20).

This street was repaired several times and reached its final form in the early sixth century. It was lined with the aforementioned portico, with a mosaic sidewalk, and commercial shops just beyond this. In 515/6, Silvanus Street and an associated basilica (Silvanus Hall) were constructed along the northeast side of the civic center over the previous Roman period road and blocking the entrances to the Roman shops located along the road. As mentioned above, this road climbed out of the central valley up the plateau to the amphitheater residential complex. The Roman road to the north of the amphitheater was repaved at a higher level, blocking the previous entrance to the amphitheater. Inscriptions mention the paving of this road and the laying of a new pipe in the year 522. Roads outside the civic center were also redone, as the road leading to the west gate towards Legio was repaved sometime during the Byzantine period.

The layout of roads is an important difference between the late antique and earlier Roman periods. While the Roman roads were generally straight

*Figure 4.19* Palladius Street facing north towards the Tell (Photo by Carole Raddato).

*Figure 4.20* The mosaic sidewalk of Palladius Street (Photo by Jennifer Ramsay).

and angles were disguised with tetrapylons, arches, or other monuments, the late antique builders were willing to employ curved roads that followed terrain, rather than cutting through the town's topography, as at Gerasa. Silvanus Street is a good example of this, which curved from the civic center to the new southern residential area.

In the fifth century, a large trapezoidal agora was constructed over the ruins of the basilica and the previous Roman temple. Porticoes with decorated mosaics were built along the inside walls of the agora. It was remodeled at the beginning of the sixth century, perhaps in response to the constructions just across Palladius street. In the reign of Anastasius, the governor Theosebius and the *protos* Silvinus (a different person from Silvanus) embarked on a transformation of the northern part of the civic center. They replaced the mosaic and some of the shops in the center of Palladius street with a new semi-circular plaza, which they named "the Sigma" (Figure 4.21).

*Figure 4.21* The Sigma (Photo by Carole Raddato).

This semi-circular plaza contained twelve new shops or offices, each richly decorated with colorful mosaics with a portico covering the entrances and sidewalk in front of the shops. In order to construct this plaza, the builders removed portions of the nearby wadi bed and the structures standing on it, which included the odeon, already abandoned at the time of the Sigma's construction.

Another example of the changing nature of the city is the fate of the hippodrome, which was converted in the fourth century into an amphitheater that reduced it in size to about one-third of its original size. The remains of iron grills were still visible blocking the entrances to cells that likely held beasts for the games, proving the structure's new purpose. By the fifth century, the entrances to the amphitheater were narrowed, and when the street was built on the north side in the sixth century, the entrance was completely blocked.

Literary sources, such as Epiphanius, describe Scythopolis as a Christian, though Arian, city in the fourth century, but there is little archaeological evidence to suggest that the city had converted to Christianity by then. One suggestion that paganism was dying by the late fourth century is the lack of evidence that any of the temples were rebuilt or restored after the earthquake of 363 (though there isn't much evidence that they were damaged by the earthquake either). Looking at the two entrances to the Tell suggests, however, that the city had turned away from paganism. While the Propylon off the Northern Street was restored, the one which connected the civic center to the Temple of Zeus was rebuilt as an industrial complex with pools and water pipes. Similar evidence of the use of former pagan structures for industrial purposes is known from Gerasa and Petra. The other structure that was not directly restored after the earthquake, the basilica, was discovered with an altar depicting Dionysus and Pan. Tsafrir and Foerster believe that the basilica was not restored because of the changing religious and social nature of the city. Pagan rituals were no longer practised, whereas shops and churches took on the commercial and social roles that the basilica once provided.

More evidence of the Christianization of the city was the discovery of several statues, including one of Aphrodite, buried in the abandoned caldarium (hot room) of the eastern bathhouse and the burial of a life-size statue of Dionysus and other statues under Silvanus Hall. As the eastern baths were demolished as part of the construction of Silvanus Hall, these purposeful burials took place around 515/16.

Evidence of Christianity is abundant throughout Tell Iztaba, including three churches and the Monastery of the Lady Mary (Figure 4.22).

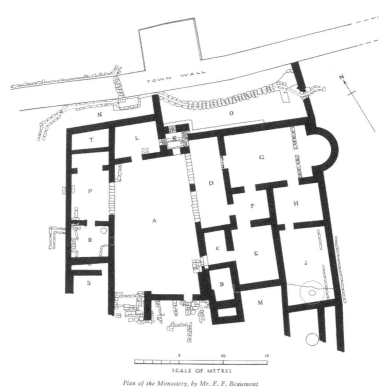

Plan of the Monastery, by Mr. E. F. Beaumont

*Figure 4.22* Plan of the Monastery of the Lady Mary at Scythopolis (Fitzgerald, G. *A sixth century monastery at Beth-Shan (Scythopolis)* (Philadelphia 1939), Plate 2. Courtesy of the University of Pennsylvania Museum Archives).

This monastery was built just within the northern city wall probably in the mid-sixth century. One church was also located within the city wall located 400 m east of the Monastery. Two churches are known to the north of the wall, one was built to the northeast of the city in 522 in the Monastery of Abba Justinus. Currently, no Christian structure has been discovered inside the civic center of the city nor from before the sixth century, although it is possible that the large putative temple to the north of the theater contained an undiscovered church.

At some point, the massive Roman-period temple on the Tell was demolished, clearing the way for the construction of residential structures on almost the entire surface of the Tell. It is possible that the temple was destroyed by the earthquake of 363, and the church was constructed on the site only after a significant period perhaps after 200 years. This may be supported by the fact that the central portion of the church was constructed over a deep two-meter fill of Roman and Hellenistic remains. Spolia from third and fourth century buildings, presumably destroyed by the 363 earthquake, were used in the church's construction. A stylistic examination of the columns of the church (now in the University of Pennsylvania Museum) suggests that the church was constructed in the late fifth or early sixth century (Figure 4.23).

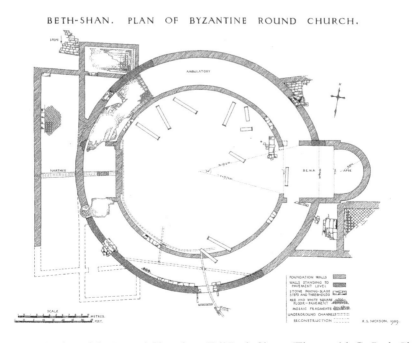

Figure 4.23 Plan of the Round Church on Tell Beth-Shean (Fitzgerald, G. *Beth-Shan Excavations 1921–1923: The Arab and Byzantine Levels* [Philadelphia 1931], plan between pp. 18 and 19. Courtesy of the University of Pennsylvania Museum Archives).

This church is similar to several churches in Jerusalem, especially the Rotunda in the Church of the Holy Sepulchre. This church consists of two concentric circular walls with the traditional eastern-facing apse projecting outside these walls. The outer wall has been interpreted as a circumambulatory. An oblong narthex projects beyond the circular walls to the west. Because of the small size of the walls, it is thought that only the circumambulatory was roofed. Access to the church likely originated from the street mentioned below into a courtyard outside the narthex.

Large mansions were constructed on the northeastern terrace of the Tell. Excavated mosaics floors indicate that these structures were elaborately decorated. A four-meter wide paved street led from the northwest of the Tell where there was a gate to the church, which was constructed at the very end of the Byzantine period. The road winds through the Tell, following local topography. This road was later blocked by the construction of early Islamic period residential structures. The Byzantine period site also had a large rectangular open roofed structure near the church (perhaps associated with the church) and a large storeroom. The structures in this period appeared wealthy, many with mosaic floors and roofs supported by columned arches; however, later constructions from the Islamic period have obscured the original layout of the buildings (Figure 4.24).

An earthquake seems to have heavily damaged the city in the late sixth century or the early seventh century. It caused severe damage to the city that was never repaired. For example, Silvanus Hall was leveled and the portico of the Byzantine agora and sigma were irreparably damaged. It is also possible that the columns of Palladius Street fell at this time. The last known repair of the street occurred sometime after 565 CE, helping to date the earthquake to no later than the mid-sixth century.

Scythopolis is mentioned in the Islamic accounts of the conquest, where it is reported that the inhabitants of the city tried to halt the Muslim advance by damaging the irrigation canals to flood the surrounding area. This did not prevent the city from being captured, but there is no archaeological evidence of damage in the city due to the Islamic conquest (or of the Persian conquest two decades prior). According to the Islamic accounts, the city was required to give half of all houses to the conquerors, but it is unknown how or if this was done.

With the passing of control of Scythopolis from the later Roman to Islamic authorities, the town lost much of its importance. While it had been the capital of a wealthy province under the later Roman Empire, the Islamic conquerors completely transformed the provincial government of the Near East, moving the capital of the region to Tiberias. Scythopolis, now known as Baysan, was just another city in the Jund al-Urdunn, as this new province was called. This transformation meant that there was no longer imperial money to improve the city, though the major monumental features of the city remained in use and standing for over a century until destroyed in the earthquake of 749 (Figure 4.25).

*Figure 4.24* Plan of the Tell showing the Byzantine and early Islamic levels (Fitzgerald, G. *Beth-Shan Excavations 1921–1923: The Arab and Byzantine Levels* [Philadelphia 1931], end plate. Courtesy of the University of Pennsylvania Museum Archives).

Although the changes that took place in the city in the early Islamic period are hard to date, there are numerous obvious trends. First, many of the monumental structures were occupied by industrial pursuits. This included the domed chamber of the frigidarium (cold room) of the eastern bathhouse, the theater which was used for ceramic production, the western bathhouse that contained a large number of open-air ovens (tabuns), the Byzantine agora that had numerous pottery kilns, and the entrance to the amphitheater which also had large pottery kilns. Along almost all the streets, shops had encroached onto the sidewalks, dramatically narrowing

*Figure 4.25* Example of earthquake damage at Scythopolis (Photo by Carole Raddato).

the size of the thoroughfares. Makeshift buildings were constructed in what were previously public spaces, such as in the plaza in front of the Central Monument. Walls were built along Valley Street, narrowing it significantly.

In the Early Islamic period, the Tell's plan was completely altered. The circular church, the Byzantine period road, and residential complexes were all replaced with a planned community, which had two roads that intersected in a right angle at the southwestern sector of the Tell. These roads ignored the topography of the Tell and ran in straight lines. Not much dating evidence was recovered from the site, but the most recent evidence suggests that this early Islamic period remodeling occurred prior to the earthquake of 749. An early Arabic inscription dated to 806 CE confirms that the church destruction occurred sometime prior to that date.

There was also some remodeling of the civic center during the early Islamic period. In the middle of the eighth century, a long line of shops was constructed on top of the remains of Silvanus Hall. These builders removed and then rebuilt the Byzantine arcade by reusing the marble bases, shafts, and capitals. Just behind the shops, another portico was erected, with an arched passageway connecting the new suq with the rear portico. A large mosaic was discovered which contained the *shahada*, the Muslim declaration of faith, and another mosaic declared that the complex was built during the reign of caliph Hisham ibn Abd al-Malik [724–743] by the governor Ishaq bin Qasbisa. Sometime later, the roof tiles of the portico were removed and makeshift shops were constructed across Silvanus Street from the new suq. The street was also not being cleaned as deposits of trash up to 10 cm were discovered along it.

So far, no mosque has been discovered in the civic center, unlike at Gerasa, for the Umayyad period. It is possible that an earthquake damaged the sigma, as it was deserted around 700 CE when building elements were removed and used nearby. The area of the sigma became a cemetery in which approximately four hundred Muslim burials were discovered. Nearby Palladius street was covered by alluvial soil. The columns from the street were placed in the former roadbed at ninety-degree angles to the road to support run off agriculture in the street.

Tsafrir and Foerster describe the city under its Umayyad rulers as having lost a sense of civic or collective identity. They recount the looting of structures, from the roof tiles of Umayyad suq to the pavers of the sidewalk on Silvanus Street. I've already mentioned above how Palladius street was used for agricultural purposes and building materials of the sigma were completely dismantled for use in private structures. In addition, many buildings especially in Tel Iztaba were abandoned, and the settlement appears to be less dense than the sixth century. There appears to have been no municipal authority to prevent individuals from scavenging materials from still-standing structures or prevent the closure of streets. Yet, there are many signs of civic vitality, and it is possible that Tsafrir and Foerster's understanding of the city is misguided. The growth of industrial activities suggests that the city became more functional rather than ornamental. The building of the suq by Hisham ibn Abd al-Malik indicates that commerce was still an important part of the economy. The city was not the same as it was during the earlier period, but that may indicate that the idea of the city, instead of staying static, changed to be relevant for the conditions of the Near East in the seventh and eighth centuries CE.

## Conclusion

Both cities were devastated on January 18, 749 CE. At Gerasa, the earthquake of 749 caused substantial damage to the city. For example, the church of the Bishop Isaiah was destroyed. It was still in use at this point as repairs to the roof and walls were occurring at the time of the earthquake, and the portico was altered and the western door was blocked. In the iconoclastic wave that hit the entire Near East, human portraits and animal mosaics were carefully removed and replaced with blanks or mixed up, showing that the mosaics were not destroyed but well cared for.

After the earthquake, the courtyard of the Temple of Artemis became an industrial zone. A potter's kiln in the forecourt of Temple of Artemis made lamps (two lamps had Christian themes, the Baptism of Jesus and Daniel in the Lion's den). The altar of the temple was destroyed to make room for this kiln. Occupation continued in the Umayyad house, where the structure was remodeled after the earthquake to create three dwellings entered from opposite sides. Pottery production, with further industrial uses, continued on the Zeus esplanade. Evidence of continuity is clear from most regions of the city after 749, suggesting that while the earthquake damaged many large structures, the inhabitants of the city rebuilt their shops, industrial complexes, and houses, and continued life in the shadow of the ruined buildings. New evidence collected in the last decade indicates that there was a large Mamluk period structure built in the north-west section of Gerasa, indicating that settlement in the city continued much longer than previously believed.

At Scythopolis, destruction is found throughout the city. One example is the pronaos façade and columns of the city-center temple, which remained standing until this earthquake, despite the fact that the temple had gone out of use by 404 CE. There was no effort to rebuild the monumental civic buildings, but local residents seem to have quickly rebuilt homes on top of the debris and settled amongst the rubble. Large numbers of shops were also destroyed. Some were later looted, but not all. Two shops still contained gold and silver coins and jewelry that were not retrieved after the earthquake and found by archaeologists. The main civic center of Scythopolis was largely abandoned, with the exception that a congregational mosque and residences were built inside the large temenos to the southwest of the Tell. Settlement during later periods concentrated in the southern residential zone with occasional occupation (during the Crusader period, for example) on the Tell.

The explosion of construction activity in the second century CE both at Gerasa and Scythopolis leads to the question: who paid for these constructions? At both cities, inscriptions indicate that the funds for these new buildings came from rich inhabitants of the cities themselves. This is one reason I've been able to give such precise dates for the building of structures at Gerasa, because the men who paid for the structures proudly proclaimed their involvement in doing so and almost universally included the date of construction in inscriptions. The building inscriptions and dedications to the deities of the city mention the names of dozens of local citizens and provide information about the city offices that were responsible for maintaining the city in the Roman period. In that period, it appears that Gerasa and Scythopolis were more like Apamea than Antioch.

In Scythopolis, some inscriptions from the Roman period mention the role of the *boule* (city council) in erecting columns or statues in honor of citizens who provided for the city, but most inscriptions mention donations by rich individuals, such as Cassiodorus who was described as "the temple builder." One individual who donated the base of a torch to light the Northern Street mentioned that he contributed to the city out of the sense of *philotimia* ("a love of honor"), which in this period was bound up with pride in donating to embellish the city.

In the fourth century, in these cities, the contributions of private individuals largely disappeared, with the exception of church contexts. In addition, the imperial authorities, particularly provincial governors, appeared as the most important benefactors of cities. In Scythopolis, the *boule* and *demos* (people) completely disappeared from inscriptions, though a local official, the *protos* Silvanus, is mentioned in conjunction with the provincial governor (the archon) in two inscriptions.

There is ample evidence from Scythopolis of imperial involvement in building in the late antique period. The nymphaeum in the civic center was restored by the governor Artemidorus around the year 400. A governor, Palladius, was responsible for building the stoa and mosaic sidewalk on Palladius street. Two inscriptions mention the role of provincial governors in restoring the city wall. The governor Severus Alexander constructed the entrance hall of the western baths in 499/500, and another governor built the exedras in the western baths, probably in the early sixth century. The road and drainage pipe just north of the amphitheater was installed by the governor Flavius Orestes in 522. The money to build Silvanus Street and Silvanus Hall came from the emperor Anastasius, through the benefaction of two members of the imperial court resident at Scythopolis – Sallustius and Silvanus – as did the money for building the extension of the Byzantine agora. One exception is the portico in the western baths, in which Nysius Sergius bragged he built "without touching public money." However, he was also the governor of the province, so not necessarily a private citizen!

The reigns of Anastasius [491–518] and Justin I [518–527] were the peak of construction in late antique Scythopolis. Tsafrir and Foerster argue that two events – the Samaritan revolt of 529 and the plague of 541/2 – dramatically damaged the city. The only problem with this interpretation is that there is little evidence of either event having a large impact on the city. There is no archaeological evidence of the revolt as causing damage in Scythopolis, though a thousand pounds of gold were allotted for the entire province of Palaestina Secunda for repairs. The one known casualty was Silvanus, who was responsible for obtaining the emperor's support for the construction of Silvanus Street and Silvanus Hall; and he was lynched by a Christian mob in 529 because he was a Samaritan.

There are few imperial officials mentioned in building inscriptions in late antique Gerasa, and none of the constructions are extant (one may have been a portico near the South Tetrapylon). Instead, there are eleven different bishops mentioned in mosaic inscriptions as builders of churches, baths, a jail, and repairs to structures. The earliest of these bishops is Exercecius in 359 who built an unknown structure, whereas the latest is Genesius in 611 who built his eponymous church. The most active bishop was Paul who in 531 was responsible for the prison, the churches of Procopius, Saint John, Maria and Soreg, the Synagogue church, and for repairs in the Cathedral.

Bishops were now the only local elites who were mentioned in building inscriptions at Gerasa. They constructed churches, but also public baths and even a jail! Although there are no Christian buildings known from the civic center of Scythopolis, inscriptions in the Monastery of Abba Justinus built in 522 and a hospital for lepers built by the bishop Theodorus in 558/9 indicate that church officials were responsible for building in Scythopolis as well.

The transition from local benefactors to imperial and church authorities in the construction and maintenance of public buildings is a sign of changing culture in late antiquity. Christianity taught that its adherents should seek the treasures of heaven rather than civic fame or wealth in this life. One response to these changing beliefs was the decline of inscriptions, which served only for an individual's aggrandizement. Such boasts became passé in a Christian world. Another impact was that funds which used to go to secular buildings were diverted to the Christian churches. Wealthy individuals donated money and objects, like silver bowls and plates, to their local churches. In this way, bishops came to control large amounts of wealth. Some of this money went to overhead, some to social services (such as alms for the poor and support for widows), and some to the construction of new churches. Since fewer local funds were committed to maintaining civic life, the imperial authorities had to step in. Provincial capitals, like Scythopolis, received a disproportionate amount of funding, as befitting their status and the attention of the local governors, but inscriptions at cities like Gerasa show that they too received attention from the imperial government.

The next chapter uses the cities of Jerusalem and Caesarea to further examine these trends. Jerusalem became a major pilgrimage destination in the fourth century with the legalization of Christianity. Jerusalem's connections to Jesus meant that the city attracted financial patronage from all over the Mediterranean world, but especially from the emperors and their families. This caused the economy of the city to boom, which brought a dramatically increased population. Caesarea came to be the most important city in the southern Levant for the Roman imperial administration. The governors who resided there in the Roman period and late antiquity constructed numerous buildings. The city also attracted wealth, both through taxation and the functioning of the imperial apparatus. Caesarea also was the most important port for pilgrims seeking the spiritual benefits of Jerusalem. The next chapter demonstrates that Christianity and the imperial administration had a profound impact on these two cities, but other historical factors, such as the Jewish Revolt of the first century CE and the Islamic conquest, also dramatically influenced the way these cities evolved.

## Suggestions for further reading

*ARAM* volumes 4 (1992) and 23 (2011) focus entirely on the Decapolis.
Avi-Yonah, M. "*Scythopolis.*" *Israel Exploration Journal*, 12(2), 1962, 123–134.
Browning, I. *Jerash and the Decapolis.* (London 1982).
Kennedy, D. *Gerasa and the Decapolis.* (London 2013).
Khamis, E. "Two Wall Mosaic Inscriptions from the Umayyad Market Place in Bet Shean/Baysān." *Bulletin of the School of Oriental and African Studies*, 64(2), 2001, 159–176.

Lichtenberger, A. and R. Raja (eds.). *The Archaeology and History of Jerash: 110 Years of Excavations.* (Brussels 2018).
Mazar, A. *Excavations at Tel Beth-Shean 1989–1996, Vol. I. From the Late Bronze Age to the Medieval Period.* (Jerusalem 2006).
March, C. *Spatial and Religious Transformations in the Late Antique Polis: A Multidisciplinary Analysis with a Case-Study of the City of Gerasa.* (Oxford 1981).
Rattenborg, R. and Blanke, L. "Jarash in the Islamic Ages (c. 700–1200 CE): A Critical Review." *Levant,* 49, 2017, 1–21.
Tsafrir, Y. and Foerster, G. "Urbanism at Scythopolis-Bet Shean in the Fourth to Seventh Centuries." *Dumbarton Oaks Papers,* 51, 1997, 85–146.
The investigation of Late Antique and Islamic Jerash can be found at: http://miri.ku.dk/projekts/djijp/ and http://projects.au.dk/internationaljerashexcavation/ complete with reports, maps, and images.
Walmsley, A. and Damgaard, K. "The Umayyad Congregational Mosque of Jarash in Jordan and its relationship to early Mosques." *Antiquity,* 79, 2005, 362–378.

# 5 Judea and Palestine (Jerusalem and Caesarea)

The New Testament is not kind to King Herod of Judea [r. 37–4 BCE], who was accused of ordering the deaths of all newborns in the city of Bethlehem in an attempt to kill Jesus and prevent him from becoming the king of the Jews (Matthew 2:1–18). His Jewish subjects didn't like him either, for he was not seen as truly Jewish. His father was an Idumaean whose family had been forced to convert to Judaism in the late second century BCE, while his mother was Nabataean. He was also considered particularly cruel because he murdered his favorite wife and three of his sons. On top of this, he was a Roman collaborator. In 40 BCE, the Roman Senate selected him as king of Judea, and he won his throne only with support from Mark Antony.

Herod supported Mark Antony's losing side in the Roman civil war against Octavian. In 31 BCE Herod met Octavian and pleaded that he would be as supportive of Octavian as he had been to Antony. Herod won over Octavian by this argument, and Octavian not only accepted Herod as king of Judea but also granted him additional lands to control. Herod demonstrated his support for Octavian in many ways, but one of the most visible was the founding of a new city, Caeserea, on the Mediterranean coast. In 27 BCE, Octavian was renamed Caesar Augustus. By naming the city Caesarea and the port Sebaste (Greek for Augustus), Herod confirmed his loyalty for everyone in the Roman world to see. To further demonstrate his connection to the Romans, he constructed a massive Temple to Rome and Augustus on the acropolis near the Harbor, where all visitors to the city would have seen it (Figure 5.1).

Herod was a profligate builder. His constructions in Antioch, described in Chapter 3, transformed that city and possibly developed the template for colonnaded streets in the Near East. He also built a palace in Jericho and two massive fortress-palaces at Herodium and Masada. But, he is well-known for new constructions in Jerusalem, such as the famous Second Temple.

Of all the cities in the world, perhaps none needs fewer introductions than Jerusalem. Holy city of the three Abrahamic religions – Judaism, Christianity, and Islam – Jerusalem may be the most written-about city in the world, and today, it is perhaps the most contested. Followers of all three religions have built structures in the city both for their own religious purposes and to stake

*Figure 5.1* The Temple of Rome and Augustus at Caesarea (Drawing by Anna Iamin. Courtesy of Kenneth Holum and Marsha Rozenblit).

a claim to the holy ground in the city against the others. For Judaism, Jerusalem was the location of the original temple to their God, built according to tradition by King Solomon. During the reign of Herod, the largest temple in the entire Near East was constructed on the site known as the Temple Mount. To Christians, the city was the site of Jesus' last days and the location where he was crucified and subsequently resurrected. Constantine [312–337], the first Christian ruler of the Roman Empire, constructed the Church of the Holy Sepulcher on the putative location of Jesus's tomb. For Muslims, Jerusalem is not only the location where the Jewish prophets and Jesus walked – for Islam honors these figures as well – but also where Muhammad rode into heaven during his Night Journey in the year 620 CE. During the reign of Caliph Abd al-Malik [685–705 CE], the al-Aqsa mosque and the Dome of the Rock were built to commemorate this Night Journey on the ruins of the Temple Mount (called the al-Haram ash-Sharif, "the Noble Sanctuary," in Arabic). Three rulers, three religions, three different polities: yet all were engaging in "propaganda of stone" in the city (Figure 5.2).

Jerusalem is located a few hundred meters east of the watershed between the Judean Hills and lowlands to the west and the more arid Judean desert to the east. In late antiquity, the remote and dry nature of the eastern desert made it ideally suited to Christian monks and monasteries. It lies about 60 km from the Mediterranean Sea, but only about 30 km from the Dead Sea. In antiquity, Jerusalem was surrounded by forests of olive, almond, and pine trees.

*Figure 5.2* The Dome of the Rock and Dome of the Chain (Photo by Young Shanahan, CC attribution license).

Today, what is called the Old City is enclosed with city walls from the Ottoman period (sixteenth century CE) that do not match exactly with any of the ancient/medieval city walls. This often confuses ill-informed visitors, including many of the first western explorers of the city. The Old City is divided by tradition into four quarters – Jewish, Christian, Armenian, and Muslim – with the Temple Mount (al-Haram ash-Sharif) separate and currently administered by an organization supported by the Kingdom of Jordan (Figure 5.3).

Ancient Jerusalem spread over several hills – the Temple Mount in the east, the eastern hill just to the south of the Temple Mount (called the City of David), and the western hill (today called Mount Zion) – and was bounded by valleys on the southern and eastern sides. The western hill and Temple Mount were separated by the Central Valley, called the Tyropoeon Valley (Valley of the Cheesemakers in Greek), in antiquity, which runs into the Kidron Valley. The Kidron Valley bounds the eastern edge of the Temple Mount and runs south, where it meets the Hinnom Valley, which in turn surrounds the western hill on the western and southern sides. The famous Mount of Olives lies across the Kidron Valley from the Temple Mount. The area north of the Old City is of a higher elevation than any of the hills of the city. For this reason, and the fact that the valleys protected the southern, eastern, and western sides of the city, Jerusalem has always been attacked from the north, for example, in 70 CE when the Romans sacked the city. Settlement at Jerusalem began on the eastern hill because of the nearby

*Figure 5.3* Photo of Jerusalem taken from the Mount of Olives. The Dome of the Rock is in the center and the Ottoman period city wall can be see surrounding the Old City (Photo by Jennifer Ramsay).

Gihon spring in the Kidron Valley, which is the only perennial source of fresh water. Another spring, the En Rogel, only intermittently produced water and became a well in the Crusader period.

Jerusalem's earliest history has traditionally been recounted using the Hebrew Bible, which states that King David conquered the city from a group known as the Jebusites. The earliest extra-biblical reference to Jerusalem appears in the Amarna letters from circa 1350 BCE and again in Assyrian documents from around the year 700 BCE. Jerusalem, and the southern Hebrew Kingdom of Judah of which it was the capital, survived the Assyrian period and lasted until the Babylonian destruction of the city in 587 BCE. Few of the earliest remains of Jerusalem have been discovered in archaeological investigations because of later destructions and constructions throughout the city. For example, it is suspected that much of the pre-587 BCE city was located under the Temple Mount. Therefore, the evidence of the Iron Age city largely comes from locations outside of the current city walls of the Old City. For example, there are remains of a large stepped stone structure (glacis) from the eighth century BCE, and several houses from the seventh and sixth centuries BCE on the eastern hill. Sometime prior to 587 BCE, the city expanded to the western hill, which was likely surrounded by a city wall.

Although Herod was also responsible for the initial planning and construction of Caesarea, its period of peak prosperity came much later. The city benefited from the Jewish War and many Roman veterans were settled there. Roman governors routinely resided there even before the city became capital of the province of *Palaestina*. In late antiquity, a massive Octagonal Church stood on an elevated platform instead of the Temple to Rome and Augustus, indicating the conversion both of the imperial rulers and the city to Christianity. Caesarea profited from the legalization of Christianity in the Roman Empire, as it became the chief port for pilgrims on their way to and from Jerusalem.

Caesarea is located on the Mediterranean Sea, approximately halfway between the modern cities of Tel Aviv and Haifa. As a city on the Mediterranean coast, it lay on the most important road leading from Syria down to Egypt. Other roads from the city went to Scythopolis directly to the east and Jerusalem to the southeast. It came to be the most important port in the area, despite the fact that this strip of coastline lacked a natural harbor. Herod ordered the construction of an artificial harbor and brought in Roman engineers who were able to make a type of cement that hardened underwater.

Caesarea sits on a very fertile coastal plain. Ancient authors, such as the sixth-century historian Procopius, described the incredibly lush agricultural surroundings of the city as "the best land in the world" (*Secret History* 11.30). As Procopius was from the city, he would have known well how rich its hinterland was, even if his comment was that of a proud citizen.

The location of Caeserea quickly proved its value. Several of Herod's successors lived at the site, as did most of the early Roman governors of Judea. In late antiquity, Caeserea was the capital of the province of Palaestina (later Palaestina Prima) and home (or origin) of many influential people, such as Origen, the great third century Christian theologian, Bishop Eusebius, the prolific Christian author and originator of the genre of Ecclesiastical history, and Procopius, the most important historian of the sixth century. With the legalization of Christianity and the origins of pilgrimage, Caesarea's economy boomed as it was the most important port with access to Jerusalem.

## Hellenistic period

### *Jerusalem*

There is ample evidence of the destruction of the city in 587 BCE, both literary and archaeological. Arrowheads and stone balls were found in excavations in the late 1970s, and several excavated buildings both inside and outside the city walls were completely burned. No bodies were found, thereby suggesting that the city was destroyed after its people had been removed.

It is unknown how many people lived in Jerusalem during the Babylonian captivity, but in 539 BCE, the Persian ruler Cyrus [c. 559–530 BCE] conquered Babylon and allowed members of the exiled Hebrew community to return to Jerusalem to rebuild. According to several Biblical verses, a second temple was completed in 515 BCE. Since it lay in the same spot as Herod's later constructions, there are no known remains of this temple. According to the book of Ezra (3:12), it compared very unfavorably to Solomon's temple. This makes sense as the community, even after the return of the exiles, would have been impoverished and in the process of rebuilding the city and its economy. By 445 BCE, the city wall was repaired as attested in the book of Nehemiah and the discovery of repairs to the pre-587 BCE city wall. Beyond these scant finds, little is known about the city during the period of Persian domination.

Jerusalem was conquered by Alexander, who may have bypassed the city, even though Josephus recounts a story that Alexander visited Jerusalem on his way to Egypt (*Antiquities* 11.325-31). After Alexander, the land of Judea was first ruled by the Ptolemies of Egypt. After 200 BCE, the Seleucids took charge. We hear little about the region until the reign of Antiochus IV [175–164 BCE], who began pursuing cultural and religious policies that he hoped would restore Seleucid power, such as promoting Greek culture to the indigenous peoples. Most of the inhabitants of Syria seemed willing to adopt Greek culture and become members of the ruling class, including important people in Judea, such as the high priest Jason who petitioned to enroll the people of Jerusalem as citizens of Antioch (II Mac 4:9). These actions and others, such as opening a Greek-style gymnasium in Jerusalem, led to the Maccabean Revolt and independence of Judea from the Seleucids. The Maccabees founded a dynasty known as the Hasmoneans that lasted until 37 BCE (Figure 5.4).

Very little of the Hellenistic city has been discovered, and only a few information is known about the plan of the city in this period. It is assumed that Herod's constructions on the Temple Mount covered the previous temple and any structures that would have stood nearby (as on an acropolis). Sources indicate that Antiochus IV built a fortress called the "Akra" (Greek for high point) that overlooked the Temple mount, much as Herod's later fortress the Antonia, but it has never been located. A seam in Herod's eastern Temple Mount platform wall has been suggested as a possible location for the fortress, but this has not obtained scholarly acceptance. This fortress might have been located either to the north of the Temple Mount, where the ground is higher in elevation, or on the southern end, which would have required an elevated platform. Another fortress, the Baris, was built at the northern end of the city to protect those approaches by John Hyrcanus I [135/34–104 BCE], but no remains have been found of this fort either. Finally, a palace was built by Aristobulus II [67–63 BCE], likely opposite the still-extant Western (Wailing) Wall, but again no remains of it exist. His successors Hyrcanus II [Ethnarch from 47–40 BCE] and Herod seem to have used

*Figure 5.4* The Kingdom of Judea at its greatest extent (Ball, W. *Rome in the East*. [Routledge 2016, 2nd edition], Figure 2.6).

the palace, and it is mentioned in the sources that describe Pompey's visit to Jerusalem in 63 BCE.

Portions of the Hellenistic city wall have been excavated in several places of the southwestern hill, indicating that the Mount Zion was included inside the city walls. Several towers were found in the courtyard of the citadel (now called the Tower of David). They had two phases, one from the middle of the second century BCE and another from the early first century BCE. In the early Hellenistic period, the city wall surrounding the City of David was built on a higher elevation compared to the earlier city walls. Two towers flanked the much earlier stepped glacis sometime during the Hellenistic period.

Josephus mentions that there was a "second wall" built to encompass a northern suburb running in an arch from the gate of Gennath to the Temple Mount. The beginning and end points of the wall are known, but there is no archaeological evidence of its exact course. However, it seems likely that the wall enclosed most important market of the city, which was located in the northern part of the Tyropoeon Valley.

In conclusion, the city was clearly growing, as the construction of the "second wall" attests. After winning independence, the Hasmoneans may have used the Akra as their palace until the construction of the Baris and later the palace of Aristobulus II. The City of David and Mount Zion were enclosed in the city walls, and the temple stood on the Temple Mount.

## *Caesarea*

Prior to the development of Caesarea, there was an earlier settlement known as Strato's Tower, founded in the fourth century BCE by a Phoenician king (Straton or Strato). While some Hellenistic period finds have been discovered from the northern edge of the Herodian community, whatever existed of this settlement has been largely obscured both by Herod's reworking of the settlement and even later development, such as the Crusader castle located in the center of the site. A small villa from this period was discovered near the expansion of the late antique northern walls (called Field Site G). Some remains of a harbor quay also have been found from before the time of Herod. One would assume that the site possessed a tower (some scholars suggest there was a lighthouse instead of a tower), but the only discovered Hellenistic tower dates to either c. 100 BCE or later. So, while there is clear evidence that a Hellenistic settlement existed at the site, there is little substantive archaeological evidence of it. It seems to have been quite small and based around the later inner harbor.

In 259 BCE, a Ptolemaic official named Zeno visited the town, and his account suggests that Strato's Tower was a prosperous port. In the second century BCE, a local tyrant named Zoilus took control of the town, and likely was responsible for building city walls around it. The town was then captured by the Hasmonaean ruler Alexander Jannaeus [103–76 BCE] in a failed campaign to conquer the strategic port of Ptolemais (modern Acre). A source from a few hundred years later mentions that when Jannaeus took control of the town, the non-Jewish inhabitants of Strato's Tower were forcibly replaced with Jewish colonists. It was later made an autonomous city by Pompey in 63 BCE, and his lieutenant Gabinius was said to have "rebuilt" it.

## The Roman period

As a result of Pompey's reorganization of the eastern Mediterranean in 64/3 BCE, the Kingdom of Judea became a client state of the Romans, and the Romans reserved the right to choose its ruler. In 40 BCE, the

144  *Judea and Palestine (Jerusalem and Caesarea)*

Romans decided to back Herod as king. After convincing Octavian to keep him as ruler, Herod embarked on an expansive building campaign in Jerusalem and throughout his kingdom, including the construction of the town of Caesarea. In Jerusalem, he left his mark throughout the city, with a new fortress, palace, and an especially grand temple (the Second Temple) (Figure 5.5).

Yet, Herod did not transform the actual city plan of Jerusalem but instead he worked within the already established civic plan. After the Romans annexed Judea, inexperienced and hostile Roman officials made life for the average person there difficult, eventually sparking the Great Jewish Revolt in 66 CE. The revolt was devastating to Judea and the Jewish population. The Roman armies, led by three legions, killed thousands and completely destroyed the city of Jerusalem, burning it to the ground in 70 CE.

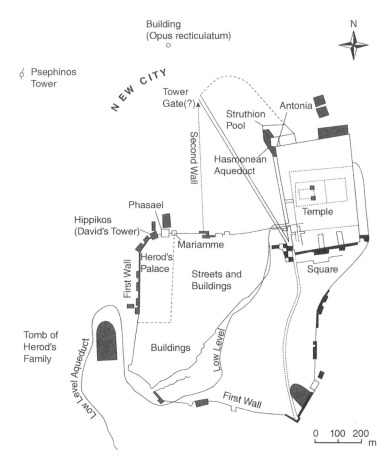

*Figure 5.5* Jerusalem in the time of Herod (Ball, W. *Rome in the East*. [Routledge 2016, 2nd edition], Figure 2.8).

Perhaps no two cities experienced such different circumstances as a result of the same event. The violence of the First Jewish Revolt began with the killing of up to 20,000 Jews in Caesarea, resulted in the complete destruction of Jerusalem, and led to the rise in importance of Caesarea. From this point forward, Caesarea would remain the most prominent city for the imperial administration of the southern Levant. Jerusalem, of course, was venerated by Christians and Jews and was heavily patronized by Christian emperors, but it lost its political role until the twentieth century.

The ruins of Jerusalem were sparsely inhabited until the reign of Hadrian [117–138], who decided to construct a new, pagan city on the site, which he named after himself and the Capitoline hill in Rome, Aelia Capitolina (Hadrian's full name was Publius Aelius Hadrianus Augustus). Coins now attest that work on the site began before 132 BCE, the year the Bar Kochba Revolt (sometimes called the Third Jewish Revolt) began, thus suggesting a causal link between Hadrian's decision to construct this new community and that revolt. While the archaeology of this period of the city's history is the most obscure, it is clear that the plan of the later Byzantine city dates to this re-founding.

## *Jerusalem*

Herod's constructions changed Jerusalem but did not dramatically change its urban plan. His new temple (the Second Temple) was an incredible expansion from the previous one. The outer Temple platform largely survived the Roman period destruction, including its access points, but nothing survives of the Temple itself. Descriptions of the Temple given by Josephus and the *Mishna* (one of the first Rabbinical texts) are contradictory, and archaeologists have proposed several different reconstructions of the temple. It is known that the platform was extended to the north, west, and south. In the northern part of the site, the rock had to be removed, whereas large portions of the southern and western expansion required massive substructures to level the new platform. This doubled the surface area of the Temple Mount to 14.4 hectares, which made it the largest temenos in antiquity. Discoveries in the 1990s suggested that the southern expansion of the Temple platform occurred sometime in the early first century CE (Figures 5.6 and 5.7).

The edge of the platform was bounded by doubled naved halls in the west, north, and east. The southern hall consisted of a three-naved basilica known as the "Royal Stoa." Jews and non-Jews used a large area of the temple platform for commerce, which is most memorable from Jesus's encounter with the moneychangers in there. There was a portion of the platform that was only for Jews, both men and women, marked by a fence and inscriptions in Greek and Latin forbidding non-Jews to enter. Another courtyard was to be entered only by Jewish men. Finally, the Temple stood facing east or aligned with the line of the walls. Some reconstructions place the Temple in the center of the platform, whereas others reconstruct it off-center.

146  *Judea and Palestine (Jerusalem and Caesarea)*

*Figure 5.6* Model of the Temple of Jerusalem built by Herod in the Holy Land Hotel, Jerusalem (Ball, W. *Rome in the East*. [Routledge 2016, 2nd edition], Plate 2.15).

*Figure 5.7* The "Wailing" Wall, the only surviving portion of the Temple of Jerusalem from the time of Herod (Photo by Jennifer Ramsay).

Although the Temple Mount remained the most famous of Herod's constructions in the city, he was known to have constructed or rebuilt several other public buildings, such as a new fortress, a new palace, a theater, an amphitheater, and a hippodrome. Unfortunately, there is little archaeological evidence of these constructions. Sometime between 37 and 31 BCE, Herod rebuilt the Baris fortress and renamed it the Antonia after Mark Antony. Josephus provides a detailed description of the Antonia (Jewish War 5.5.238–245), but only a part of a wall is archaeologically attested. Like the Baris, it was situated at the northwest corner of the Temple Mount, which both provided a location to monitor the Temple Mount and to guard it from the northern vulnerable side. No remains of the theater, amphitheater, or hippodrome have been found. According to Josephus, the theater was built inside the city, whereas the amphitheater was built "in the plains," and most scholars think that the hippodrome was located to the south of the city, outside the city walls. It has been suggested that the amphitheater and hippodrome were the same building, and that they might have been built out of wood.

Herod's palace was located in the "Upper City." It was built just to the south of the three towers of the Hasmonean period on Mount Zion. There are no surviving remains of the palace, but Josephus provided a detailed description of it. There were three square towers to the north of palace, but these do not match up with the surviving towers in the area (discussed above). The structure now called the Tower of David is sometimes identified as being one of the three towers of Herod's palace. The palace itself stretched to the south and was surrounded by a wall containing decorative towers. Inside there were two buildings, one named for Caesar (Augustus) and the other for Agrippa (Augustus's confidant), built around inner courtyards with ponds in the classical Mediterranean model. Some of the substructures for this palace were excavated, but no standing remains have been discovered.

The City of David largely lay outside of the city walls in this period. Most of the structures built there included domestic complexes and *miqva'ot* (ritual baths), which should be associated with the purification rituals required to enter the nearby Temple complex. Only one massive, monumental structure has been discovered there. Possibly, it was the palace of the former royal family of Adiabene, which Josephus describes.

There was a stepped pool, called the Pool of Siloam, located at the foot of the City of David near the location where the Tyropoeon Valley flows into the Kidron Valley. This pool has been interpreted as the site of public immersion rituals, likely connected with the nearby Temple Mount, as a stepped road led from this pool up to the Temple Mount, which then continued north along the western edge of the Temple Mount. The pool was surrounded by a small courtyard, attesting to its public function, and its steps reveal that it was worn down by constant uses. Northeast of the pool, and thus, in the City of David, a ruined building was discovered including an inscription mentioning a synagogue.

A terraced domestic complex, with an associated private *miqveh* (ritual bath), was found facing the pool on the lowest slopes of the Western Hill. These were constructed into the cliff faces, demonstrating that people exploited the local topography. The excavated remains show that there were several houses built stepped one on top of each other, with three separate dwellings per level. A stepped, paved path ran to the south of the complex up the Western Hill (possibly this was only for residents to reach their apartment). This path connected to the road that ran from the Pool of Siloam to the Temple Mount.

Prior to the discovery of this domestic complex, it was assumed that the "Upper City" (the top slopes of the Western Hill) was dominated by the elites, whereas the southern slopes of the hill, the "Lower City," were inhabited by people of relatively low means. However, the finds of this domestic complex in the "Lower City" suggested to the excavators that this distinction is invalid as they viewed this domestic complex as befitting elite occupation.

Excavations in the "Upper City" have revealed incredibly rich dwellings attesting to the wealth of this part of the city. These consisted of buildings of at least two stories (a ground floor and a basement) built around a courtyard with colored mosaic floors. The houses were clustered together on terraces that led up the slope of the Western Hill. Only one of the dwellings appears to be close in style to the standard peristyle courtyard buildings known from throughout the Mediterranean; however, many of the dwellings did have a central courtyard with more private rooms that opened off the courtyard. One called "the palatial mansion" had an area of almost 600 m$^2$. Wall frescoes were found in these dwellings of the First, Second, and Third Pompeian style. The rooms were being remodeled and repainted based on the latest styles, but one owner opted for the "throwback" First Pompeian Style. Even though this demonstrates knowledge of artisitic trends in Italy, none of the houses had depictions of humans or animals, further enhancing the identification of the buildings as Jewish. The majority of the villas contained one or more *miqva'ot* (ritual baths), attesting to their Jewish cultural beliefs.

Herod's reign and the period that followed witnessed the expansion of the population of the city, as people started to build north beyond the second wall. Although there are at present few architectural remains, there is abundant pottery from the first century CE. It has been suggested that the area to the north of the city was being used for terraced agricultural production. A Third Wall was constructed about 400 m to the north of the Second Wall. Evidence suggests that it dates to the time of Herod Agrippa I [41–44 CE], but some scholars have argued that it dates to the time of the First Revolt or from the founding of the Hadrianic city or even from the late antique period. I believe it should be linked with the growth of the city after Herod, as there is no evidence to prove a later date. Josephus notes that this part of Jerusalem was called the "New City" or "Bezetha," which he said was on the "fourth hill" of Jerusalem, which can only be the hill to the north of the current Old City. As the pottery evidence is overwhelmingly from the first century CE, it seems most likely that the Third Wall dates to that time and not from a later period.

The entirety of Jerusalem was destroyed by the Romans in 70 CE. The destruction associated with this event is well attested archaeologically, for example in the so-called Adiabene royal palace in the City of David. The entire building was completed demolished, with the top courses of the walls collapsing into the underground vaults and the complete destruction of

*Figure 5.8* Collapse from the time of the Roman destruction of Jerusalem (Photo by Carole Raddato).

the floors. Furthermore, the stepped street from the Pool of Siloam to the Temple Mount was covered in debris dated to 70 CE. A drainage tunnel ran under this street, and the excavators found that the drain covers were removed. They believed this confirms a story from Josephus that some of the people of Jerusalem fled the Roman destruction by using the drainage tunnel to escape (*Jewish War*, 6.7.370, 6.8.401). Of the dwellings discovered in the Upper City, the "palatial mansion" and the "burnt house" were both destroyed by fire in 70 (Figure 5.8).

The remains of the city were defended by the X Fretensis Legion, which would have included approximately 6,000 soldiers who also would have watched over the neighboring population to prevent further uprisings. Hadrian ordered the construction of his new city, Aelia Capitolina, sometime before 132 CE. This decision led directly to the second Jewish Revolt, named after the leader Bar Kochba. When the revolt was crushed, the legion remained at Jerusalem and was joined by veterans of the war, their families, and some Roman officials. It was at this point that the city was designed and constructed. The emperor Septimius Severus [193–211] visited the city and renamed it Colonia Aelia Capitolina Commodiana.

Scholars agree that the basic city plan of the later Byzantine city dates back to Hadrian's foundation, so the major city streets known from the later city were originally laid out in this period; however, there is little agreement about the size and extent of the Roman city. It is not even known where the legionary base was located! One interesting feature of Aelia Capitolina is that most of the building blocks were reused from structures of the Herodian period, including from the Temple Mount and its retaining walls. This is most clear at the surviving Roman gate under the Damascus Gate and the lower courses of the rebuilt tower there. According to the Madaba map, the triple entrance gate was flanked by towers. Today only the eastern gate survives, about 10 feet below the modern street level (Figure 5.9).

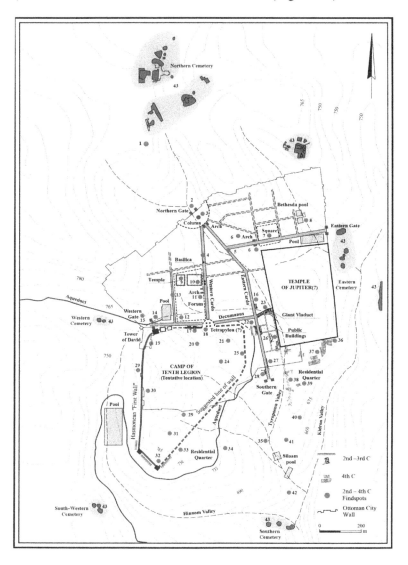

*Figure 5.9* Plan of Roman Jerusalem (Map by Shlomit Weksler-Bdolah, courtesy of Shlomit Weksler-Bdolah and the Israel Antiquities Authority).

There are several debates about the civic plan of the city, because there is so little evidence from the Roman period city. One debate concerns the location of the legionary base, another the purpose of the "Third Wall," and still another the size and extent of the city plan. I will attempt to reconstruct the city in this period as best as I can based on the archaeological remains.

First, it seems most likely that the legionary base was located on the western hill, and not on the Temple Mount. My primary argument for this is that later Christian writers, such as the Patriarch Cyril [d. 386], and the later Muslim tradition consistently describe the Temple Mount as covered in ruins. For Cyril, the destruction on the Temple Mount was proof that the Christian religion was superior to the Jewish one. That the Temple Mount was not cleared of rubble from the destruction of the Second Temple is supported by the fact that the early Muslim rulers were able to build the Al-Aqsa mosque and the Dome of the Rock there after the removal of debris. This suggests to me that the Romans had not cleared the remains of the Second Temple nor used the space to construct the barracks, walls, and other buildings that would have been required for the legion. Therefore, the most likely location of the legionary fortress was on the western hill, where Herod's palace had been located. Josephus specifically mentions that the towers of Herod's palace and the western city wall were preserved for the security of the troops stationed there. It seems likely then that the Roman legion would have reused the city wall originally built by the Hasmoneans, which ran along the western side of the hill. Several towers from this wall were excavated, as described above. One problem with this idea is that a legionary bakery and bathhouse were discovered near the Temple Mount to the southwest. However, as the legionary kiln works were located a distance from the city, it is not a necessity that the bakery and bathhouse had to be located inside the legionary fortress. Also, it is quite possible that Jerusalem only held a portion of the legion, as the kiln works at Givat Ram (2 km northwest of the Old City) and a bathhouse at Ramat Rachel (4 km south) are clearly connected to the legion.

On the other hand, literary sources suggest either that Hadrian built a temple to Capitoline Jupiter on the Temple Mount, or that there was a column with a statue of Jupiter erected there. Although no remains of the temple are visible today, the arches of a massive bridge that crossed the Tyropoeon Valley, providing access to the Temple Mount from the western hill, may suggest that the Temple Mount was in fact used during the Roman period. If this is the case, then the Temple of Jupiter must have fallen into ruins prior to the mid-fourth century. It also appears that the Temple Mount was being used as a quarry for building materials, as most of the stone blocks used to construct both the Roman and late antique city likely originated from the Herodian constructions on the Temple Mount, again suggesting that the Temple Mount was largely unoccupied.

A second debate concerns the size of the Roman city and its shape. Traditionally it was argued that the Roman city was roughly the same size as the current Old City. Nahman Avigad, noting that there were virtually no Roman remains from the current Jewish quarter, suggested that only the northern half of the Old City (north of the modern David Street) made up the Roman city. Jodi Magness has argued that the shape of the city was square, and that the third wall, mentioned above, was constructed by Hadrian as the farthest extent of the city. She argues that a dedicatory inscription found near the third wall belonged to a triumphal arch and thus furnishes evidence of the Roman construction of this wall. Furthermore, burials from this period are all located north of the third wall. She argues that the third wall was, thus, intended as an encircling, northern city wall of the city that was abandoned around the turn of the fourth century.

I strongly disagree with Magness's reconstruction of the city. First, consider the parallel with Gerasa in Chapter Four. There the triumphal arch of Hadrian stood apart from the city wall (though it could have represented a planned extension that was never carried out). The city began at the city walls, whose southern entrance led to the oval plaza. Jerusalem also had an oval plaza (now the plaza inside the Damascus gate) as depicted on the sixth-century Madaba Map, just inside the city walls. The northern edge of the Roman city wall is followed closely by the modern Old City wall, and a Roman period gate can be seen just beneath the modern Damascus Gate. Additionally, as mentioned above, the remains from between the Old City wall and the Third Wall are almost exclusively from the first century CE, suggesting that the Roman settlement did not extend beyond the north of the Old City wall.

It seems best to reconstruct the city as limited in size to the northern half of the Old City, so north of the modern David Street/Street of the Chain (roughly the modern Christian and Muslim quarters) as argued by Avigad. The Roman city wall on the north side roughly corresponds to the line of the current Old City wall. Just inside the northern gate, there was a semicircular plaza, from which several streets ran off. The western cardo ran to the south, and an eastern cardo ran to the southeast (these are the two streets that appear on the Madaba Map). The eastern cardo ran approximately 90 m west of the Temple Mount along the path of the current Ha-Gai Street. Ancient sections of this street are still visible and used today. Both cardos intersected with the decumanus, which was along the line of the modern David Street/Street of the Chain and ran from the Jaffa Gate to the Temple Mount.

The Roman forum was located to the west of the western cardo and north of the decumanus. Within this forum there was temple of Venus and a basilica. Elements of the basilica (columns from the original cardo, the triple arched gate, and façade) are perseverved in the Russian Alexander Hospice.

*Judea and Palestine (Jerusalem and Caesarea)* 153

*Figure 5.10* The Ecce Homo arch marking the entrance to the eastern forum (Photo by Carole Raddato).

To the east of the eastern Cardo and north of the Temple Mount was another forum (called the eastern forum) that is associated with the Ecce Homo arch and the Lithostrotos pavement. This forum was built directly over the Antonia fortress. Both were entered through free-standing triple gates (the Ecce Homo arch is one example), like the Roman gate now under the Damascus Gate. Near the eastern forum was a temple of the healing god Asclepius, which reused the Bezetha pools, which previously had been used to wash animals for slaughter at the Second Temple. A Mithreaum was likely located in the caverns near these pools. These structures, dedicated to the god Mithras, were always underground. Roman soldiers especially favored the worship of Mithras (Figure 5.10).

In 2017, archaeologists discovered the remains of the theater just to the west of the Temple Mount under Wilson's arch. Research is just beginning, but the archaeologists believe that it was never finished or used. It appears to have been designed to hold about 200 people, making it possible that it was an odeon or *bouleuterion*.

In the period of the early Roman Empire, therefore, the city of Jerusalem went through extensive changes as the city was substantially monumentalized under King Herod, destroyed, and then refounded by the emperor Hadrian. From this point, the plan of the city of Jerusalem largely followed the Roman streets. Any visitor to today's old city, therefore, is not walking through the city of Jesus, but rather, the city of the Roman occupiers.

## Caesarea

As described in the introduction, Herod designed the city of Caesarea to curry favor with the Emperor Augustus. The work to transform the small settlement of Strato's Tower into a Greek city and major port took years. Herod built a large palace on the site, which he and his successors used. After 6 CE, when Herod Archelaus was removed from power, the Roman governors, such as Pontius Pilate (as an inscription attests), could normally be found at Caesarea. These governors used Herod's palace, as the account of the Paul's arrest in 58 CE demonstrates (Acts 21–25). The future emperor Vespasian used Caesarea as his base during the Jewish Revolt and rewarded the city for its loyalty with the title of Roman colony. Roman governors continued to use the city as their chief residence, and it became the most important Roman city of the new province of Syria–Palaestina, as the province was named after the Bar Kochba Revolt in the mid-second century. By the middle of the third century, the coins of the city proudly proclaimed that it was "Caesarea Metropolis Provinciae Syriae Palaestinae" (Caesarea, the metropolis of the province of Syria–Palestine) (Figure 5.11).

Herod's new city completely replaced the previous community of Strato's Tower and was intended to be a Greek city from its outset (though there was a substantial Jewish community there). As such, it was laid out according to Hippodamian principles, as Josephus notes. The city contained five streets that ran completely straight from north to south with eleven running east-west, forming dozens of street blocks (insulae). The standard insula there measured 80 m east-west and 120 m north-south. A main cardo ran from the gate to Ptolemais in the north down to the gate to Joppa in the south. Three additional gates opened to the east, with roads that eventually led to Scythopolis, Neapolis, and Jerusalem. The main decumanus ran from the north side of the Temple of Rome and Augustus to the eastern gate. The earliest evidence of colonnaded streets at Caesarea dates to the second century, which is odd since Herod was responsible for the first colonnaded streets at Antioch. The question of why he did not colonnade the streets at Caesarea is unanswered. Most of the discovered column capitals date to the late second or early third century, suggesting that most streets were provided with columns only at this late date.

Herod provided the city with an incredibly large territory (*chora*, in Greek) that is estimated to include 100,000 hectares, much of it incredibly productive land. Its territory stretched almost 35 km from north to south and in some places 27 km inland. Most of the landowners lived within the city. Some of these were Greek-speaking local non-Jews, and some were veterans of Herod's armies. A large portion of the hinterland was inhabited by Samaritans, who paid rents to the city-dwelling landowners. Many Jews lived in the city until the time of the Jewish Revolt – one source mentions that 20,000 of them were killed in pogroms at the start of the war.

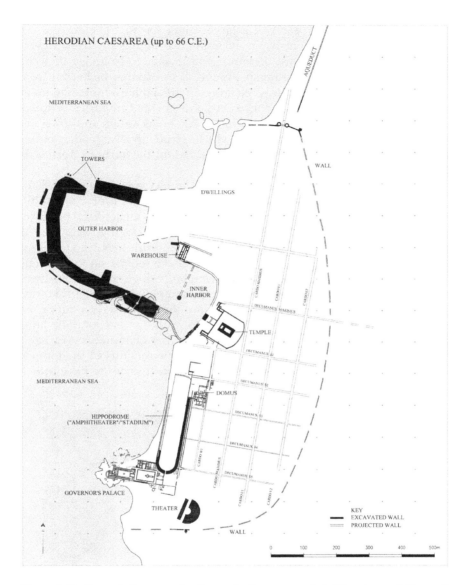

*Figure 5.11* Plan of Caesarea in the early Roman period (Courtesy of Kenneth Holum and Marsha Rozenblit).

The coastline for dozens of miles near Caesarea lacks adequate shelter for vessels, so one of Herod's chief ambitions was to create a harbor at Caesarea that would allow it to become the most important port in the area. In order to accomplish this task, Herod employed Roman engineers with the technology to "set" concrete underwater. The port had two harbors, a smaller inner one and a larger outer harbor. The currents in the Mediterranean flow north past Caesarea, bringing silt from Egypt. The southern breakwater was, therefore, constructed to be longer than the northern one, and the resultant gap allowed ships to enter the harbor from the north. The resulting port was the largest artificial harbor created up to that point. Herod ordered the construction of horrea (granaries or warehouses, horreum in the singular) on top of the breakwaters and towers at the entrance to the port. A lighthouse, which Herod modeled on the famous wonder of the world in Alexandria, was placed on the harbor's northwest corner (Figure 5.12).

The most prominent landmark in the entire city was the temple dedicated to Rome and Augustus (see Figure 5.1). It was built on a small hill (like the temple at Jerusalem) that was expanded with an artificial platform (a constructed acropolis if you will) supported by arches that were used as horrea. The platform was accessible on all sides, with massive staircases leading to it from ground level. It is clear that the temple sat at an angle that is offset from the Hippodamian civic plan, which means that there must have been a reason for positioning the temple platform in this way. The temple itself was built in the Roman, not the Greek style, on a raised podium with a frontal-facing orientation towards the harbor. The altar of the temple was surrounded by walls, much like the famous Ara Pacis constructed in Rome by Augustus. There are few remains of the temple, but some of its foundations have been discovered. It seems to have been a

*Figure 5.12* Example of a horrea at Caesarea (Photo by Jennifer Ramsay).

hexastyle temple in form, with Corinthian columns of up to 20 m in height. Thus, it is clear that the reason why the temple platform was constructed at an odd angle was to make the temple front visible to any ship or visitor approaching by sea.

The area around the inner harbor consisted of a series of horrea. Just south of the temple platform were also a number of vaults that served as horrea. It is unknown where the agora was located, although north or west of the temple platform seems most likely.

The area to the south of these warehouses was designed as Herod's prestige quarter of the city. In close proximity to one another, Herod built a hippodrome, a theater, and his palace. It is possible that Herod modeled the association of these buildings on Rome, with Augustus's house on the Palatine, the Theater of Marcellus, and the Circus Maximus serving as inspiration. The areas south and east of the hippodrome were originally uninhabited.

The hippodrome was constructed just south of the Temple of Rome and Augustus along the seashore to the location of the palace (see Figure 2.32). Herod staged chariot races here to inaugurate the city in 10/9 BCE. Recent archaeological evidence suggests that the hippodrome was severely inundated by a tsunami in the early second century CE. The southern half of the hippodrome was converted into an amphitheater. After this amphitheater was abandoned, the entire complex was used as trash dump until it was completely filled in and built over in the late antique period. South of this hippodrome and just inside the Herodian city wall, a Roman-style theater was constructed that could seat about 3,500 people. The orchestra was painted in colorful geometric designs, and the stage possessed an ornamented *scaenae frons* with three niches (Figure 5.13).

*Figure 5.13* Remains of Herod's Palace at Caesarea (Photo by Carole Raddato).

Herod also had a large palace constructed on a rocky embankment that extended into the sea, which was located south of the harbor and just inside the original city walls. This Promontory Palace consisted of several chambers that became more private as one moved deeper inside. One entering the palace from the north led into the most public space, the audience hall. From there, one would have entered a peristyle courtyard located to the south. This led west into a *triclinium* which then led onto a peristyle courtyard with a massive fish pool in the center. The sides were flanked with several rooms. Moving west down a passage, one entered into a semi-circular peristyle courtyard. One approached the most private of spaces from this courtyard through an eastern entrance. This palace was later used by the Roman governors of the province, and the building underwent occasional renovations. For example, the central audience chamber was re-floored four times, at least twice with mosaics, and an apse was placed in the dining room. In addition, a bathing facility was subsequently added.

The close connection between the palace and the hippodrome was deliberate, as Herod and the Roman governors used the hippodrome for dispensing justice. For example, according to Josephus, Pontius Pilate set up his tribunal in the hippodrome ("the great stadium") to gather the Jews who were protesting Roman actions in Jerusalem (Jewish War 2.172).

Although the city plan was completely laid out during the time of Herod, large portions of the site inside the city walls seem to have remained unoccupied. Monumental building within the city is attested during the rest of the Roman period. For example, an inscription mentions that Pontius Pilate built a temple to the emperor Tiberius, although the temple itself has not been found. Archaeological evidence shows that a nymphaeum was built in the northwest corner of the temple platform during the reign of the emperor Claudius [41–54 CE] or shortly thereafter. Hadrian visited the city and ordered the construction of a temple in his honor. In addition, a second hippodrome was built at this time outside the Herodian city walls to replace the one that had been covered by the tsunami. The western aqueduct was also constructed during the time of Hadrian, possibly indicating that the city's population was expanding beyond the ability of the eastern one to supply the city.

After the First Jewish War, Roman veterans were settled at Caesarea on the land of the massacred Jewish inhabitants. In doing so, the city became a Romanized bastion in the Near East. As a *colonia* of Rome, the inhabitants received Roman citizenship, and the influx of Latin-speaking soldiers added to this Romanness. Inscriptions mention the new Roman character of the city. For example, the famous Maioumas inscriptions, which were written in Latin, praise the actions of a *decurian* (Latin for town councilor) Marcus Flavius Agrippa. He was a priest, an ambassador for the city, and one of two *duumvirs*, the city equivalent of the Roman consuls. With three names, this is the standard nomenclature of a Roman citizen. The appearance of "Flavius" suggests that he (or an ancestor) received Roman citizenship from Vespasian or Titus, both of whose names were Titus Flavius Vespasianus.

The most prominent building project of the Roman governors was the large praetorium constructed in the first insula south of the temple platform. Latin inscriptions mention several Roman procurators who were in charge of the finances of the province. This praetorium contained a large basilica audience hall that was built on top of four vaults. The buildings continued to be used into late antiquity (see Figure 5.18).

The impact of the increased population can be seen in the expansion of the city to the east of the hippodrome (termed the South-west zone). A large north-south depression was filled in with local materials and civic trash. The latest coins in the fill dated to the time of Nero, suggesting that this project was intended to level out the ground of this sector of the city for Roman veterans of the Jewish War. The western portion of this area was built up and leveled to the height of the eastern cavea of the hippodrome. On top, two parallel lines of columns were erected, creating a gallery. The excavators discovered several streets, all paved for the first time in the later part of the first century CE; however, there seem to have been unpaved roads before this period, suggesting that the city grid was in fact designed by Herod and laid out throughout his entire walled city. At the end of the first century CE, Cardo W1 was a narrow road, with no sidewalks of columns. In the first half of the second century, at least one of the roads in this area (Decumanus S3) was reconstructed with marble colonnades. Around the same time, a public bath was constructed near the hippodrome, with a configuration implying that the hippodrome was still in use. An unexcavated (but heavily quarried) amphitheater built outside the Herodian city may be related to the settlement of these Roman veterans.

Another indication of the presence of Roman veterans is the discovery of a late first century Mithraeum in Vault 1 under the warehouses south of the temple platform. Like the more famous ones found at Ostia (Rome's port), this one has benches on both sides of the underground vault. There was an altar on the eastern end. The benches, altar, walls, and vault were all covered with plaster. The back wall would have been decorated in wood with a half-sun with rays of the sun radiating outward. Two apertures in the roof allowed light to shine onto the altar in mid-June. The vault was painted in blue to represent a darkened sky. A medallion was discovered here that shows the central feature of the faith, the Tauroctony, when Mithras slayed the Bull of Heaven.

## Late antiquity

In late antiquity, Jerusalem became one of the most important cities in the entire empire not because of its strategic location but because of its religious connections to Jesus and the origins of the Christian faith. With the consolidation of power by Constantine I [312–337] and his adoption of Christianity, the city of Jerusalem became the focus of intense imperial patronage and increasingly large numbers of pilgrims. This process began with the visit of Constantine's mother Helena in 326 and her "discovery" of Jesus' final resting place, now the location of the Church of the Holy

160  *Judea and Palestine (Jerusalem and Caesarea)*

Sepulcher. The city grew expansively throughout the period of late antiquity, and the very public patronage of Christian structures by emperors, church members, and believers, remade the city as a Christian hub. The city surrendered peacefully to the Muslims, who took the opportunity afforded by the ruins of the Second Temple to remake the Temple Mount.

Caesarea also benefited from the legalization of Christianity. The city became the most important port for pilgrims who wished to visit Jerusalem. In addition, as capital of the Roman province, and most important Roman city in the southern Levant, it benefited from imperial patronage and the wealth of being an administrative center. Its economy and population boomed throughout the fourth-sixth centuries. Unlike Jerusalem, however, the Roman government held Caesarea against a long Muslim siege. When the city was finally captured, many of its inhabitants had already fled, and the city no longer remained prosperous.

### Jerusalem

The layout of late antique Jerusalem followed the plan of the Hadrianic city. A representation of this city on the sixth-century Madaba Map shows the semi-circular plaza that opens from the Damascus Gate, and the two cardos. The western cardo is shown lined with columns and roofed with red tiles on both sides, but the eastern one only has the columns and portico on the east side (this is likely just a function of the representation, since archaeological finds have demonstrated that both sides were colonnaded). Several churches are shown including the Church of the Holy Sepulcher, Justinian's Nea (New) Church, and the Hagia Sion on Mount Zion (Figure 5.14).

*Figure 5.14* Jerusalem on the Madaba Map (Photo by author).

One of the major features of Jerusalem on the Madaba Map is the fortification wall that ringed the city. Portions of this wall have been excavated, for example at the City of David, near the end of the Tyropoeon Valley, and at the southern slope of the western hill. These excavations reveal that the wall was built by the early fourth century, around the time the X Fretensis legion moved to the city of Aila on the Gulf of Aqaba. This wall was much thinner than previous city walls, at only 3 m thick.

Excavations of the western cardo on the southwestern hill in the modern Jewish quarter suggest that the pavement of the cardo was laid down during the late antique period on a fresh site, suggesting that the western cardo in the Roman period did not extend into the southwestern hill, supporting my view of the city described above (Figure 5.15).

These excavations showed that the cardo in this area was divided by two rows of columns. The central portion of the street of approximately 12 m in width was unroofed, and there were two approximately 5-m-wide sidewalks that flanked the main street. It is thought that wooden beams provided a roof and shelter from the sun over the sidewalks. The western sidewalk was bounded by a wall of dressed stones with some shops at the bottom of the hill, but the eastern side held many shops – some constructed from stone and others cut out of bedrock. The eastern cardo was generally narrower, and the pavers were secondary use stones dating to the Second Temple period. Shops were also excavated in some locations along the street. Fill from beneath the southern portion of this street dated the street to the late antique period, providing further evidence that the original street plan did not include this area.

*Figure 5.15* Reconstruction of the western cardo from late antiquity (Photo by Carole Raddato).

The evidence from the street excavations, therefore, suggests that the Roman city did not stretch south of the Decumanus (David Street/the Street of the Chain). If the southwestern hill was the location of the X Fretensis legionary base, then that area would have been deserted by the early fourth century when the legion was transferred to Aila. Pottery and other artifacts suggest that a new city wall and the roads in the Jewish quarter were constructed in the early fifth century. The roads linked the southern gates with the heart of the city, which was centered around the Roman decumanus. The extension of the eastern cardo would have happened at this time as well (Figure 5.16).

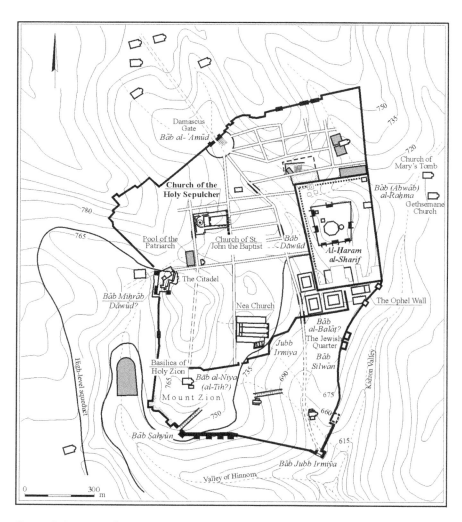

*Figure 5.16* Map of Jerusalem showing the late antique churches and early Islamic buildings on and around the Temple Mount (Map by Gideon Avni, plan courtesy of Israel Antiquities Authority and Gideon Avni).

The visit of Helena in search of the locations of Biblical events marks the beginnings of the city as a Christian pilgrimage destination. As mentioned by several authors, but chiefly Eusebius (*Life of Constantine*, 25–4), Helena ordered that the temple of Venus in the western forum be destroyed because local tradition described it as the location of Jesus's burial. While digging below the temple, excavation discovered a cave and pieces of wood that were identified as the "True Cross". On this spot, Constantine ordered that the governors of the eastern provinces construct a church worthy of their savior, which became known as the Church of the Resurrection, but it is now better known as the Church of the Holy Sepulcher. Churches were also built on the Mount of Olives and in Bethlehem at this time.

The Church of the Holy Sepulcher was originally constructed as two structures, the Martyrium Basilica, of which little survives today, and the Anastasis Rotunda, which is largely extant. The builders leveled the topography but left a large stone, identified as Golgotha, looming to a height of 5 m over the church. One entered the complex through an entrance off the western cardo, which brought one into a peristyle courtyard of trapezoid shape. Three entrances then led into the basilica. The basilica had four rows of columns, which divided it into a central nave with four aisles. Unlike most churches of the period, the apse was directed westward to the Rotunda. From the basilica, one entered another courtyard, where Golgotha stood in the southeastern corner. Further west was the Rotunda constructed around the location thought to be Jesus's tomb.

In 394, the Church of Hagia Sion (Holy Zion) was built on the western hill to serve as the veneration site for the Last Supper and Passover celebrations. Not much evidence of the church has been discovered, but the discovery of some of its foundations allows its location to be pinpointed. In the middle of the fifth century, a church was constructed to facilitate pilgrims who wanted to visit the Siloam Pool. The eastern cardo had already been extended when this church was built.

Justinian ordered the construction of the Nea (New) Church of Mary Theotokos (mother of God), and it was dedicated in 543. This required dismantling of a portion of the western cardo and the construction of a new and much wider courtyard because the church was recessed from the street. The construction of this church required adding underground vaults to support it, and excavations have confirmed the vaults and the dating of the church to the time of Justinian from an inscription. Very little of the church was found in excavations, but portions of two flanking apses and part of the southeastern corner were found. It was a large basilica-style church constructed in order to accommodate the large numbers of pilgrims who were visiting the city. At about 300 m in length, it was the largest church in Palestine. By the sixth century, the temple of Asclepius had been converted to a church, and the heated pool became associated with the miracles of Jesus at the pool of Bethesda. This church was, therefore, also connected to pilgrimage visits. One must imagine that those pilgrims needed hostels, food, goods, and souvenirs of their pilgrimage, greatly enhancing and stimulating the economy of the city.

Evidence suggests that the city was booming economically and in terms of its population throughout late antiquity. The city continued to expand north and east of the city walls. This is especially clear in the area just north of the Damascus gate, where several monasteries were founded and occupied into the ninth or tenth centuries. Despite this expansion of population, few domestic structures have been excavated from the city. For example, several dwellings were found flanking the eastern cardo on the western slope of the City of David. They were, interestingly, not established according to the city plan. Excavation of these structures showed that they were built in the fourth and fifth centuries. They were designed as two-story peristyle houses made of smoothed stones and plastered with frescos. The floors were either of beaten earth or paved. Dwellings from the late sixth century were more integrated into the city plan. These were also two stories high, with rock-cut storage or workrooms. Like earlier Herodian period dwellings, these lacked the peristyle columns but incorporated an open-air courtyard. These houses had at least some floors that were decorated with mosaics in geometric and floral patterns with an occasional Biblical quote. Several courtyards had evidence of industrial activity, such as dyeing and tanning. Some of the houses had clear evidence of cooking stoves and kitchen utensils, and one even had a latrine in a private courtyard.

In the early seventh century, first the Persians and later the Muslim Arab armies took control of Jerusalem and the Near East. Because late Roman imperial ideology was so focused on Christianity, the Persians were especially pleased to conquer the city, and in 614 CE, Jerusalem fell to them. According to sources at the time, this conquest was quite destructive to city buildings and monuments, especially churches, and to the Christian population. Several mass burial sites have been discovered, which may date to the Persian conquest (at least one contains a thousand bodies); however, there is no evidence that there was massive destruction of the city(though it is possible that the Nea Church was destroyed at this time). Recent excavations in the Givati parking lot in the City of David along the eastern cardo have revealed a Roman administrative building that was likely destroyed in 614, and the possible destruction of residences at the same time. Even if there was damage to many buildings, most of those buildings were rapidly repaired or rebuilt, so that the Persian conquest had little impact on the city plan – unlike, in contrast, the destruction of the city in 70 CE by the Romans.

When the Muslims conquered Jerusalem in 638, there was no military confrontation at the city, no destruction, and no mass killings. The Patriarch of the city, Sophronius, negotiated with the Caliph Umar, who visited the city as a pilgrim. Umar refused to pray at the Christian churches out of fear that he would create a precedent that would lead Muslims to take over those sites for themselves. Instead, he noted the ruins on the Temple Mount and saw that Christians had used the site as their garbage dump as a way to insult the Jews. It is said that Umar ordered the clearing of the Temple Mount and the construction of a wooden mosque on the site of the current al-Aqsa Mosque.

The archaeological record compares favorably to the literary sources, as there is no evidence of destruction to the city or transformation of the churches into mosques. In fact, there is very little evidence that the Muslim occupation impacted the city plan, except for a few prestige building projects, such as on the Temple Mount and the nearby palaces. The city continued to expand as the population continued to increase. Some of the residential complexes in the City of David were continuously inhabited throughout the late Roman and into the early Islamic period (although some were destroyed presumably during the Persian conquest). Evidence from the monasteries north of the Damascus gate show there was continued construction in the seventh and eighth centuries and that Armenian Christians were moving to the city.

As visible in other cities from the same period, the cardo and decumanus became narrower because of the construction of shops along the streets. Instead of representing some sort of "decline" from the Greco-Roman period, this should be seen as increased vitality of city life. Excavations of some of the alleys in the Old City show that the modern streets where laid directly on top of the late antique streets, showing a continuity of the urban and street plan. Christian building in the city continued. For example, a church was built adjacent to the Church of the Holy Sepulcher. Yet, nearby was also a mosque, attributed to Umar, that had an Arabic inscription forbidding non-Muslims to enter. One change is that large numbers of Jews were allowed to return to Jerusalem. They established themselves in a quarter in the southern part of the city, in order to be close to the Temple Mount.

The most visible change to the city was the construction of the Haram al-Sharif complex on the Temple Mount and associated nearby buildings. In 691, under the Caliph Abd al-Malik, the Temple Mount was transformed into a propaganda showpiece for the new Islamic regime. He may have been motivated by a rival claimant to the Caliphate who was in charge of Mecca at the time, or perhaps he wanted to build a structure to compete with the beautiful Christian churches in the city. Two major complexes were built on the Haram al-Sharif, one associated with the Dome of the Rock in the center of the platform, and the Al-Aqsa Mosque in the south-western corner, which was believed to be the site from which Muhammad stepped off the earth into heaven.

The Dome of the Rock (Qubbat al-Sakhra) is an octagonal structure, thought to be modeled on the rotunda of the Holy Sepulcher, the Golden Church at Antioch, the round church at Scythopolis, and the Octagonal Church at Caesarea. By using the Holy Sepulcher as a model, Abd al-Malik attempted to surpass Jerusalem's most important religious landmark. And, just as the churches at Caesarea and Scythopolis dominated those cities' skylines, so has the Dome of the Rock dominated Jerusalem ever since (see Figure 5.3).

The first task prior to construction of the Dome of the Rock was to restore the enclosure wall of Herod's Temple Mount and to restore tunnels and entrances. An artificial platform and associated stairways were built for the foundation of the Dome of the Rock to compensate for the gently sloping terrain. Of the eight sides of the Dome of the Rock, one could enter only through four, directed to the north, south, east, and west. Each of the walls has seven arches, with five center arches containing windows. Inside sits a rock that Muslims associate with Adam, the potential sacrifice of Ishmael by Abraham, and Muhammad's journey to heaven. Inscriptions, which run along the walls, attack the Trinitarian Christian concept of God and emphasize His oneness. The structure is capped by a dome equal in width to its height, clad in a layer of gold, like the Golden House in Antioch (see Figure 5.2).

A much smaller domed structure, the Dome of the Chain (Qubbat al-Silsila), lies near the eastern entrance of the Dome of the Rock. This structure is also octagonal and was originally open on all sides. The interior consists of two rows of concentric columns and a mihrab (prayer niche which faces Mecca) added at a later date. It is thought to commemorate the location where Solomon chained the earth to Heaven and is the location of judgment at the end of time in the Islamic tradition.

The al-Aqsa Mosque (Al-Jami al-Aqsa) was constructed between 708 and 711 as attested on papyri from Egypt. The original structure was a quadrangle, which faced south towards Mecca. The interior of the structure contained a wide nave with seven aisles on both sides, separated by columns. It was clearly designed using the plans of Christian basilicas but was wider than the previous churches which typically had only two aisles. It was, therefore, designed to accommodate a large number of worshippers. An earthquake in 749 destroyed the structure, excluding the mihrab, but it has been rebuilt several times since with slightly different variations.

Six large palaces were discovered just south and southwest of the Haram al-Sharif, possibly dating to the time of the construction of the Dome of the Rock and of the Al-Aqsa mosque. Each of these structures were extensive, with wall painting and stucco. These decorations are simple geometric and floral designs, and quite unlike that found in the Desert Castles of Jordan, which were also built as palaces for the Umayyad dynasty. The foundations of these structures reached up to nine meters below ground level. Among these buildings was the governor's residence, a *diwan* (financial office), and a bath complex (*hamman*). The governor's residence connected to the Al-Aqsa mosque via a walkway. These structures were also destroyed in the 749 earthquake and subsequently rebuilt, and were abandoned only at the end of the eleventh century.

Evidence of manufacturing in the seventh century has recently been published from the Givati parking lot excavation. The eastern cardo had been expanded into the City of David down to the Pool of Siloam, and a large administrative building was built there. However, this space had been abandoned sometime in the seventh century, and even some of the pavers of the cardo were removed. For a few decades from the mid- to late seventh century, this location was used to manufacture lime from limestone and marble – the nearby buildings from earlier periods were dismantled and left in piles, providing ready materials. Tchekhanovets argues that this site was chosen for manufacturing lime because of its close proximity to the Temple Mount and the Umayyad constructions there. If true, most of the lime produced at this manufacturing center was used to construct the buildings discussed in the previous paragraphs.

## Caeserea

In the third century, one of the most prominent citizens of Caesarea was the Christian theologian Origen. From c. 230–250, he lectured, wrote, and collected a large library. The city was already known for the education one could acquire, and Origen fit into this intellectual world, even if his competition came from education Latin and Greek speaking pagans. He produced a vast literary output, including a copy of the Bible called the Hexpla, which contained two versions of the Hebrew Bible and four Greek translations in six parallel columns. Christian scholars came from all over the Mediterranean to consult it, and he developed a wide circle of students. In 250/1, he was arrested and tortured by agents of the emperor Decius who had declared that all people must sacrifice to the emperor. As a particular devote Christian, Origen refused, and later died from his wounds.

Fifty years later, during the Great Persecution [303–313] launched by the Emperor Diocletian, Caesarea was site of numerous Christian trials, as all those arrested for being Christian in the province were transported there for trial, torture and/or execution. However, the legalization of Christianity in 312 and Constantine's conquest of the east in 325 had profound changes for Caesarea, just as they did for Jerusalem. Caesarea's port quickly became crowded with ships carrying pilgrims, bringing supplies for the growing region, and in turn exporting wine from the region visited by those same pilgrims. The population in Caesarea and the economy in generally were booming throughout the fourth through sixth centuries (Figure 5.17).

Evidence of this expansion is clear from the construction of a new city wall in the late fourth century. This wall runs approximately 2,500 m in a semi-circle around the city from sea to sea, enclosing about three times as much territory as the Herodian city. Every sector of the city that has been excavated has revealed extensive late antique remains. Archaeologists have suggested the population of the city might have approached 30,000 people within the expanded city walls.

Despite the death of thousands of Jews in 66 CE, by the third century, a Jewish community had returned to Caesarea. Jewish rabbis are known in the city between the third and fourth centuries from the Jerusalem and Babylonian Talmuds. The only structural archaeological evidence is a synagogue that was used in the fourth through sixth centuries, which was discovered to the north of the Crusader wall. It was 9 m wide and 18 m long with columns decorated with menorahs and mosaic pavements. Just outside the eastern city walls, excavators discovered a Jewish cemetery from the fifth and sixth centuries.

Even though the columns of the colonnaded streets date largely to the early second century, the excavators have determined that most of the paved streets date to the late antique period. This suggests that the streets were paved multiple times, with the late antique streets replacing the previous streets, but reusing the old columns. One of the best excavated is Street II from just south of the Crusader fortifications. There, a third-century street was discovered 1.5 m below the sixth century one. The street itself

168  *Judea and Palestine (Jerusalem and Caesarea)*

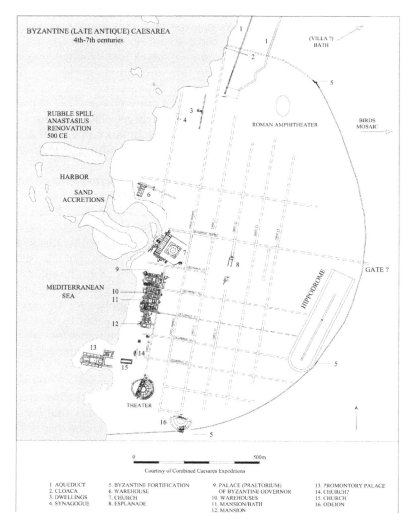

*Figure 5.17* Plan of late antique Caesarea (Courtesy of Kenneth Holum and Marsha Rozenblit).

was paved with two lines of diagonally placed stones that formed a "V" pattern, flanked on two sides of columns (the capitals were reused from the third century road). Manholes provided access to the sewer below. Each side of the street had a large sidewalk covered with mosaic pavements and roofed. Shops, houses, and public buildings were accessible behind the sidewalls, in this case, the Archives Building. Other streets, such as the east-west Street 4, were paved for the first time in the sixth century. Streets were even being renovated as late as the late sixth or early seventh century, which is evident from the street which ran in front of the horreum north of the inner harbor.

This horreum was built about 400 CE, possibly as a storage location for the imperial *annona* (redistribution of taxes in kind for the army and bureaucracy). This was a large structure, 20 × 45 m, built on top of an earlier horreum and constructed with thicker walls than the other horrea in the city. A central corridor ran down the middle of this warehouse and rooms opened off the sides, which contained storage areas for dry and liquid goods. The warehouse continued in use until the early seventh century.

Caesarea in late antiquity was the most important administrative center in Palestine, and archaeological evidence has confirmed the presence of a large number of bureaucrats who worked there. A large administration building, called the Archives Building, was identified as a result of inscriptions in the mosaic floors. The building contained seven rooms around a central court where the tax records of the provincial administration were housed. Inscriptions mention important officials, such as a *magister* and *noumerarios*, who supervised the staff, which may have consisted of over 200 individuals. This building was only a part of a larger complex which the excavators have identified as the praetorium, originally built in the Roman period. This complex took up an entire *insula*, and in addition to the revenue office, housed the governor's mansion and a small bathhouse. This complex was altered in major and minor ways throughout the sixth and early seventh centuries (Figure 5.18).

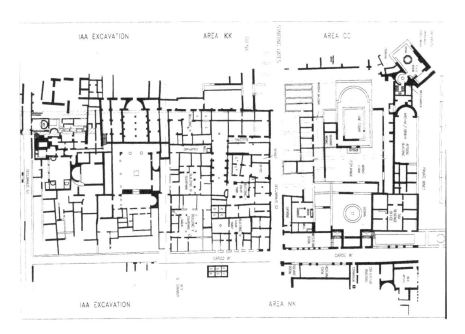

*Figure 5.18* Plan of the praetorium with Archives Building and adjoining warehouses (Courtesy of Kenneth Holum and Marsha Rozenblit).

To the south of the praetorium, there was an insula that contained six warehouses. Each one was able to store liquid and solid commodities, and included subterranean storage areas for grain. Each one had a small room with a mosaic floor, which was identified as the business office. Across an alleyway, the excavators discovered a large urban villa that took up half an insula. This *mansio* (urban villa) contained a private bath, a dining room with an apse, and a peristyle courtyard. The floors were paved with multi-colored marble tiles. Across a road from this *mansio*, there was another insula with another warehouse and *mansio*. This *mansio* had a staircase that led out to the beach on the harbor. And just south of this was another warehouse with another *mansio*. What this demonstrates is that at Caesarea, there was no distinction between commercial and private space, or "zoning" laws in a modern city. Instead, all such activities took place in close proximity, even next to the houses of the wealthiest individuals. One might speculate that the *mansio* owners also owned the warehouses located in the same *insula*, but there is no explicit evidence that this was case. It does highlight, though, the close connection between the landowners and the source of their income – rents extracted from the hinterland.

Sometime at the end of the third century or the beginning of the fourth, an earthquake struck the city. It is unknown how much damage the city received, but it seems that the temple platform was damaged. New evidence indicates that a bathhouse was constructed directly in front of the temple platform, suggesting that the temple was no longer being used. Some sort of structure was built on the temple platform in the fifth century that was dismantled to build the Octagonal Church.

At the end of the fifth century, there is clear reconstruction work visible in the archaeological record. The vaults were repaired, likely in preparation to build the famous Octagonal Church, constructed around the year 500. Although termed the Octagonal Church, its plan is actually two concentric octagons within a square. Although much of the Octagonal Church was constructed using reused materials, the columns were carved from newly imported stone. A small chapel was also built over the nymphaeum when the Octagonal Church was built. The bathhouse in front of the platform was destroyed, and a large horreum was built in front of it (Figure 5.19).

Kenneth Holum attributes the changes in this area to the revitalization of the harbor under Anastasius. He argues that these two events were coterminus and occurred around the year 500. Anastasius' actions helped restore the safety of the harbor, allowing more ships to dock there. At this time, a monumental staircase was constructed from the inner harbor to the Octagonal Church. In this way, all Christians who entered the harbor on pilgrimage would be able to immediately disembark and begin their stay in the Holy Land at the Octagonal Church. Although it is unknown to whom the church was dedicated, recent arguments have suggested Philip the Evangelist mentioned in Acts (21:8–9).

*Judea and Palestine (Jerusalem and Caesarea)* 171

*Figure 5.19* Artists depiction of the Octagonal Church (Drawing by Anna Iamin. Courtesy of Kenneth Holum and Marsha Rozenblit).

Literary sources note several churches at Caesarea (at least 10), even though there is little archaeological evidence of them, beyond the Octagonal Church and a small chapel to St. Paul. At least nine *martyria* are mentioned as being in the city or just outside the city walls. These commemorated famous Christians from the city, including Saint Procopius who died during the Great Persecution, providing inspiration for a very common name in Caeserea, such as that held by the eponymous sixth-century historian.

By the late antique period, trash had accumulated to the point that the original hippodrome was now at the same level as the gallery built in the late first century. At this point, the area was built over and integrated into the city plan. The marble gallery, which still appears to have been in used, was dismantled, and walls for non-monumental buildings were constructed in their place. Streets were laid over the fill layer, and new pavement was laid along the entire street length to level it and put in a new sewer line. The sidewalks of Decumanus S3 were annexed into private buildings. New insulae were thus made, and one of which had a large public bath. Each of these insulae were subdivided with alleys that led to dead ends – that is, one could not traverse the alleys between the cardos and decumani. Many of the alleys had stone thresholds, which would have allowed the insulae to be closed off from the outside – an early "gated" community if you will!

In the late sixth century, the outer walls of the theater's cavea were used to construct a *kastron* (fortress). Stones from the theater were then used to build projecting towers. This suggests that the theater was out of use by this time. In addition, the hippodrome also went out of use in the sixth century, as the western seating was removed, and other buildings were constructed in its place. Both of these developments point to the end of some activities associated with traditional classical culture (Figure 5.20).

In the late sixth and early seventh centuries, new buildings continued to be constructed at Caesarea. One example is called the north-south oriented "Byzantine esplanade," which was located two blocks east of the Octagonal Church, and was built between 546 and 606. It consists of a marble paved forecourt with and entrance hall, steps to an upper level, and an 80+ m long mosaic pavement, flanked by shops. The archway to the steps was flanked by two statues – one of which was of the Emperor Hadrian. Both required additional stone bits to replace missing portions of the statues' bases and were restored in a rough manner. These have been interpreted as evidence that the quality of craftsmanship in the city had declined from the previous period. To the south of this structure, there was a newly built courtyard with porticos from the sixth century. Its most prominent feature was a statue of the Tyche of Caesarea. Furthermore, the street that ran just north of the inner harbor was repaved – work which required new water lines and sewer channels. Just as the "Byzantine esplanade" has been interpreted as evidence of a deterioration of building standards, there is evidence that the civic water system to the southern portion of the city had gone out of use around the early seventh century. In order to run water to the bath at the praetorium, a well needed to be dug nearby. Other buildings in the area showed a similar need for water, as wells were dug in the floors of several of the nearby warehouses. Industrial activities were discovered in the vaults

*Figure 5.20* The "Byzantine esplanade" (Photo by Carole Raddato).

*Figure 5.21* The bath in the praetorium (Photo by Jennifer Ramsay).

below the praetorium and one of the vaults was turned into a tavern and wine cellar (Figure 5.21).

Excavators have also found evidence of industrial production of ceramics from the late sixth and early seventh centuries in area C.21, which is just south of the Crusader Wall. None of the manufacturing equipment was discovered, but the evidence is incontrovertible. Dozens of examples of lamp molds were found, and pottery wasters, and molds for cosmetic boxes and figurines. Thousands of broken pottery shards were discovered on the site, attested to the large-scale production of these vessels.

Outside the city wall, near an excavated, luxurious villa, archaeologists found a well-preserved bathhouse from the sixth century or early seventh century. Containing all the traditional rooms of a bathhouse, the floors were covered in opus sectile patterns. The most unique feature of the bathhouse is its small size, suggesting it was for private, not public use. Combined with the remains of the nearby villa, with a large 11.5 × 13.4 m mosaic floor, it is clear that the wealthy lived very comfortable lives.

In the late antique period, imperial officials are commemorated for the construction of new buildings. For example, the city walls were attributed to a count and former governor of the province, Flavius Procopius Constantius Alexander. In the sixth century, the count Flacius Euelpidius and a "father of the city" Elias (possibly a Roman senator since his title was "*lamprotatos*") financed a basilica with a marble and mosaic pavement and the steps of the nearby temple to Hadrian, which had been deconsecrated.

However, the restoration of the harbor was too costly a task even for the local provincial administration, for an appeal was made to the Emperor Anastasius [491–518] to improve the safety of the harbor, which he did.

The Promontory Palace continued to be used at least until the sixth century, though it may have been in private hands. At this point, the bath complex was no longer being used, but the dining area and the private suite were still occupied, as noted by coins from the time of Justinian found on the floor. At some point after this, the palace caught fire, as attested by the burned mosaic tesserae, perhaps during the Samaritan Revolt in 555 when sources say that the governor Stephanos was killed in his *praetorium* (John Malalas, *Chronographia* 18.119). Sometime during the early Islamic period, the pool was converted into a salt-water fish farm.

Between 614 and 628, the Persians controlled Caesarea. In contrast to Jerusalem, Caesarea surrendered, and so it was not stormed. Literary sources, like those at Jerusalem, however, describe the Persians as attacking and repressing the local Christian communities. For example, the Persians used the *kastron* to imprison Christians before execution, and the Persians used the *praetorium* as their headquarters. Some evidence of destruction has been detected from the early seventh century, but it is unknown if this destruction was caused by the Persians. There is evidence of rapid rebuilding, so if the city was sacked, much of the population survived, and no mass graves have been discovered unlike those at Jerusalem. Texts from just after the Persian conquest indicate that the city was functioning much as it had before, with a wealthy class of landowners and the church responsible for the city. A church to the Persian martyr Anastasius was begun, and the texts indicate that there were at least six other churches in operation. Whatever persecution the Persians inflicted on the Christians, it didn't cause a lasting decline.

Caesarea was the last of the cities held by the Roman Empire in the Near East against the Muslims, who took the city in 640 or 641. The Muslims besieged the city for seven years, but it was supplied by the sea. The city only fell through treachery, when Muslim forces were let in through either a sewer or aqueduct. Literary sources mention that much of the population fled during the siege, or left afterwards when the Muslims allowed "Greeks" to leave and go to Constantinople.

Archaeological evidence seems to confirm that the city became rapidly depopulated around the middle of the seventh century. Evidence from area KK (south of the Crusade fort) shows that one of the wealthiest sections of the town was completely abandoned and replaced by agricultural fields, including the use of stone irrigation channels. The walls of the luxurious buildings continued to stand, but most were in a state of ruin. These walls were used as wind breaks to protect crops from the steady winds that are famous in the area. Whether this activity occurred during the Muslim siege or after is debated. Other excavations in the northern and eastern sections of the city demonstrate the same type of abandonment at exactly the same time. For example, excavations of the warehouses in Area LL demonstrate the continued storage of goods until the 630s and then the complete abandonment of the warehouses. There is, thus, ample evidence that the Muslim conquest represented a major break in the urban tradition at Caesarea. The site was not completely abandoned, but the remaining settlement was much smaller, less wealthy, and much reduced in population.

Survey work also suggests that the hinterland of Caesarea rapidly became depopulated. Reports from the Archaeological Survey of Israel for the maps of Binyamina, Ma'anit, Hadera, and Mikhmoret – all from Caesarea's hinterland – showed that the total number of sites dropped from 238 in the fourth–sixth centuries to 43 in the eighth through tenth centuries. Although this evidence comes from surveys, which means the sites have not been systematically excavated or conclusively dated, two sites from Caesarea's hinterland have in fact been examined in detail and both show abandonment after the Muslim conquest. One, the "Mound of the Crocodiles," flourished from the fourth to seventh centuries but was abandoned by the end of the seventh century. A large villa at Horvat 'Aqav shows destruction in the early seventh century (possibly from the period of Persian occupation), restoration, and then complete abandonment in the mid-seventh century.

## Conclusion

Jerusalem and Caesarea were significantly impacted by historical events. Jerusalem, which had developed organically and without Greek styles of planning prior to the Jewish Revolt, was completely leveled and replaced with a Hippodamian-style city plan. Topography, in this case, the two hills, dictated that there would be two main cardos instead of the one seen at sites like Antioch, Apamea, and Gerasa. In this way, the design of the city was more in line with Scythopolis, whose topography dictated its unique street plan. The Roman colony at Jerusalem appears to have been relatively small until the legalization of Christianity and the subsequent growth of pilgrimage traffic and imperial patronage. The population increased dramatically in late antiquity, leading to the extension of the city plan to the south. The city's association with Muhammad meant that the Muslims were also interested in the city for its religious significance, and the Islamic rulers continued the Roman tradition of monumental construction in the city. The key to Jerusalem's prosperity – its religious significance and resulting patronage by the ruling elite – remained key throughout the entire period of this book, except for the brief period following the destruction of the Jewish city and the legalization of Christianity.

These historical events also influenced Caesarea's development. Herod was so successful at building Caesarea in the Greek style and showing his loyalty to the Romans that the city was favored by the Roman administration. Imperial officials could often be found at the city. For example, the future emperor Vespasian stayed there with two Roman legions in the winter of 67/68 CE while planning the strategy to put down the Jewish Revolt. Many of his legionaries were settled there after the war, increasing the population and adding to its *Romanitas*. Caesarea was, thus, different culturally than the cities in the surrounding region for its Roman rather than Greek, Syrian, or Jewish make-up. However, such differences were subtle. Latin was used more extensively in the city, especially in the Roman period, than in most other places of the Near East though Latin continued to be the language of government in late antiquity. The unexcavated amphitheater (and the amphitheater built out of the ruined hippodrome) could be further evidence of the city's Romanness. Other than these features, Caesarea looks like almost every other city we have examined, both in terms of its Hippodamian plan and its buildings. True, no other city boasted a Temple of Rome and Augustus, but most other cities had temples dedicated to either living or deceased emperors (such as Antioch and Petra).

With the destruction of Jerusalem, Caesarea became the most prominent city in the southern Levant. After the legalization of Christianity, Caesarea's economy became even more diverse. Trade flourished as pilgrims visited the city on their way to Jerusalem, and people in the Mediterranean wanted the goods from Palestine, most especially wine and religious souvenirs. However, the Muslim conquest of the Near East removed Caesarea's entire reason for being. The city lost its administrative importance and could not rely on providing services or imperial cash for its prosperity. In addition, fewer pilgrims visited Jerusalem from the Mediterranean world, and there was less commerce between Muslim and Christian territories in subsequent centuries. The Muslim conquest, therefore, led to the near abandonment of the city.

This chapter began with Herod, King of Judea and client of the Romans. Herod was exceptional for his building activities, but he was just one of a number of rulers in the Near East who owed their thrones to the Romans. One example, a contemporary of Herod, was Aretas IV [9/8 BCE–39/40 CE], ruler of the Nabataean Kingdom located to the east and south of Judea. The Nabataeans were a people who had become wealthy conveying incense and myrrh from southern Arabia. Their capital of Petra is famous for its beautiful rock cut tombs. Their kingdom was annexed by the Romans in 106 CE and became just another city of the Roman Empire in what became known as the province of Arabia.

The Nabataeans controlled the semi-arid region between Judea and the Arabian Peninsula. Their kingdom and the province of Arabia served to defend the southeastern frontier of the Roman Empire. Many other peoples were located on the edge of the Empire. A prime example is found in the people of the city of Palmyra, who controlled trade between the Roman Empire and their rivals to the east, the Parthians. Their city celebrated the merchant activities which made them rich. The buildings, most famously the Temple of Bel, incorporated traditional Greco-Roman architecture with unique innovations. The next chapter explores the cities of Petra and

Palmyra as examples of cities founded on the edge of Greco-Roman influence, in an attempt to understand if the distance from the core of Greco-Roman influences impacted civic planning and urban life.

## Suggestions for further reading

Avni, G. and G. Stiebel (eds.). *Roman Jerusalem: A New Old City.* (Portsmouth, Rhode Island 2017).

Bieberstein, K. *A Brief History of Jerusalem: From the Earliest Settlement to the Destruction of the City in AD 70.* Abhandlungen des Deutschen Palästina-Vereins 47. (Wiesbaden 2017).

Golar, K. and G. Avni (eds.). *Unearthing Jerusalem: 150 Years of Archaeological Research in the Holy City.* (Winona Lake, Indiana 2011).

Golar, K. and H. Bloedhorn. *The Archaeology of Jerusalem: From the Origins to the Ottomans.* (New Haven 2013).

Magness, J. *The Archaeology of the Holy Land: From the Destruction of Solomon's Temple to the Muslim Conquest.* (Cambridge 2012).

Patrich, J. (ed.). *Studies in the Archaeology and History of Caesarea Maritima: Caput Judaeae, Metropolis Palaestinae.* (Leiden 2011).

Porath, Y. et al. *Caesarea Maritima I: Herod's Circus and Related Buildings.* (Jerusalem 2013).

Raban, A. and K. Holum (eds.). *Caesarea Maritima: A Retrospective after Two Millennia.* (Leiden 1996).

Richardson, P. *Herod: King of the Jews and Friend of the Romans.* (Columbia 1996).

Tchekhanovets, Y. "Recycling the Glory of Byzantium: New Archaeological Evidence of Byzantine-Islamic Transition in Jerusalem." *Studies in Late Antiquity*, 2(2), Summer 2018, 215–237.

# 6 The desert fringe (Petra and Palmyra)

The rediscovery of Petra in 1812 is a colorful tale. Now famous as one of the "New 7 Wonders of the World" and from its inclusion in several movies – such as *Indiana Jones and the Last Crusade* (1989) and *Transformers: Revenge of the Fallen* (2009) – Petra's location had in fact been completely unknown for hundreds of years. The last literary source, which mentioned it, dated to 1276 – already 500 years after the city had been abandoned!

On August 22, 1812, John Lewis Burckhardt became the first westerner to visit the ruins of this rose-red rock carved city. He did so despite the great danger to his life. The locals believed that foreigners were magicians and treasure hunters and attacked anyone who got too close to the city, so Burckhardt disguised himself as an Arab pilgrim who wanted to sacrifice a goat at the tomb of St. Aaron (Haroun in Arabic), which was located near the ancient site of Petra. He dressed in the local style and named himself Sheikh Ibrahim Ibn 'Abd Allah. He traveled to the town of Wadi Musa and convinced some of the inhabitants there to show him the way to the tomb of St. Aaron. The quickest path from Wadi Musa to the tomb was down the 1.2 km Siq, which led to the ancient city of Petra. Arriving into the heart of Petra, Burckhardt described in his journal several of the famous landmarks of the city, such as the Treasury (Al-Khazneh, likely built in the reign of Aretas IV), the theater, and the Qasr al-Bint (a temple likely dedicated to the chief Nabataean god Dushares). When his guides began to get suspicious that he was in fact a treasure hunter, he cut his explorations short and traveled to the tomb of St. Aaron and made his sacrifice (Figures 6.1 and 6.2).

Burckhardt lived in the Middle East for several years before "discovering" Petra. He was mostly based in Aleppo and studied the Arabic language and Middle Eastern customs so he could blend in. During this time, he visited other ancient sites, such as Baalbek, home to the largest extant temple in the Near East, and Palmyra (Tadmor). Palmyra had previously been "discovered" by westerners, and like Burckhardt's visit to Petra, early attempts to visit Palmyra were dangerous (Figure 6.3).

In 1678, a group of merchants from Aleppo who worked for the British Levant Company attempted to visit the city, but they were captured by the local Emir who let them leave only after they gave him all of their possessions. The first

*Figure 6.1* The Petra Siq (Photo by author).

*Figure 6.2* The Treasury (Al-Khazneh) in Petra (Photo by author).

*Figure 6.3* View of Palmyra at sunset (Photo by Greg Fisher).

expedition that succeeded in studying the remains of the city wasn't until 1691. The first travelers to visit the site found that parts of it, especially around the Temple of Bel, were inhabited. The first pictures of Palmyra show that the temenos of the Temple of Bel was completely crowded with mudbrick domestic structures. These houses were removed in the 1930s by the French Mandate government in order to allow archaeologists to access the site (Figure 6.4).

Both Petra and Palmyra flourished in a generally inhospitable desert zone. Palmyra was located in the middle of Syrian Desert approximately half way between the Euphrates River and Damascus. It owed its existence to the springs that produced an oasis filled with palm trees (hence the name!) (Figure 6.5).

The most important spring was the Efqa, which lies beneath Jebel Muntar to the southwest of the city. The highlands near Palmyra receive enough rain for limited agriculture, and this rain was responsible for the springs and underground aquifer at Palmyra. The Wadi al-Qubur also runs from the northwest to the southeast of the site. It would have filled with water during the intermittent rains each year. The first century CE Roman writer, Pliny the Elder, mentioned that the springs allowed the cultivation of fields near the city, but that it was a virtual island in its isolation because of the desert.

Petra, on the other hand, is located in the Shara mountain range to the east of the Wadi Araba. It received more rain than Palmyra, but this rain needed to be harvested, stored, and protected. The spring in Wadi Musa also provided the city with water, as the surviving pipes in the Siq demonstrate. Agriculture was possible in the area around Petra. Research conducted around Jebel

The desert fringe (Petra and Palmyra)  181

*Figure 6.4* Photograph from the 1884 Wolfe expedition showing the mudbrick houses built inside the temenos of the Temple of Bel (Photographs of Asia Minor, #4776. Division of Rare and Manuscript Collections, Cornell University Library).

*Figure 6.5* The Temple of Bel as seen from the oasis (Photo by Greg Fisher).

Haroun (the traditional site of Aaron's tomb), located 3 km southwest of Petra, shows that the Nabataeans built dikes, dams, and irrigation channels that served to channel and control water for the production of plants. These structures were maintained, reused, and expanded into late antiquity.

Both cities were important for their role as commercial centers. The Nabataeans controlled overland trade networks that connected the Mediterranean Sea with the southern Arabian Peninsula, through which they brought incense and myrrh and some other luxury items from the Red Sea. Petra was also home of an extensive perfume and ceramic manufacturing center. Although they faced competition from merchants operating out of Egypt via the Red Sea, the overland trade routes seem to have continued at least into the third century CE, at which time the perfume industry also seems to have collapsed. This means that caravan traffic continued even after the Roman annexation of Petra and the Nabataean Kingdom in 106 CE.

Palmyra, on the other hand, was located between Roman territories and those controlled by the Parthians and later Sassanian Persians. The city and its merchants formed a link between these two rival empires. The Palmyrene merchants maintained their own soldiers, but some served in the Roman military. Palmyrene troops served at the Egyptian Red Sea port of Berenike, for example and at Dura Europos on the Euphrates River. Palmyrene merchants are also known to have operated deep into Parthian territory, with evidence that they traveled to the head of the Arabian Gulf. The first century CE Roman writer, Pliny the Elder, copying an earlier lost work, even mentioned that Petra and Palmyra were connected by desert trade routes.

The Nabataean people first appear in the historical records in the decades following the death of Alexander the Great, when they are described as merchants who had made large profits trading incense and myrrh. They are described as nomadic, but they had created a fortress, known as Petra, where they could retreat for protection. It is unknown if this source refers to the later site identified as Petra or another site known as Sela (both Petra and Sela mean "rock"). The writer Strabo, active during the reign of Augustus, describes the Nabataeans differently, as a people ruled by a king who built houses out of stone. Archaeology supports these (admittedly few) literary sources and shows that the Nabataeans underwent a process of settlement during the Hellenistic and early Roman periods. During the early Roman period, the Nabataean kings began monumentalizing their capital, Petra, so that by the second century CE, when the Romans assumed direct control of the Nabataean Kingdom, the city was already well developed.

Petra's topography made it an excellent location as a refuge against the Nabataeans' enemies, especially the Hasmonean Dynasty in Judea. It was surrounded by mountains and was only easily accessible through the 1.2 km long cleft in the mountains known as the Siq. These mountains, such as Umm al-Biyara and Jebel ad-Deir, provide breathtaking views of Petra and the surrounding region and gave the Nabataeans a workable and beautiful material for the carving of tombs. Hundreds of tombs are known from the site, but only a couple dozen are extensively decorated. The Siq not only provided an entrance for humans into Petra, but it also allowed water (both from the spring in Wadi Musa and from rain) to rush down into the city. Rains, even today, quickly become flash floods, and the Nabataeans had to develop a system of dams and cisterns to prevent dangerous flood waters from rushing into the city. As archaeology shows, they were not always successful. The suburb of Gaia was located outside the Siq, but this has largely been obscured by the modern town of Wadi Musa. Kilns for making the distinctive Nabataean pottery have been found in this area (Figure 6.6).

The Treasury (Al-Khazneh) marks the end of the Siq and the beginning of Petra itself. Continuing to the right, a visitor to the site entered into a street flanked by tombs, leading down to the theater (see Figure 2.29). At this point, the path curves slightly north and opens to the monumental city center tucked in a valley between several mountains. A continuation of the Wadi Musa runs roughly east to west just north of the colonnaded street, which terminates at the Qasr al-Bint temple complex. As in other cities, the colonnaded street was flanked by monumental structures, with domestic complexes located farther from the civic center to the north and the south. Tombs can be seen carved into all the nearby mountain ranges. It is truly one of the world's most spectacular sites! (Figures 6.7 and 6.8).

Palmyra appears in ancient records as Tadmor as early as the Bronze Age. As one of the only sources of water in the desert between Syria and the Euphrates, one would expect humans to be attracted to the site. Archaeology has shown that there were religious services conducted around the Efqa Spring as early as the 11th century BCE. There is very little literary evidence

*Figure 6.6* Rockcut tombs along the path to the theater (Photo by author).

*Figure 6.7* The Qasr al-Bint, a temple likely dedicated to the chief Nabataean god Dushares (Photo by author).

*Figure 6.8* The "Royal Tombs" from left to right, the Palace Tomb, the Corinthian Tomb, and on the far right, the Urn Tomb (Photo by author).

of the city even up to the beginning of the Roman period, when Mark Antony is described as raiding the city in 41 BCE. He found the city deserted, for the Palmyrenes had moved all of their wealth across the Euphrates River. This suggests that Palmyra was not a large or monumental city in this period. Archaeology south of the wadi, however, questions the validity of this idea.

By the middle of the second century CE, the city had developed extensively and had several monumental structures. It seems that the earliest community was located to the south of the wadi. The later, monumental, city was situated to the north. A city wall originally enclosed both sides of the wadi. A later wall, built during the reign of Diocletian in the late third century CE, only encompassed the northern half of the city. The remains south of the wadi have been relatively unexplored compared to the north, but seem to have been abandoned at the end of the third century CE. This corresponds with the famous revolt of Zenobia and the reconquest of the city by the emperor Aurelian. Modern gardens lie over most of the southern remains. The northern half of the city is organized around the Grand Colonnade that runs roughly north-west from the Camp of Diocletian to the southeast to the Temple of Bel. A necropolis is located to the west, southwest, and southeast of the city (Figure 6.9).

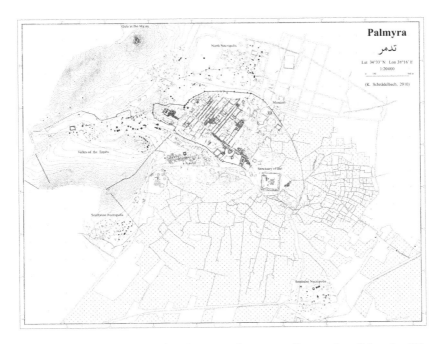

*Figure 6.9* Plan of the city of Palmyra and surrounding region (Map by Klaus Schnädelbach, originally published as Schnädelbach, K. *Topographia Palmyrena, 1 Topography*. Documents d'archéologique Syrienne XVIII. [Damaskus 2010]. On commission by Dr. Rudolf Habelt GmbH, Bonn).

## Hellenistic period

As mentioned earlier, Palmyra rarely appears in historical sources prior to Pompey's annexation of Syria; however, recent archaeological research shows that the city possessed permanent buildings as early as the third century BCE. Petra and the Nabataeans, on the other hand, appear frequently in literary sources beginning in the middle of the second century BCE because of their rivalry with the kingdom of Judea. By the middle of the second century BCE, the Nabateans had spread over a large portion of western Jordan, southern Israel, and the Sinai Peninsula. They started minting coins around the end of the second century BCE, indicating that they were adopting the ruling and economic culture of the Hellenistic age and declaring themselves as an independent state. Around 93 BCE, the Nabataeans captured the territory of Moab and the area around the Decapolis. A decade later, the Seleucids invaded but were turned back. The Nabataeans then acquired their largest amount of territory, which included Damascus. They held the city for almost fifteen years before losing it to Tigranes of Armenia (Figure 6.10).

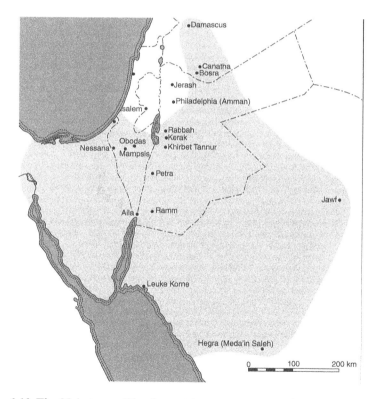

*Figure 6.10* The Nabataean Kingdom at its greatest extent (Ball, W. *Rome in the East*. [Routledge 2016, 2nd edition], Figure 2.9).

## Petra

It is not known when the Nabataeans began to settle at Petra, but this likely occurred sometime near the beginning of the Hellenistic Period. Some scholars have suggested that the first Nabataean settlement at Petra may have been on the mountain of Umm al-Biyara (which lies on the western end of the later civic center) as their original refuge. In the early twentieth century an Edomite village was excavated there, but this had been abandoned for over 200 years prior to the Hellenistic period. There are ample Nabataean remains on the site, which have been recognized as a possible palace of the Nabataean kings from the late first century BCE/early first century CE. It is possible that earlier Nabataean remains will be found in the future, or were destroyed by earlier excavations looking for the Edomite settlement.

One problem in determining the earliest settlement at Petra is that the Nabataeans underwent a slow process of sedentarization. They may have slept in the numerous caves or camped under the stars for decades (or longer!) in the area of Petra before building permanent structures. Excavations conducted in the early 2000s under the shops along the colonnaded streets and in the temenos of the Qasr al-Bint temple revealed that the Nabataeans were building permanent structures at Petra in the fourth or late third century BCE. These were built directly on the alluvial plain of the wadi using water-worn stones taken from the nearby wadi. Fire pits were found near these structures, which might indicate food preparation or other industrial activity. Because the soundings that excavated these structures were so limited, the remains can be interpreted in many ways. For example, they may be storage areas because they consisted of stone and clay dividers on top of clay floors. The Nabataeans may have camped next to them and used them to store goods while traveling. The caves (and some of the rock-cut structures too) may have been used at this early stage for storage and living. Alternatively, these structures could be domestic in nature and reflect the first permanent settlement in Petra. However, the discovery of imported fine ware pottery under the Qasr al-Bint indicates that an elite population lived in the area or nearby. Later structures built on top of these earliest structures indicate that there was continued occupation of the site throughout the Hellenistic period. There is ample evidence of ground leveling and a fine quality of construction. These structures, dated to the third to first century BCE from excavations under the Qasr al-Bint, were aligned on the same orientation as those located to the east under the shops along the colonnaded streets. There were open spaces between the structures, suggesting that the development of the town was at an early stage.

Excavations on the ez-Zantur ridge just south of the civic center revealed further evidence of the transition from a nomadic to settled way of life dating to the first century BCE. In the earliest strata, dated from the beginning of the first century to the end of the first century BCE, archaeologists discovered a series of layers that alternated between sterile sand and layers that contained trash. These alternating layers were interpreted as evidence of seasonal occupation of the site. By the end of the first century BCE, a small stone structure was constructed next to the tent camp (Figure 6.11).

Another problem with understanding the evolution of settlement at Petra is that very few of the tombs have inscriptions attesting to their construction date and there is little other diagnostic evidence. Most of the tombs cannot be dated conclusively because they lack inscriptions and are dated based on stylistic features and comparison to another Nabataean site – Hegra (modern Mada'in Saleh in Saudi Arabia) – where such inscriptions do exist. The earliest surviving tomb inscription at Petra mentions a *triclinium* constructed at the beginning of the first century BCE. The Nabataeans had by this time already adopted the *triclinium* for use in funerary occasions, and several rooms with that layout are known from funerary contexts in the city. The range of influences in tomb decoration is vast, spanning everything from ancient Assyria to Parthia to Alexandria to Italy. While dating based on architectural comparisons is universally recognized, it is possible that some tomb owners would have wanted designs that were not currently in

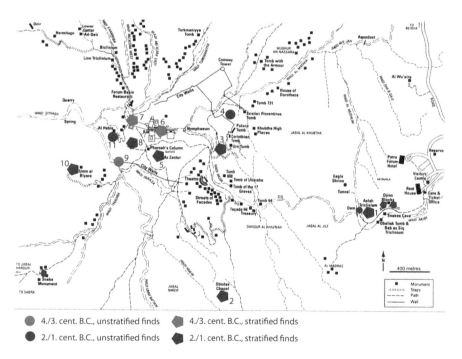

*Figure 6.11* Location of Hellenistic period finds in Petra (Plan by Sebastian Hoffman).

*The desert fringe (Petra and Palmyra)* 189

style (see for example, private houses in Jerusalem where the owners purposely selected unfashionable decoration styles). This suggests that we should perhaps be wary of using decoration styles as conclusive evidence for dating of these structures.

*Palmyra*

Despite the small number of written sources from the Hellenistic period that describe Palmyra, new archaeological excavations indicate that there was a major settlement there by the beginning of the third century BCE. A geophysical survey conducted in the late 1990s and more recently satellite imagery revealed streets and housing blocks. Several roads can be seen that ran roughly east-west. The roads south of the wadi do not follow the same orientation as the Roman roads north of the wadi, suggesting that the ones to the south and north were not part of a unified plan. Excavations south of the wadi have demonstrated that buildings in the Hellenistic period were constructed with both mudbrick and ashlar stone construction. For example, a large building was discovered from the second century BCE, which was constructed using very wide mudbrick walls. The walls were covered in frescos of fish and other marine themes. A later large courtyard-oriented structure was built on top of this building in the Roman period. The intersection of two streets was also excavated. One of these streets had water pipes running under it, obviously to supply water to the area (Figure 6.12).

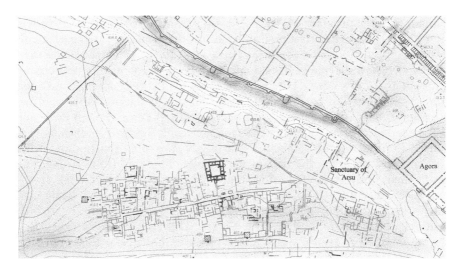

*Figure 6.12* Plan of Hellenistic Palmyra based on geophysical survey (Map by Klaus Schnädelbach, originally published as Schnädelbach, K. *Topographia Palmyrena, 1 Topography*. Documents d'archéologique Syrienne XVIII. [Damascus 2010]. On commission by Dr. Rudolf Habelt GmbH, Bonn).

Unfortunately, without more excavations in the area it is impossible to know what the urban plan of the Hellenistic period city was. The reason for this is that settlement south of the wadi continued until the late third century CE, at least in the two limited locations that have been currently excavated, so we cannot be sure that the buildings found through the ground penetrating radar date back to the Hellenistic period. If they do, however, some features stand out. First, there was not a city plan at this time. There were at least two major streets, but the secondary roads are irregular and appear to be placed wherever there was open space. Second, houses arranged around courtyards are quite evident, but are not arranged in standard insulae. Some houses are arranged along the main streets, but others are not.

## The Roman period

In 62 BCE, the Roman governor of Syria, M. Aemilius Scaurus, decided to attack the Nabataeans. The Nabataean king, Aretas III [85–62 BCE], bribed Scaurus with a large amount of money in return for accepting him as king of the Nabataeans. From this point until 106 CE, the Nabataeans were clients of the Romans, who had the final say over who ruled the kingdom. The Nabataeans sided with both Julius Caesar and Octavian during the Roman civil wars, but occasionally quarreled with Roman governors, even recapturing Damascus for a period during the reign of Aretas IV (9 BCE–40 CE). Later, the Nabataeans supplied troops to the future emperor Vespasian during the Jewish Revolt, securing his acceptance of their kingdom.

It is unknown why the emperor Trajan decided to annex the Nabataean Kingdom as the province of Arabia, or if the transition of power was violent or peaceful. Immediately upon annexation, the Romans altered elements of the monumental civic center at Petra as a means to demonstrate their rule. After the annexation, developments in Petra become more obscure because of a lack of sources, but archaeology of the Petra-Gaza road indicates that the incense and perfume trade continued into the mid-third century. Roman soldiers and governors were occasionally at Petra, though the legion was based farther north at Bostra. One governor, Sextus Florentinus, was buried in an elaborate tomb in Petra in 129 (probably reusing an earlier tomb). Petra obtained the title of metropolis of Arabia from Trajan, and was called Hadriana Petra after Hadrian's visit to the Near East. In the early second century, it obtained the title of Roman colony, and then a little later, the title "mother of colonies" (*metrocolonia*), a title it shared with only Antioch and Palmyra, and possibly Emesa. This evidence all suggests that Petra remained one of the most important cities in the Near East even after its annexation in 106.

In the middle of the first century BCE, Palmyra may have aided the Parthians against the Romans, perhaps leading Mark Antony to raid the city (although other sources suggest he was mainly motivated by plunder). His raid did not result in any lasting damage, but does suggest that the city had already developed an extensive trading network. That the people of the city are reported to have fled across the Euphrates River suggests good relations with the Parthians.

Augustus made peace with the Parthians in 20 BCE, removing the prospect of war between the two empires for a time. By the death of Augustus in 14 CE or just after, Palmyra was probably considered a part of the empire. Even at later dates, however, the city seems to have possessed an incredible amount of autonomy. Merchants from Palmyra operated throughout the Roman Empire and in Parthian territory. The Palmyrene merchants were held in especially high esteem by the kingdom of Mesene (vassals of the Parthians), located in the southern part of Mesopotamia. One Palmyrene citizen was even appointed governor of Thilouna (modern Bahrain) by the king of Mesene. The new economic opportunities attracted settlement to the burgeoning city. Tribal groups (Arabs?) from the surrounded desert and steppe areas began to settle at the site, rapidly increasing the city's population in the first century CE.

Palmyra was able to take advantage of the Pax Romana to greatly expand its wealth and prosperity. After peace was made with the Parthians, a century went by before Trajan invaded Parthia and disrupted the Palmyrene trade network for brief moment. Hadrian's policy of peace with Parthia seems to have restored trade for some time. Hadrian himself visited the city in 130/31, perhaps granting its inhabitants some tax benefits, and the city adopted the name Hadriana Palmyra. As at other cities, the visit of Hadrian corresponded with increased civic enthusiasm. Construction began on the Grand Colonnade and the theater and the cella of the temple of Baalshamin was finished in 132. In the third century, Palmyra was advanced to the rank of metrocolonia and was visited by the Emperor Severus Alexander in 235 CE.

Wars between the Romans and the Parthians under Marcus Aurelius and the Severan dynasty weakened the Parthians to the point that they were overthrown in 224 CE. As discussed in previous chapters, the Persians, especially under Shapur I, were a much more dangerous threat to Roman interests in the Near East than the Parthians. When the Emperor Valerian was captured by the Persians in 260, an elite member of Palmyra, Septimius Odenathus, collected remnants of the Roman army, peasants from Syria, and Palmyrene troops in order to resist the Persian occupation. He was so successful that the Emperor Gallienus granted him the impressive title "restorer of the entire world." In 267, Odenathus was murdered, but his wife, Zenobia, and son took control of Palmyra. Zenobia moved quickly. Whereas Odenathus operated independently, he still deferred to the Roman emperors. Zenobia, on the other hand, launched an invasion of the province of Arabia, conquered Egypt, and advanced on Anatolia. She even claimed the title of Augusta for herself and Augustus for her son. The emperor Aurelian marched from the west, defeated the Palmyrene forces in several battles, and put Palmyra to siege. Zenobia tried to flee to the Persians, but was captured.

The city surrendered in 272, and Aurelian was lenient, but the city revolted again in 273. This time, Aurelian returned with a fury, destroying substantial parts of the city, especially south of the wadi, and killing many people.

## Petra

Petra's city plan as it developed in the Roman period was based around one axis that ran roughly parallel to the wadi Musa. While we should not assume that the earliest known remains mentioned above were in fact the earliest settlement in Petra, they do show that even at this early date that the city extended down to the wadi Musa. By the middle of the second century CE, the road south of the wadi had been transformed into a sacred way leading to the Qasr al-Bint and was paved and colonnaded. The city was not designed on a grid plan as the local topography, with the hills flanking the valley bed of wadi Musa, did not allow for a Hippodamian plan (Figure 6.13).

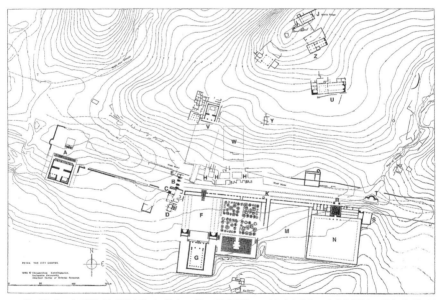

Map of the city center of Petra, May 2001. **A:** Temple of Dushares ("Qasr al-Bint"); **B:** Temenos Gate; **C:** South Tower; **D:** "Baths," "College of Priests" or "Palatial Residence"; **E:** North Tower; **F:** Lower Temenos of the Great Temple Complex; **G:** Great Temple and Its Upper Temenos; **H:** Bridges; **J:** Ridge Church; **K:** Colonnaded Street; **L:** Pool Complex ("Lower Market"); **M:** "Middle Market"; **N:** "Upper Market" ("Agora"); **P:** "Byzantine Tower"; **R:** "Trajanic" Arch; **S:** South Nymphaeon; **T:** North Nymphaeon; **U:** The Petra Church; **V:** Temple of the Winged Lions or Temple of Al-ʿUzza ("Gymnasium") **W:** "Royal Palace"; **Y:** Area A; **Z:** Blue Chapel.

*Figure 6.13* Map of the civic center of Petra (Map courtesy of Talal Akasheh, Hashemite University, Chrysanthos Kanellopoulos, the American Schools of Oriental Research, and American Center of Oriental Research, Amman. Originally published in Kanellopoulos, C. and T. Akasheh. "The Petra Map." *Bulletin of the American Schools of Oriental Research*, no. 324, 2001, pp. 6–7. The original article can be accessed at www.jstor.org/stable/1357628).

Over time, the hills to the north and south of the city developed into extensive residential zones. The southern hills, such as Katute and ez-Zantur, are the location of several excavated domestic structures. On the other side of the valley, the lower North Ridge held monumental buildings, but the upper ridge was originally used as a necropolis in the first centuries BCE/CE before domestic structures sprang up after the Roman annexation. City walls, probably from the first century BCE or CE, contain the city to the north and south sides. Just south of the southern city wall was the town's dump, which has been partially excavated.

Petra is most famous for its city center, but the surrounding iconic landscape suited the creation of ritual locations or palaces with stunning views. One example is the palace constructed on top of Umm al-Biyara. This palace, which appears modeled on those built by Herod such as Masada and Jericho, overlooks the civic center but is isolated from it. Other examples are the numerous high places of sacrifice throughout the mountains and the stunning ed-Deir tomb up over 800 steps from the civic center. Some of these religious centers existed during the Hellenistic period, such as the earliest phase of the "Obodas Chapel" located a kilometer south of the theater.

Another example is the temple at the top of Jebel Haroun, which was later replaced by a Christian monastery. At the foot of the Jebel was a sanctuary dedicated to the Egyptian goddess Isis with an open-air biclinium, and there was another temple to Dushares further down the wadi. The Nabataean kings also built monumental structures in some of the surrounding villages. For example, at Beidha (colloquially known as Little Petra) about 10 km north of Petra, archaeologists discovered a Dionysian Hall with a courtyard and a banquet hall, constructed with Ionic and Corinthian capitals. Dating to the mid-first century BCE, the structure further reveals the extent to which the Nabataean kings had adopted Hellenistic culture.

Research in Petra over the past twenty years shows that the reign of Aretas IV [8 BCE–40 CE] was instrumental in transforming the urban character of Petra. His reign overlapped the final years of Herod of Judea, and it seems likely that the Nabataeans were aware of Herod's building projects and the prestige that those brought to him. The works of Aretas IV demonstrate that he was interested in imitating Herod in transforming Petra into a Hellenistic capital worthy of an important Near Eastern kingdom (Figure 6.14).

The most famous construction of Aretas IV is the Treasury (Al-Khazneh). The date of this tomb has been long debated, but excavation under the current ground level in front of the façade suggests that the tomb does in fact date to the time of Aretas. The Treasury is an amazing artifact of Hellenistic influence on the Nabataeans. It has architectural parallels, such as the broken pediment flanking the *tholos* (a round structure with a roof), to buildings in Alexandria and across the Near East, Greece, and Italy. Because the central figure is a representation of a goddess (identified as either Tyche, Aphrodite, Isis, or another), it is possible that the tomb was built in honor of Aretas's first wife Hulda.

*Figure 6.14* The Treasury (Al-Khazneh). The grate at the bottom covers the earliest tombs (Photo by Carole Raddato).

The Qasr al-Bint temple stood at the western end of the civic center and is the obvious focal point of the city. Strangely, the temple does not face towards the sacred way (compare for example, the Temple of Artemis at Gerasa). This could be explained by the fact that the temple was originally entered from the north instead of the east, or that the temple faced the mountains that were connected to Dushares. Another explanation is that an earlier temple from the first century BCE stood on the same spot with the same orientation (Figure 6.15).

The cella of the Qasr al-Bint temple was likely completed in the reign of Aretas IV in the early first century CE. All of the domestic structures under the Qasr al-Bint were demolished sometime in the mid-to-late first century BCE and the ground leveled. The choice of the location is clear. At the foot of the el-Habis mountain and the end of the Wadi Musa, any building constructed on the site would become the focal point of the city.

It is commonly thought that the Qasr al-Bint was dedicated to the chief Nabataean god Dushares, but because the temple possesses three *cellae*, three deities may have been worshipped there. The middle *adyton* (platform) likely housed a Nabataean betyl (stone block used in Nabataean religion to represent their deities), whereas the flanking side chambers could have just given access to the roof via stairs. Complicating matters is that inscriptions from the temenos (built in the early second century CE) mention Zeus Hypsistos, the Tyche of Petra and probably the goddess Aphrodite. One of the gods worshipped there may also have been syncretized with Helios (likely Dushares), as a frieze depicting this god was discovered in the temple.

*The desert fringe (Petra and Palmyra)* 195

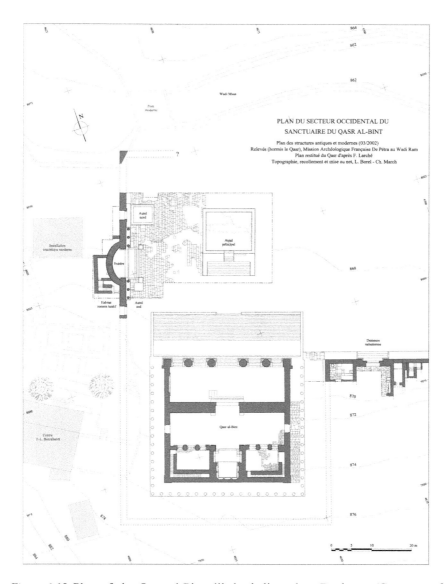

*Figure 6.15* Plan of the Qasr al-Bint, likely dedicated to Dushares (Courtesy of François Larche).

Around the same time or just before the Qasr al-Bint cella was built, the street was first monumentalized. Excavations have shown that there was an east-west colonnade near the (later) Temenos Gate that has been dated to the last half of the first century BCE. It may or may not have stretched the length of the road.

196  *The desert fringe (Petra and Palmyra)*

Another large temple, the Temple of the Winged Lions, was built in the late first century BCE or early first century CE, also possibly during the reign of Aretas IV (Figure 6.16).

This temple was built to the north of the wadi and likely had access to the main street, provided by a bridge. The famous eye betyl was discovered in the temple, which was dedicated "to the goddess ..." possibly al-Allat, al-'Uzza (syncretized with Aphrodite and consort of Dushares), or Isis. Petra's most

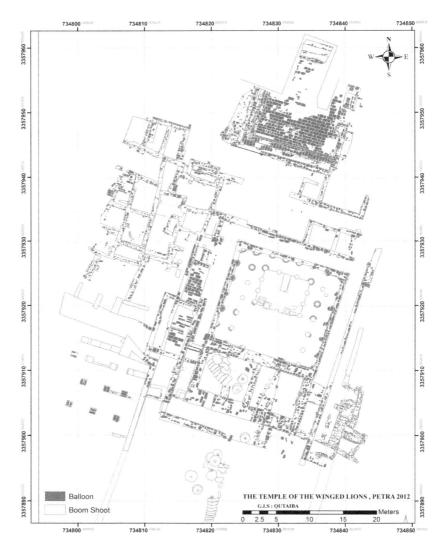

*Figure 6.16* Plan of the Temple of the Winged Lions (Plan by Qutaiba Dasouqi, courtesy of the Temple of the Winged Lions Cultural Resource Management Initiative).

*The desert fringe (Petra and Palmyra)* 197

*Figure 6.17* Photo of the Great Temple (Photo by author).

extensive Nabataean religious inscription, dated to 37th year of Aretas IV (27/8 CE) was discovered in the temenos wall. A building termed the "Palace," though possibly a temple, lies directly to the east of the Temple of the Winged Lions (Figure 6.17).

New interpretations suggest that the Petra "Great Temple" was built as an audience chamber for the Nabataean Kings at the end of the first century BCE. Its monumental entrance (propylaeum) is located just before the temenos gate of the Qasr al-Bint. There are two artificial platforms connected by staircases. The lower level is surrounded by a double row of columns in the front with triple-columned rows on the east and west sides, whereas the rear contains two exedrae that flank the staircases to the upper level. Sculpture in the Great Temple reflects both classical, Greco-Roman forms (eight panels with the gods and goddesses and a head of Tyche) and Nabataean style aniconic betyls. The expansion of the Great Temple in the first century CE with the construction of the lower level reflects Roman influence as it copies design elements of the Forum of Caesar. Directly to the east of the Great Temple, the Nabataean rulers built a large garden and pool complex, which was in line with Persian ideals probably at the beginning fo the reign of Aretas IV. Both the Great Temple and the garden complex were intended to display the majesty of the Nabataean rulers (Figure 6.18).

The theater was also constructed at the end of the first century BCE and the beginning of the first century CE. Seating was largely carved directly out

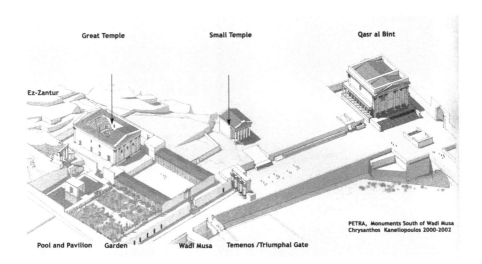

*Figure 6.18* Digital reconstruction of the civic center of Petra south of Wadi Musa (Drawing by Chrysanthos Kanellopoulos, courtesy of Chrysanthos Kanellopoulos and ASOR. Originally published in Kanellopoulos, C. "A New Plan of Petra's City Center." *Near Eastern Archaeology*, vol. 65, no. 4, 2002, p. 254. The original article can be found at www.jstor.org/stable/3210854).

of the mountainside, making it one of the most spectacular monuments of the city. The theater cut into previous rock-cut tombs. Only the front rows were constructed and not carved. There are in total 45 rows of seats. The entrances were carved out of the mountainside, with masonry arches built over them. The stage and *scenae frons* were freestanding and constructed out of local stone (see Figure 2.29).

Although the civic center and the fabulous rock cut tombs have attracted the majority of the attention of scholars and visitors, some domestic structures have been excavated, from both the north and south sides of the civic center. In addition to these stand-alone structures, some of the rock-cut tombs were in fact rock-cut houses! The caves across from the theater, for example, are widely considered to have been houses. They seem to have been extremely suitable for dwellings, as Judith McKenzie describes. She notes that the caves were warm in the winter and cool in the summer (1990, 107).

After the monumentalization of the civic center, residential areas were clustered on the ridges to the north and south of the civic center. The earliest houses excavated on the Katute and ez-Zantur ridges just south of the civic center appear to date to the first century CE. A house excavated on Katute was built using even courses of masonry, which was covered with stucco on the inside walls. The house itself was arranged around a courtyard, but several of the rooms were accessed only through a succession of other rooms.

Four houses were excavated nearby on ez-Zantur. The earliest of these (EZ-1) dates to the early part of the first century CE. It originally covered the entire terrace, making it a large complex. Built out of local stone, even the floors were paved. It was clearly a structure built to impress. The public rooms were arranged around a peristyle courtyard, demonstrating a knowledge of standard Hellenistic house planning. The private rooms, however, follow local topography and do not conform to a standard housing plan. This structure burned in the early second century. Another large domestic structure was discovered on a terrace below Ez-Zantur (EZ-4). Although not all of it was excavated, it also appears to have covered the entire terrace. It too was paved with stone slabs, but also decorated with opus sectile floors and painted stucco. Three rooms – an exedra flanked by two rooms – appear to have been modeled on palaces in the eastern Mediterranean.

The North Ridge held monumental structures, such as the Temple of the Winged Lions on the lower slopes, but the upper slopes were originally the site of a necropolis. Dozens of shaft graves have been discovered there and several have been excavated. By the early first century CE, a residential area had sprung up in this area. The structures were built out of stone and continued down the slope towards the civic center. A Painter's Workshop and Marble Workshop were discovered near the Temple of the Winged Lions, and were clearly used for the construction and maintenance of the nearby monumental structures.

In the early second century, the inner-city wall was constructed, which cut through some of the northern residences and reused the walls of others. Occupation returned to the area until the 363 earthquake, though the areas nearest the city wall were used as a trash dump. In the second century, the ridge stopped being used for burials. Further west on the ridge, excavators found an urban villa, which dated to the second century and contained its own bath complex with beautifully carved marble statues of Aphrodite and Cupid. It was built directly adjacent to the inner-city wall, which collapsed on top of the villa during the 363 earthquake.

While it is unknown why the Romans decided to annex the Nabataean Kingdom in 106 CE, its impact on the city can easily been seen through recent archaeological evidence. Excavations revealed that just after the Roman annexation, the Qasr al-Bint temenos was enlarged and rebuilt. A large platform was built north of the temple, extending into the Wadi Musa, which diverted the wadi bed to the north. The pavings of the temenos and the Temenos Gate date to this same renovation. The street was transformed at the same time. Stone paving up to 18 m in width was placed over two prior street levels of sand and gravel. Although shops along the front of the Upper Market were built prior to this time, a new staircase was built for the Upper Market (and possibly the Great Temple) and the shops were expanded. Many of the shops contained two stories, and it thought that the second stories were used for storage or sleeping. If the colonnades did not run down the whole street in the prior phase, they were constructed at this point along both sides of the road. There do not seem to have been any shops along the north side of the street along the bank of the wadi (although there may have been some in front of the "palace"). It is also possible that the nymphaeum on the north side of the street was built at this time. An ornate bath complex was rebuilt at the same time on the remains of a previous one next to the Great Temple. Some repairs and renovations were done on the island pavilion in the garden complex.

The Romans made changes that were clearly ideological in nature. One such change occurred in the Great Temple, where an odeon was constructed. This apparent transformation of a previous Nabataean audience hall into a bouleuterion would have visibly demonstrated the end of the Nabataean dynasty and the new rule of the Roman emperors based on independent cities controlled by local elites. Another indication of Roman rule is the Small Temple, located between the Great Temple and the Qasr al-Bint. The Small Temple has been interpreted as a temple of the imperial cult. Inscriptions discovered inside the temple commemorate the reigns of Trajan, Alexander Severus, Elagabalus, and possibly others. Later changes at the Qasr al-Bint, such as the construction of a new exedra with statues of the emperors Marcus Aurelius and Lucius Verus, further demonstrate the changed political circumstances.

As Andrade has recently demonstrated, the expansion of Roman authority led directly to the transformation of local governments and the creation of new civic councils. The transformation of the Great Temple and the building of the Small Temple would have underscored the changed political structure of the city from monarchy to communal and Roman governance (128–146, 233–239). Despite the political transformation, in the words of Burns,

> the Roman takeover of Petra in AD 106 provides no clean break, as the choice of urban forms or architectural templates had already increasingly sought to give the city a more Roman look... [i]t was, however, the colonnaded axis which by the early second century was adopted as the clearest signal of the city's status as a major center under Rome.
> (Burns 115)

Petra is mentioned only occasionally in the historical accounts of the second and third centuries. There is little evidence that the Persian invasions, which so heavily damaged the more northerly Syrian cities like Antioch, had any impact on Petra, which lay far from the zone of conflict. The city likely came under the control of Palmyrene forces, but there is no conclusive evidence that the city was fought over or resisted. Archaeological evidence suggests that the Petra perfume industry disappeared sometime in the third century, and this seems to be supported by the gradual abandonment of the Petra-Gaza road stations. Sometime between the end of the second century and the end of the third century CE, the pool and garden complex went out of use, and the pool was converted into a reservoir. Portions of the Great Temple were being used as a trash dump by the late second or early third centuries. Evidence suggests that the Qasr al-Bint was also damaged or neglected by the end of the third century. It has been suggested that some of these developments were linked to the expansion of Palmyrene control over the Near East or the subsequent Roman reconquest, but it is also possible that they reflect the changing economic situation of the Near East and the overall decline of trade in the third century due to political instability. Unfortunately for Petra, the long-distance trade that enriched the city in the Nabataean period and Roman periods never returned. The city continued to be important in late antiquity and was capital of a Roman province, but it never again obtained its world-renowned status.

## *Palmyra*

Like the other cities in this book, the Roman period represented the pinnacle of building at Palmyra, but there are some major differences. The first is that the civic center was originally built fronting a wadi, rather than a colonnaded street. When citizens of the city decided to construct a monumental street (the Grand Colonnade) following the example of other cities, the builders had to make significant deviations from the standard. For example, the available land was located north of the wadi. Because many of the earlier monumental buildings faced the wadi to the south, these buildings backed up to the later monumental street, rather than facing it. As we will see, the irregular design of the rear of these buildings meant that the colonnaded street could not run straight, but required both alterations of previously used space as well as bends in the design of the road.

The small-scale excavations south of the current wadi have shown that there was a continuity of settlement there from the third century BCE until the late third century CE. The large building based around a courtyard was originally built near the time of Pompey's annexation of Syria and continued through several phases until its destruction at the end of the third century CE. Based on the ceramic finds, excavators have interpreted this structure as a caravanserai. Imported wares from Parthian territories make up a large percentage of the finds. This building measures 40 m by 40 m and had a large propylon on the south side.

In this early city, the focus was on a road that ran along the northern edge of the wadi. All but two of the early monumental structures on the northern bank were aligned towards the wadi to the south. These structures include the famous Temple of Bel, the Temple of Nebu, the Agora, and the Tariff Court. Corresponding buildings from the southern side of the wadi are not extant, except it is known that a Temple of Arsu was built across from the Agora. All buildings to the north of the wadi were enclosed in a wall built during the rule of the emperor Diocletian, whereas the southern half of the city lay in ruins after Zenobia's Revolt. Excavation of the southern part of the wadi is in its infancy, so presumably, there would have been additional monumental buildings on the southern side as well (Figures 6.19 and 6.20).

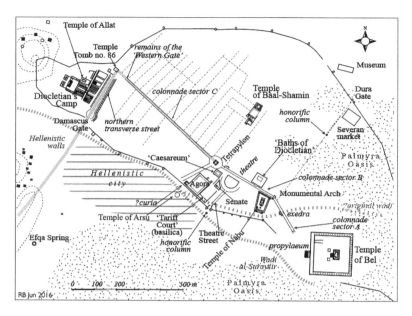

*Figure 6.19* Map of Palmyra (Burns, R. *Origins of the Colonnaded Streets in the Cities of the Roman East*. [Oxford 2017], Figure 10.05).

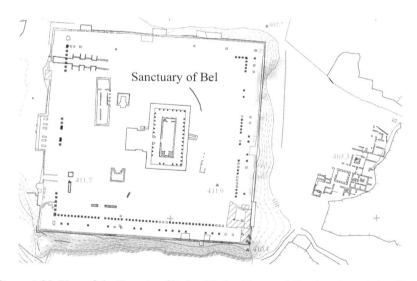

*Figure 6.20* Plan of the Temple of Bel, with the House of Cassiopeia and the House of Achilles located to the east (Map by Klaus Schnädelbach, originally published as Schnädelbach, K. *Topographia Palmyrena, 1 Topography*. Documents d'archéologique Syrienne XVIII. [Damascus 2010]. On commission by Dr. Rudolf Habelt GmbH, Bonn).

The Temple of Bel was the first of the major monuments constructed in the city (see Figure 1.2). From inscriptions, it is clear that individuals from the city paid for the initial construction of the cella, which was finished in 32 CE. The temple's entrance faces directly west towards the wadi and the Efqa Spring. The temenos wall is monumental and gives the appearance of a fortress. The massive propylaea was converted into a citadel in the twelfth century, so its current appearance is not representative of its previous grandeur. In antiquity, a staircase would have led to a portico with eight Corinthian columns. The four interior sides of the temenos were surrounded by porticos formed by massive Corinthian columns. The west side consisted of one aisle, whereas the other three sides had two aisles made from two rows of columns. A ramp in the northwestern side of the temenos interior allowed cattle to be led to the altar for slaughter (Figures 6.21–6.23).

While the huge fluted Corinthian columns would be at home in the cella of any classical temple, the entrance to the cella is uniquely located in the wider side. The clear intention of the designers was to provide space at either end of the cella for two cults to be worshipped, instead of a standard Greco-Roman temple with one cult (or its triad) in the rear of the temple. The design is even stranger still, because the roof of the temple is not arched, but flat, and stairs led to the roof.

Only two major monuments from the earliest period of development were not built near the wadi. One was the Temple of Baalshamin, begun in 23 CE, whereas the other was the Temple of Allat, originally built in the

*Figure 6.21* Temenos wall of the Temple of Bel (Photo by Greg Fisher).

*Figure 6.22* Columns at the rear of the cella of the Temple of Bel (Photo by Greg Fisher).

*Figure 6.23* Adyton of the Temple of Bel (Photo by Greg Fisher).

first century BCE (see Figure 1.3). Like the Temple of Zeus in Gerasa, the Temple of Baalshamin was reconstructed several times, first finished in 67 CE, with the extant sanctuary completed in 132. The earliest temple on the site possessed a series of courtyards much like the sanctuary dedicated to Baalshamin in Siʻa in southern Syria. Originally, there was no *cella* in the temple. In the second phase, columns were added to the middle courtyard, but it was only in the third phase that a temple was built inside the middle court. The cella itself is surrounded by Corinthian pilasters, and the adyton is divided into three parts.

The Temple of Allat originally consisted of a small chapel and temenos from the late first century BCE (see Figure 6.33). In the second and third centuries, it was consistently rebuilt and monumentalized. The later Camp of Diocletian was built around the temple, preserving it, perhaps because the goddess Allat was often equated with warrior goddesses such as Athena or Minerva.

The late first century CE was a time of extensive building and transformation in the city, which corresponded with increased Roman attention given to the city. For example, the governor of Syria, Marcus Ulpius Traianus (father of the emperor Trajan) completed a road from Palmyra to the Euphrates River. The earliest inscriptions from the Agora indicated that it was built at the same time in the late 70s or early 80s CE. Attached to the Agora was a small chamber likely used in the imperial cult. At the same time a basilica (the Tariff Court) was begun, but never completed. The first evidence of the boule of Palmyra is dated to 74 CE. A temple dedicated to Belhammon was built on top of Jebel Muntar in 89 CE. Two temples were begun facing the wadi, the Temple of Nebu, north of the wadi, and the Temple of Arsu, south of the wadi. The structures along the wadi are built at different angles from each other, suggesting that they were attempting to follow the course of the wadi instead of being built on a unified plan (Figure 6.24).

Construction in the city reached its peak during the second century CE. A completely new section of the city was laid out on a grid plan just to the north of the established city center. The first transverse street in the west was the double the size of the later streets. As it led to the gate to Damascus, the ample size of the street likely was intended to facilitate the loading and unloading of caravans. This construction begun before that carried out on the Grand Colonnade, as inscriptions attest to work on it between the years 110 and 179 CE. The second transverse street runs south from the oval plaza that connected Sections A and B. It connected to the oval plaza at an odd angle, likely because it ran to the Temple of Arsu across the wadi. The third street follows the walls of the Tariff court from the theater to the (later) city wall and might be dated to the third century CE. The fourth street runs north from the Monumental Arch to the gate to Dura-Europos, with the Suburban Market being the most prominent feature. Other than the Grand Colonnade, there are no few streets that run east-west in the northern half of the city. In addition, the width between the north-south roads was highly variable. This means that there were no standard insulae in this part of the city (Figure 6.25).

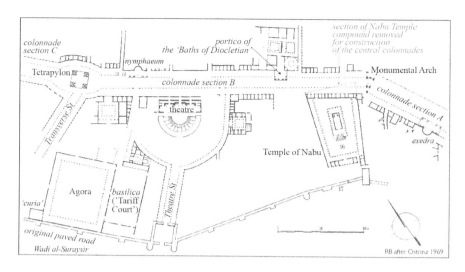

*Figure 6.24* Detailed view of the civic center of Palmyra (Burns, R. *Origins of the Colonnaded Streets in the Cities of the Roman East.* [Oxford 2017], Figure 10.09).

*Figure 6.25* Columns along the Grand Colonnade (Photo by Greg Fisher).

After Hadrian's visit to Palmyra in 129/30, construction on the Grand Colonnade began, possibly at imperial suggestion. It runs from the Camp of Diocletian in the northwest to the Temple of Bel in the southeast. Scholars divide the sections of the Grand Colonnade into three sections. Section C runs from the western gate (constructed before 200) down to the civic center. Inscriptions attest to the construction of columns from the mid-second to early third centuries. Section C joins with Section B at an oval courtyard, which was constructed to disguise the fact that the two sections were twisted about ten degrees off the same axis. A tetrakionion, probably built during the reign of Diocletian like at Gerasa, was an attempt to further disguise the awkwardness of the intersection (Figure 6.26).

If the entire road followed the route of Section C to the Temple of Bel, it would have run straight through the cella of the Temple of Nabu and portions of the theater. Section B was, therefore, routed to pass behind the theater.

But changing the angle of the road didn't eliminate all of the problems because the backs of the existing buildings were uneven. Portions of the temenos of the Temple of Nabu were removed in order to make space for the road. The space between the rear of the Agora and uncompleted basilica of the Tariff Court was filled in with structures possibly related to the civic government. The inscriptions from this section date to the period between 224 and 271, with the majority clustering around the period of Odenathus.

*Figure 6.26* The tetrapylon (a tetrakionion) at the intersection of Sections C and B (Photo by Greg Fisher).

Section A runs from the civic center to the Temple of Bel. The variance in direction from Section B is even more extreme compared to Section A and B, at 29 degrees. To hide this unsightly interruption in sight lines, a Monumental Arch was constructed that showed its face directly to both Section B and A. To do this, the arch has a trapezoidal shape. This section was never completed, with the last columns dated to 219. The arch was built sometime after 212. This section approaches the entrance to the Temple of Bel at an odd angle, further demonstrating that the Grand Colonnade was planned long after the major buildings of the civic center (Figure 6.27).

The beginning of construction on the Grand Colonnade at the site after Hadrian's visit indicates how important colonnaded streets had become in the Near East. In order to build the Grand Colonnade, significant changes had to occur to several of the previously built monumental structures along the northern edge of the wadi. But, strangely, the work doesn't seem to have been a major priority for the city as construction only occurred intermittently, and none of the three sections of the Grand Colonnade were actually completed. The width of the street varies, even within the three sections. Some stretches have shops along the street, whereas others do not. The sidewalks vary in width as well. Everything suggests that the Grand Colonnade was not built according to a grand plan, but rather, donors (whether individuals, tribal units, or the *boule*) made decisions as they saw fit. Building

*Figure 6.27* The monumental arch connecting Sections B and A as seen from the Temple of Nabu (Photo by Greg Fisher).

the transverse streets may also have diverted interest and funds from the Grand Colonnade.

Although most of the archaeological work has concentrated on the monumental center of Palmyra, it is clear that domestic complexes were incorporated into the city plan during the development of the grid in the northern half of the city. Each sector of the northern half of the city was filled with residential buildings. Most of the excavated buildings from the Roman period are elite structures. They appear to conform to the typical Mediterranean style house with rooms surrounding a peristyle courtyard. One important characteristic of these houses is that their shape is adjusted to fill all available space, even if this does not follow a standard grid plan. Domestic structures in the civic center conform to the available space. For example, houses were squeezed in between the Theater and the Temple of Nabu and between the Temple of Nabu and the Grand Colonnade.

In the Eastern Quarter of the city near the Temple of Bel, two villas were discovered – the House of Cassiopeia and the House of Achilles – so named because of the mosaics found therein. Both structures were built at the beginning of the third century and attest to the prosperity of the upper class in that period. The Eastern Quarter seems to have held plenty of open space for expansion even down to the time of Zenobia (see Figure 6.22).

In the middle of the second century, construction continued. The Temple of Nabu was still under construction, the Temple of Allat was begun, and the Temple of Baalshamin and the theater were completed soon thereafter. In the late second century (and beyond), construction continued on the Grand Colonnade, but the city began to reach is completed state. The Temple of Allat was finished and the baths dedicated to Aglibol and Malakbel were built. The last evidence of work on the Temple of Bel is dated to 175 CE. The Suburban Market, built in the early third century, was constructed along the fourth transverse street near the Dura gate.

Strangely, the expansion of Palmyrene power in the mid-late third century is not well attested with monumental structures. The only evidence of this period is that the majority of columns along Section B mention Odenathus and his supporters. The works of Herod or Aretas IV these are not. It is possible, however, that any monuments that honored Odenathus and/or Zenobia (and their son) were destroyed or that their palace lies beneath or incorporated into the Camp of Diocletian.

Just as Petra is surrounded by its amazing tombs, so is Palmyra. An extensive necropolis surrounds the city on the northwest, southwest, and southeast sides. The so-called "Valley of the Tombs" is the most well-known, located to the northwest. The Palmyrenes built three types of tombs: tower tombs (from 9 BCE–128 CE), *hypogea* (underground tombs, dated from the first century CE until the mid-third century), and temple or house tombs (built between 143–254 CE). The tower tombs are just that – ornately decorated towers (Figure 6.28).

*Figure 6.28* Tombs at Palmyra (Photo by Greg Fisher).

The temple or house tombs replaced the tower tombs as the main burial sites of the elite. In these and the *hypogea*, the dead were not buried but placed in sarcophagi or niches, which were occasionally arranged as a triclinium much like Nabataean practices. It has been suggested that the abandonment of the tower tombs for the hypogea and temple/house tombs represents Greco-Roman influence on the citizens of Palmyra.

Indications of the industrial production of textiles were discovered in contexts from the age of Augustus from the southern half of the city. Evidence included a large pot containing red dye, and over 20 loom weights. Although this evidence is limited, it is more than survives from most of sites from this period.

## Late antiquity

In late antiquity, both Petra and Palmyra were no longer as important as they had been during the Roman period. Petra, having been the chief city of the Nabataean kingdom, retained its importance in the Roman imperial administration until the end of the third century. Then, in the later fourth century, it once again became capital of an imperial province; however, the trade, which had been the lifeblood of the city no longer, flowed through it. The extreme independence that propelled Palmyra onto the world's stage in the third century was never regained. Even more troubling for the city, the conditions that allowed the Palmyrene merchants to flourish had disappeared and never returned. In 297 CE, when Diocletian made peace with the Persians, they agreed that the city of Nisibis would be the only point of exchange between the empires, relocating trade to the north.

Whatever caused the changes in Petra at the end of the third century CE, the city did not regain its importance in trade in the fourth century. Those trade routes had shifted either farther south, to Aila at the tip of the Red Sea, or west, to Egypt. And, for much of the fourth century, Petra was not a significant city for the imperial administration. This changed at the very end of the fourth century, when Petra became the capital of a new province, called Palaestina Salutaris (later known as Third Palestine). The most important historical event of the fourth century was an earthquake in 363 that caused extensive damage to the city but it was not abandoned at this point. The papyri from the Petra church demonstrate that the city was still proudly proclaiming its titles from the second and third centuries in the sixth century. Petra doesn't appear in any sources related to the Muslim conquest, suggesting that it was no longer important or inhabited at that time.

There were major changes to the city of Palmyra in late antiquity. The city south of the wadi was destroyed and abandoned after Aurelian crushed Zenobia's bid for power. Constructions on the Grand Colonnade and the Theater were abandoned. Damage has been reported from several areas of the northern city, such as the Temple of Allat and the Theater. However, the city of Palmyra commanded a strategic location against the Persia, and emperors at the end of the third century worked to make the city more defensible. Aurelian based a legion of Roman soldiers at the city. Under Diocletian, the city wall that surrounded the northern half of the Roman city was refortified with projecting towers. The late antique city, much reduced in population and size from before, was largely limited by the extent of this wall. Furthermore, a military camp was built in the far western side of the city, just inside the city wall. Many churches and at least one mosque have been discovered at Palmyra. It appears in many early Islamic sources, suggesting that it retained some of its importance.

## Petra

There are little detectable changes to the city until May 19, 363 CE, when an earthquake struck a large portion of the Near East. Damage is recorded at many of the most important archaeological sites in Petra, including the theater, two houses on the Ez-Zantur ridge, and throughout the civic center.

There was major damage to the city center, though several buildings there were likely already abandoned. The Qasr al-Bint was definitely destroyed before the late fourth century, when a dwelling was constructed on top of the temple's *exedra* in the west *temenos* wall. It had already gone out of use by the end of the third century, but it too was damaged by the 363 earthquake. The Temple of the Winged Lions was still in use until it was destroyed. The outside walls and some of the columns of the temple complex survived the temple's destruction.

Like the Qasr al-Bint, the Great Temple appears to have been abandoned prior to the 363 earthquake and then completely destroyed by it. Later, in the later fourth and fifth centuries, the complex was used for lime manufacturing in the south East Triple Colonnade and *exedrae*. Substantial ash layers were discovered, and drains and other industrial features were constructed. The pool and garden complex next door was also abandoned and used as agricultural fields. The Small Temple was also destroyed by the 363 earthquake. Prior to the earthquake, it appears to have been looted, and the inscriptions smashed before this date. If the structure was indeed abandoned prior to the 363 earthquake, then it is probable that the building was damaged at the same time as the neighboring Qasr al-Bint, possibly during the Palmyrene Revolt, or when the Great Temple went out of use (Figure 6.29).

The earthquake played a major role in the transformation of the Colonnaded Street. Portions of the street were left in ruins and not cleared of debris. Shops were built using debris and spolia in the public portion of the street and sidewalks. The flood prevention mechanisms must have been damaged and not repaired, as archaeologists have found ample evidence

*Figure 6.29* Collapsed columns from an earthquake at the Great Temple (Photo by author).

of flooding in the shops that faced the street. Overall, the results of the earthquake were devastating to the civic center of the city. The majority of the major buildings from the Roman period were destroyed or damaged, yet the Colonnaded Street remained active as the commercial center. By the late fourth centuries, lime manufacturing can be detected at the Great Temple. It is likely the location was chosen because of the abundance of marble architectural remains and statues from the destroyed buildings, which were then turned into lime for plaster for construction elsewhere in the city. Of the major buildings, only the theater appears to have been repaired and used for its original purpose, but at this time, the niches, which previously held statues of pagan gods, were filled in, and the *scaenae frons* was left in ruins. This suggests that the theater continued to be used, but that the public commemoration of pagan and imperial cults was discontinued.

The 363 earthquake affected the areas outside the civic center as well. On the North Ridge, the earthquake destroyed the city wall, which collapsed on top of the urban villa. The domestic structures to the east of this villa were also damaged. In both cases, there was no later occupation of the site. This is confusing, because this area is located directly next to the three churches on the ridge and, before excavation was thought to be the heart of the late antique city. The domestic complexes on the ez-Zantur ridge also suffered damage. The mansion EZ-IV was completely destroyed and not reoccupied. Two houses built on the ruins of the first century house at EZ-I were damaged by the earthquake, but repaired and occupied until the fifth century. These houses reused many elements of the first century house, dividing the courtyard between them. Nearby was a bakery with two ovens.

Three Christian churches have been discovered in Petra to date, all from the fifth or sixth centuries, suggesting a late conversion of the population. Literary sources describe pagan rituals in the fourth century, but all known temples were destroyed by the 363 earthquake. A miraculous story is told about Petra in which the holy man Barsauma brought a flood that helped convert the people of Petra in the early fifth century. This story might suggest that there were large numbers of pagans at the city, or it may just be a tall tale told about Barsauma to enhance his apparent sanctity. Such exaggerations were common in the Christian literature of the time.

The first archaeological evidence of Christianity in the city appears in 446 when the Bishop Jason converted the Urn Tomb into a church (Figure 6.30).

The famous church at Petra was constructed in the mid to late fifth century and continued in use until the end of the sixth century, as the Petra Papyri indicate (see Figure 2.25). Two other churches, the Ridge Church and the Blue Chapel, were built at the same time or slightly later. All three of these churches stand on the North Ridge, which overlooked the remains of the civic center. Additionally, the first church at the monastic complex on Jabal Haroun appears to have been constructed in the later fifth century. At

214  *The desert fringe (Petra and Palmyra)*

*Figure 6.30* The Urn Tomb, converted into a church in 446 CE (Photo by author).

an unknown date (perhaps not in late antiquity), the tomb known as the ed-Deir (monastery) was used by monks (four lived there in the late nineteenth century) (Figures 6.31 and 6.32).

Petra in the late sixth and early seventh centuries was a much-reduced town. The shops along the Colonnaded Street started to be abandoned around the end of the fifth century and were finally abandoned by the early seventh century. Even the paved street of the Siq went out of use in the mid-eighth century. No disasters or invasions were responsible for the end of urbanism at Petra, instead the process was gradual and lasted for centuries. Even after the civic center was abandoned, people continued to live in small villages in the region up to the time of the Crusader occupation of the site.

When the city was abandoned, pilgrims continued to pay homage to Saint Aaron (the tradition continues until today and was the reason why Burckhardt was able to visit the city). The monastic church on Jebel Haroun remained in use as an ecclesiastical structure into the late Umayyad or early Abbasid period (eighth century CE). The monastic community possessed a sizable building with a large courtyard that has been interpreted as a hostel for pilgrims, but by this time, the main civic center was largely deserted.

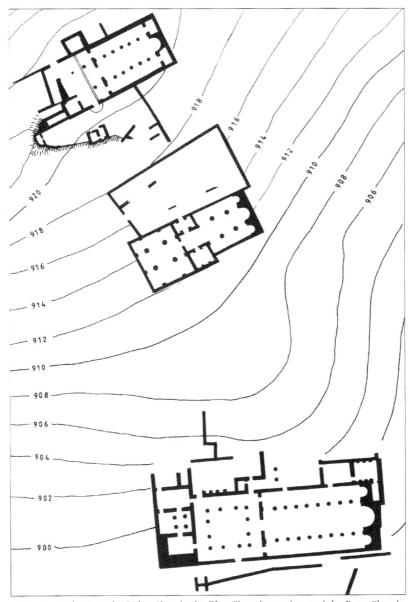

From top to bottom: the Ridge Church, the Blue Chapel complex, and the Petra Church

*Figure 6.31* The three churches on the Petra North Ridge (Plan by Chrysanthos Kanellopoulos, using the map of the Hashemite University and ACOR Petra Mapping Project. Fiema, Z. et.al. *The Petra Church*. [ACOR 2001], xii. Courtesy of ACOR).

216  *The desert fringe (Petra and Palmyra)*

*Figure 6.32* The ed-Deir (Monastery) (Photo by Jennifer Ramsay).

*Palmyra*

In the late antique period Palmyra was no longer was an important mercantile center but a frontier town, fortified against Persian invasion. The camp of Diocletian is the clearest evidence of this change. Sometime between 293 and 303, the Camp of Diocletian was constructed by the governor of Syria, Sossianus Hierocles, as a base for the *Legio I Illyricorum*. This unit, likely made up of approximately 1,000 soldiers, could not have been completely housed at the site. Excavations discovered 13 barracks blocks that contained an unknown number of rooms because of the poor state of preservation (Figure 6.33).

The construction of this camp required the destruction and removal of a large part of the northwest section of the site, except for the Temple of Allat that remained in use until the end of the fourth century. After that time, the temenos of the Temple was altered to form the Praetorium, or residence of the commander. The Camp was separated from the rest of the community by three rows of previously existing second century rooms. An imposing gate with three entranceways provided access to the Camp from the first Transverse road.

The transformation of the city from caravan city to military base is also reflected in the construction of the Baths of Diocletian by Sossianus Hierocles. Roman soldiers saw baths as one of the essential buildings of a military base, and to date no other baths have been discovered in the city of Palmyra. This bath complex was located along Section B of the Grand Colonnade, with the portico entrance built to block part of the northern half of the street. It possessed a large frigidarium, a pool, and smaller warm and hot rooms.

The constructions of the Camp and Baths of Diocletian and the destruction of the southern half of the city made an obvious statement about the

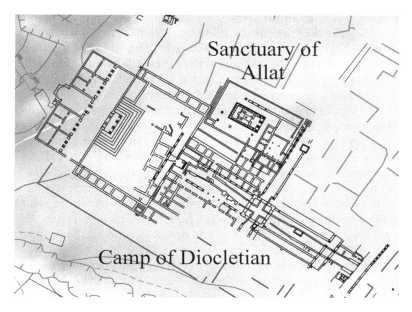

*Figure 6.33* Plan of the Camp of Diocletian, built around the Temple of Allat (Map by Klaus Schnädelbach, originally published as Schnädelbach, K. *Topographia Palmyrena, 1 Topography.* Documents d'archéologique Syrienne XVIII. [Damascus 2010]. On commission by Dr. Rudolf Habelt GmbH, Bonn).

power of the Roman authorities. The gate to the Camp was clearly constructed to impress any visitors. Roman soldiers who wished to visit the Baths would have to walk across half of the town, further demonstrating that the city was occupied by the Romans. The impact these soldiers had on the culture and economy of Palmyra is underexplored. The addition of several hundred soldiers meant that new opportunities existed for the population of Palmyra to provide goods and services to well-paid troops. This may have provided some stimulation to the economy but was not enough to replace the loss of the caravan trade.

It is unknown when the *Legio I Illyricorum* ceased to serve at Palmyra, but literary sources state that Justinian placed new units, including a *numerus* and *limitanei* (so a total of a few hundred soldiers), at the site to be commanded by the dux of Emesa. In addition, work was done to strengthen the city walls and the Camp of Diocletian shows extensive activity, such as changes to the Horreum. Along with these additions to the city, the sixth century was a time of increased church building, as will be shown below.

The Grand Colonnade remained the most important thoroughfare of the city throughout late antiquity. In the late fourth century, part of the sidewalk was reroofed. Maintenance on the main road is recorded from the fourth through sixth century. At least some of the shops along the Grand Colonnade remained in use from the second century until the eighth century. In the later fourth century, additional shops were constructed along the street in Section C. Three small Christian chapels were built near the nymphaeum and along the northern wall of the Funerary Temple perhaps to sanctify that portion of the street. Church I, built 50 m north of the Grand Colonnade, had a stone paved alley that opened onto the Grand Colonnade.

Some streets in late antiquity became much more important than in the past. For example, excavators labeled a street "Church Street" because three churches were located along it. It remained a gravel, not paved street – even after these churches were built along it. The atrium of Church III, built in the fifth century, encroached on part of the road. Previously, this street had no monumental buildings. Even though it remained a gravel path, the cluster of churches demonstrates its importance. Another street, which ran along the side of the Suburban Market, had its paving replaced in the sixth century, indicating that it remained an important road and that the market was likely still functioning.

This encroachment was not unusual in other cities, as we have seen (see for example the Propylaea Church at Gerasa), but it appears to have been a more extensive phenomena at Palmyra. In other cities, for example at Apamea, buildings generally remained confined to their insulae, but at Palmyra several buildings extended beyond their insulae and some even blocked entire streets. For example, the apse and *pastophoria* of Church IV completely blocked a street west of Church Street. A residential structure built after the early fourth century CE completely blocked a street next to the Temple of Baalshamin.

Residential structures have also been found in many of the previously open spaces. This is especially true of the temenoi of the temples. It is widely known, for example, that the temenos of the Temple of Bel became filled with houses, but the same thing happened in the Temple of Nabu and the Temple of Baalshamin. This also occurred in the Agora, and the western half of the Suburban market (the eastern half was used as cemetery for both Christians and Muslims). This trend points to increasing population density. A similar indication of population intensification comes from two houses from Palmyra, the Peristyle Building and House F. Both were elite structures in the Roman period, occupied by a single family. In the late antique period, these houses were subdivided (as seen at Apamea). This is indicated by the blocking of passageways, installing new walls, and walling in the peristyle courtyards. The new apartments were accessed by a shared courtyard rather than from the street, much like the Umayyad House at Gerasa.

Intagliata has recently argued that there is little evidence of a large group of aristocratic residents at Palmyra after the Roman reconquest of the city. While there is ample evidence of the subdivision of elite housing in late antiquity, there is little evidence of the monumentalization of houses there, such as the construction of grand entrance halls, the installation of apses in private dwellings, and the installation of new mosaic floors. The only counterevidence

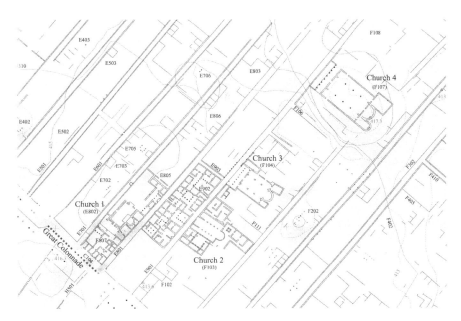

*Figure 6.34* The churches in the northwest quadrant of Palmyra (Map by Klaus Schnädelbach, originally published as Schnädelbach, K. *Topographia Palmyrena, 1 Topography.* Documents d'archéologique Syrienne XVIII. [Damascus 2010]. On commission by Dr. Rudolf Habelt GmbH, Bonn).

comes from the possible banquet hall in the temenos of the Temple of Baalshamin, which might be dated to the fourth or fifth century (Figure 6.34).

At least eight churches have been discovered throughout the city, but they are clustered in the northwest quadrant, which seems to have been the focal point of the Christian community. There were four churches in the northwest of the site. Church I had a small gravel road that led to the Grand Colonnade. This church reused a second century basilica with the addition of an apse cut into its eastern wall. The benches were constructed by spolia. The alterations occurred in the sixth century, and the church was abandoned about a century later. Three more churches were situated nearby on Church Street. Church II was built at an unknown date. It had a series of rooms including a baptistery to the east. Church III may have been constructed in the fifth century but was refurbished under Justinian. It opened onto a peristyle courtyard and at some point, the spaces between the columns were walled up. The largest church in the city was Church IV, possibly built in the time of Justinian. It was abandoned at an unknown time. Three small chapels were constructed along the Grand Colonnade. They have never been excavated, but might date to the sixth century, when Justinian is reported to have ordered the construction and repair of churches in the city.

Of the temples of the city, two may have been converted into churches. Most seem to have been occupied for residential or domestic uses. One example is the small building dedicated to the cult of the Anonymous God from the early fourth century, which reused a long mosaic paved floor from the late third century. In the second half of the fourth century, the floor was covered with plaster and the hall was divided into smaller spaces for apartments. The cult of the Anonymous God is known from hundreds of small altars throughout the city, but little is known about the god, even his name!

In addition to the previously open spaces of the Temples of Bel and Baalshamin being invested with private buildings, the cellas of both temples appear to have been converted into churches. The cella of the Temple of Bel is the clearest example, even though there is not much evidence of the church, which went out of use in the eighth century and was converted into a mosque in the twelfth. The evidence that survives suggests that either the church was oriented to the eastern wall towards the south adyton. There are paintings on the eastern and western walls that show several Christian figures, including Jesus and Mary along the western wall. Although the conversion cannot be dated with certainty, it may have occurred in the fifth century (Figure 6.35).

*Figure 6.35* Paintings of Jesus and Mary inside the cella of the Temple of Bel (Photo by Greg Fisher).

It is also possible that the cella of the Temple of Baalshamin was converted into a church, maybe in the fifth or sixth century. The evidence is complicated and ambiguous. A new entrance was cut into the west wall of the cella, which oriented the structure to the east. A porch was erected at this entrance out of the reused columns from the temple's courtyard. If a church, the porticos of the temple would have served as the aisles and the walls of the cella would have marked off the bema. One criticism of this reconstruction is that the bema would have been isolated from the rest of the church, seemly rendering the entire structure unusable for the liturgy.

There is ample evidence of the use of spolia in the late antique buildings at Palmyra. The first examples appear from the Camp of Diocletian and the Baths of Diocletian. For example, four red granite columns were reused to build the portico entrance to the Baths of Diocletian. The use of spolia continued throughout the period, with spolia appearing in Church I and Church II. Large portions of the Umayyad period suq were built using reused materials.

The capture of the city of Palmyra by Muslim forces is described in many different texts. Some state that there was strong resistance by the Roman forces in the city, whereas others claim that the city surrendered without a fight. Most mention that the walls around Palmyra were impregnable that seems be supported by the archaeological evidence that the walls remained well maintained throughout the late antique period. To date, there is no evidence of damage on the scale of the Roman sack of the city. Instead, all evidence points to a continuity of society in the seventh century.

In the early Islamic period, Palmyra was located along strategic routes through the desert. Confrontations between Muawiya and Ali are reported from the site during the First *Fitna* (the Civil War between 656 and 661, which brought the Umayyads to power) and later internal conflicts. The city was the base of the Banu Kalb tribe who generally supported the Umayyad government, but the city turned against Marwan b. Mohammad, last of the Umayyad rulers [d. 750 CE]. Literary sources claim that he destroyed the city and killed all the inhabitants, but there is no archaeological evidence to support this. By the end of the tenth century, the only inhabited section of the city was around the Temple of Bel, which is as it remained until the early twentieth century.

City life in the early Islamic period seems to have continued the trends seen in the earlier late antique city. Streets became more and more congested with structures. One example is when the Camp of Diocletian went out of use, new buildings significantly narrowed the width of the street. Another example is that a large marketplace (a *suq*) was built at the eastern end of Section C of the Grand Colonnade in the center of the previous main thoroughfare (Figure 6.36).

Enough space was left to the north and south of the suq for foot passage. Forty-seven shops were excavated that stretched approximately 170 m in length. All shops opened to the north. The marketplace was built in stages,

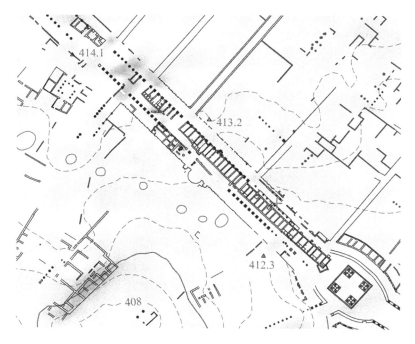

*Figure 6.36* Plan of the Umayyad suq at Palmyra (Map by Klaus Schnädelbach, originally published as Schnädelbach, K. *Topographia Palmyrena, 1 Topography*. Documents d'archéologique Syrienne XVIII. [Damascus 2010]. On commission by Dr. Rudolf Habelt GmbH, Bonn).

with the different periods of construction reflected in the way the shops were clustered. Some shops had stone floors, whereas others had plastered or dirt floors. The preexisting shops along the Grand Colonnade in this section continued to function, so the new marketplace did not replace the previous shops. This suggests an intensification of commercial activities in this section of the town.

Church II was abandoned in the eighth century. Churches I and III were abandoned in the ninth century. Church IV was abandoned at an unknown date, but it underwent extensive renovations in the early Islamic period. The nature of the alterations remains obscure. The church in the cella of the Temple of Bel was also abandoned in the early eighth century.

When the Camp of Diocletian went out of use, the area was quickly occupied by residential and related structures. This is clear from the evidence of the Via Praetoria, which demonstrates that the road was considerably narrowed by the construction of parallel walls that provided privacy to these structures. The *Groma* (a square structure marking the center of the camp) was subdivided into four rooms, each one used as a dwelling. The Praetorium was reconstructed, possibly in the middle of the seventh century after it suffered earthquake damage. At this time, the courtyard of the building was divided up into separate rooms. Some were likely residential, but others seem to be industrial, judging by the pipes and water basins in use there.

Industrial activities were detected in several of the occupied areas of the early Islamic city, such as the Baths of Diocletian, the Camp of Diocletian, and the Agora. House F was rebuilt after an earthquake in the middle of the seventh century, much like the Praetorium. In this late phase of the house, archaeologists discovered olive oil presses and storage areas. A pottery kiln was discovered in the courtyard of Church I (though it may date earlier than the Islamic period). After the abandonment of Churches II and III in the ninth century, four lime kilns were used at the churches to convert the marble into plaster.

And, as in Gerasa, a congregational mosque was placed in the heart of the civic center near the new suq. This mosque was constructed using an early Roman *caesareum* and redesigned the southern wall to serve as a qibla. Two semi-circular mihrabs were installed in this south wall. The southern row of columns from the Roman building marked the northern limit of the praying area. Four other buildings have been suggested as locations of early mosques in the city, including Church III; however, only a poorly published building from Section C of the Grand Colonnade appears to be a viable candidate for a second mosque.

## Conclusion

In 1993, excavators of the Petra Church made an amazing discovery. While digging through the remains of a fire that had engulfed the church at turn of the seventh century, they happened upon dozens of carbonized papyrus scrolls, making this one of the largest papyrus caches discovered outside of Egypt. The documents date between 537 and 593 and chiefly concern the family of Theodorus, a deacon at the church. The published documents are quite prosaic as they mainly contain information about business deals and tax liabilities. One, P. Petra 6, for example, mentions a number of items stolen by a renter from a landlord. Another describes a legal dispute over the sale of a vineyard in which the *phylarch* of the province, Abu Karib, is mentioned as an arbitrator.

Abu Karib clearly has an Arabic name. His title, *phylarch*, indicates that he was an official of the Roman Empire, which employed Arab groups (commonly called tribes) as military allies. Phylarchs and their subordinates were important for maintaining security along the desert frontier and defending the Near East against the Persians. His presence in the Petra Papyri indicates the importance of these Arab groups in the region in the later sixth century. The Petra Papyri demonstrate further influence from Arabs, as the names of some places and houses were Arabic, suggesting that the language was widely spoken in the region.

Both the Nabataeans and the people of Palmyra are referred to as "Arabs" in modern scholarship. The Greco-Roman sources routinely describe the Nabataeans as Arabs, and the kingdom of the Nabataeans was annexed as the Roman province of "Arabia." No ancient source describes the Palmyrenes as "Arab." In these contexts, the word "Arab" appears to be a label imposed by outsiders, as the word is not used in either the Nabataean or Palmyrene dialect of Aramaic to describe themselves.

There is limited evidence to suggest that some Nabataeans spoke Arabic, and the Nabataean script was the basis of the Arabic written script. In fact, the first Arabic language inscriptions were written using the Nabataean script. One of the earliest of these celebrates Imru' al-Qays, a Roman ally who claimed to be "King of all the Arabs" in the time of Constantine. It is not a coincidence that Arabs and Arabic speakers appear noticeably beginning in the early fourth century. Many scholars believe that these groups had in some way been contained or controlled by the city of Palmyra. When that city lost its autonomy at the end of the third century, suddenly the Romans and the Persians had to deal with the Arab groups directly. Alternatively, without the city of Palmyra as an intermediator between the Romans and Persians, then it was impossible for the Arab groups to maintain a neutral stance as the Near East became more polarized. Some joined with the Persians and others with the Romans (though alliances could shift at times!).

Both the Nabataeans and the Palmyrenes worshipped some gods and goddesses from Arabia, such as Allat. In Palmyra, a mixture of gods from Syria (Baalshamin), Babylon (Bel), Arabia (Allat), and their own locality were worshipped. For the Nabataeans, it was the local god Dushares who was most important. Influence from Syria and Egypt introduced Greco-Roman gods and goddesses who were often associated or syncretized with the local deities. The combination of these features impacted art and temple designs and funerary customs. For example, we have seen that the Nabataeans adopted the triclinium for funerary rituals. The Palmyrenes adopted the stylistic features of Greco-Roman temples but adapted them for their own purposes, such as the ninety-degree rotation of the Temple of Bel.

Both cities were originally organized along a wadi and both began a monumentalization program at close to the same time. At Petra, the road along the wadi was monumentalized around the early first century CE, clearly under influence of the trends in the more Hellenized regions of the Near East as begun by Herod. At Palmyra, this occurred a century later after the visit of the emperor Hadrian to the city. At Petra, the major temples and public buildings were mostly built at the same time, only to be transformed to fit contemporary Near Eastern standards upon the annexation of the Nabataean kingdom in the early second century. At Palmyra, this monumentalization continued throughout the second and third centuries in fits and starts. Temples and other buildings were constructed, as were portions of the Grand Colonnade, which was never completed. One possible reason for the difference in terms of monumentalization could be that the Nabataeans were ruled by a king who was invested in displaying the power and wealth of Petra. In Palmyra, dominated by groups of merchants and different tribes, there was not a unified vision for the city until the visit of the emperor Hadrian.

Both cities were massively transformed in late antiquity. In Petra, the 363 earthquake destroyed large sections of the public city (and some others were already in ruins). At Palmyra, the destruction after Zenobia's Revolt left the city with a much-reduced space and population. Both cities lost their important commercial connections. Whereas Petra remained the capital of a Roman province from the late fourth century, providing some imperial financial support, there is little evidence that the governor there constructed public buildings as seen at Caesarea and Scythopolis. Palmyra became important as a military base, and this helped fuel its economy until the Muslim conquest. Whereas Petra may have been abandoned (or very small) at the time of the Muslim conquest, Palmyra's population density seems to have increased in the fifth, sixth, and seventh centuries. New shops and a mosque were constructed in the heart of the town. The population only began to dwindle around the middle of the eighth century as the city slowly focused around the Temple of Bel.

## Suggestions for further reading

Browning, I. *Palmyra*. (Park Ridge, New Jersey 1979).
Fisher, G. *Arabs and Empires before Islam*. (Oxford 2015).
Intagliata, E. *Palmyra After Zenobia 275–750: An Archaeological and Historical Reappraisal*. (Oxford 2018).
Markoe, G (ed.). *Petra Rediscovered: Lost City of the Nabataeans*. (New York 2003).
McKenzie, J. *The Architecture of Petra*. (Oxford 1990).
Mouton, M. and S. Schmid (eds.). *Men on the Rocks: The Formation of Nabataean Petra*. (Berlin 2013).
Smith, A. II. *Roman Palmyra: Identity, Community, and State Formation*. (Oxford 2013).
Zuchowska, M. "Space organization and house planning at Hellenistic and Roman Palmyra." *Światowit* 9, 141–153.

# 7 Conclusion

"In imitation of Hadrian, Silvanus the most distinguished and *spectabilis* count and governor has built his own mother city...."[1] So reads an honorific inscription originally set up in Scythopolis honoring the late fourth century governor Silvanus. It is unknown if there is a connection to the later Silvanus who, in the early sixth century, was responsible for the construction of Silvanus Hall and the paving of Silvanus street, or if this was just a common name at Scythopolis. The important and interesting thing, however, is that this governor must have been responsible for some of the reconstruction of the city in the aftermath of the 363 earthquake. As we have seen throughout this work, the reign of Hadrian was especially important for urbanism in the Near East. It was under Hadrian that earthquake damage in Antioch and Apamea were repaired and this enabled the completion of the first true monumentalized colonnaded axis in those cities. He personally visited Palmyra and Gerasa, spurring both to new heights of building. He was responsible for the construction of a new city at Jerusalem. Although no specific activities from his reign are known at Scythopolis, Hadrian clearly had a reputation as a builder, even after 250 years!

It would be impossible to summarize over a thousand years of urban history in the Near East in this short conclusion; so instead, I will make some general remarks about patterns in urbanism based on the eight cities under discussion in this book and return to the three debates mentioned in the introduction. In the eight cities described in the earlier chapters – Antioch, Apamea, Gerasa, Scythopolis, Jerusalem, Caesarea, Petra, and Palmyra – some general trends can be detected in every city in the Hellenistic, Roman, and late antique periods.

Although small settlements are known at some of these cities prior to Alexander, such as at Scythopolis, Antioch, and Gerasa, Jerusalem is the only city in this book that possessed an urban life before the Hellenistic period. As far as can be known, Jerusalem developed organically in the Persian period without planning. This had something to do with topography as the hills would have made a grid difficult, but as the later Roman city shows, it was not impossible. No other cities from the Persian period in the Near East were planned, and, therefore, it is hard not to come to the conclusion that the Hippodamian grid system was brought by the Greek and Macedonian conquers of the Near East.

The grid plan in the first cities founded by the Seleucids, including Antioch and Apamea, appears to date from their founding. Of course, the earliest strata of these sites are buried under much later layers dated anywhere from three to eight hundred years later. Nevertheless, the earliest form of these cities appears to have been relatively small and functional and in no way monumental. They served primarily as Greek colonies to dominate the Near East. Scythopolis and Gerasa were founded later in the context of the rivalry between the Ptolemaic and Seleucid empires. While Scythopolis might have possessed a garrison of troops (the eponymous Scythians), Gerasa appears in the context of Seleucid expansion, having been built as either a Seleucid or Ptolemaic outpost.

The Nabataeans first appear in the context of the growth of Seleucid power in the southern Near East as well. By the third century, there was some (possibly seasonal) settlement at Petra that slowly grew into a small rooted community. The town does not appear to be planned, and the limited excavations of the earliest layers suggest that there were many open spaces in the civic center. Settlement at Palmyra may have appeared around the same time, even though the city was not written about until much later. Like Petra, the earliest settlement at Palmyra was probably not planned.

The Age of Augustus was a formative time for the Near East. With the end of Roman expansion (think Pompey's actions in the east in 64/3 BCE) and civil wars (with the death of Antony and Cleopatra in 30 BCE), peace brought increasing prosperity. Herod, Roman collaborator and King of Judea, emerges as an important shaper of Near Eastern urbanism. While he is most famous for the enlargement of the Second Temple in Jerusalem, the building of the first monumental street in Antioch (perhaps colonnaded under the emperor Tiberius), and the construction of the completely new city of Caesarea, he profoundly shaped urban aesthetic in the Near East (and beyond!). Not to be outdone, Aretas IV built extravagantly in Petra, making it one of the most renowned cities in the eastern Mediterranean. Kingdoms and cities could no longer compete militarily during the Pax Romana (without repercussions), but they could vie for honor.

The Jewish Revolt led to a number of changes in the Near East. Most famously, Jerusalem was completely destroyed, Jews were forbidden to live at the site, and the Xth Fretensis Legion was stationed there. The cities of Scythopolis and Gerasa may have been damaged in the fighting, as both began major building projects in the aftermath of the revolt. Alternatively, the monumentalization of these cities may have been a result of increased prosperity after the war. Roman veterans were settled at Caesarea after the war, greatly expanding the population and the Romanness of the city.

The monumentalization process that began in the later first century BCE and early first century CE peaked in the middle of the second century. In Apamea and Antioch, the early second century earthquake meant that both cities could be refashioned in opulent fashion. Antioch, supported by the Roman government, was rebuilt on a spectacular scale. The development of the colonnaded street at Antioch influenced subsequent developments throughout the Near East. Apamea was the first to imitate the nearby capital because the city needed renovation after the same earthquake, but it did so through local patronage. Other cities, Gerasa, in particular, followed this example as well, converting the original Ionic columns into Corinthian ones along the southern part of the cardo. Even Palmyra, though the last to develop a Hippodamian plan and colonnaded street, began these developments after Hadrian's visit in 130/31. Jerusalem, destroyed in the Jewish Revolt in 70 CE, was rebuilt as a Roman colony in Hadrian's reign. This new city was built according to a Hippodamian plan with Roman style temples and forums and two main decumani.

Throughout the second century, cities continued to build and grow. The temples of Zeus and Artemis at Gerasa are excellent examples of a city using its wealth to ornament urban life. Scythopolis was almost completely refashioned in the second century with new constructions such as the Central Monument, nymphaeum, the odeon, and the hippodrome, and the remodeling of previously built structures, such as the basilica, a bathhouse, the temple with the round cella, and the theater. After the annexation of the Nabataean kingdom in 106 CE, the city center was remodeled to demonstrate the new era of civic government instead of the monarchy.

Building slowed in the third century, perhaps because the cities were already endowed with so many monumental structures or because of the general instability of that century, but building did not cease. The suburban market at Palmyra is an excellent example of continued construction in this period.

The Third Century Crisis was devastating to many of the cities of the Near East. Antioch and Apamea were sacked by the Persians, and the southern half of Palmyra was destroyed by the Romans as punishment for Zenobia's conquest of the east. Petra may have been damaged because several important buildings such as the Qasr a-Bint and the Great Temple were abandoned. When Roman authority was restored toward the end of the third century, trade routes had changed. Petra was no longer important in long distance trade and its perfume industry had disappeared, and Palmyra also was no longer along the main trade route with the Persians. This was not the end of these cities; in the last quarter of the fourth century, Petra became capital of the province of Third Palestine, and a century earlier, Palmyra was garrisoned with imperial troops because of its strategic importance.

Late antiquity brought many changes to these cities, most importantly in terms of religion. The acceptance of Christianity by Constantine and ensuing imperial patronage of it meant that the province of Palestine quickly grew in importance because of its rich Biblical history. Constantine and his mother built the first churches in Jerusalem and Bethlehem. Pilgrims began to flock to the Near East in large numbers to visit the holy sites. Many arrived at the port of Caesarea on their way to Jerusalem. This influx of people meant a booming economy, especially in the sixth century in both cities.

It is clear that Christianity was steadily growing in the fourth century Near East, but there is little physical evidence of this growth until the fifth century when the first extant churches appear in the cities of the Near East. Pagan temples were being abandoned, attacked, and destroyed in the late fourth and early fifth centuries. Churches became the center of new communities within these cities. At Gerasa, for example, the large number of churches, especially those built around the Temple of Artemis, became the most important focal point of the entire city. In Palmyra, several churches were clustered along one road. At Petra, three churches were constructed near each other on the North Ridge. At Caesarea, the Octagonal Church was seen by all visitors who came by sea. The churches in Apamea and, presumably, Antioch (such as the Golden House) reshaped the urban environment. At Jerusalem, the churches were the focal point of an entire empire's devotion, as attested by the multiple accounts of pilgrimage to the city. Only at Scythopolis is there little evidence of Christianity in the civic center in the valley, but the church on the Tell must have been an important statement of religious belief in the city.

There is very little evidence of damage from the Muslim conquest of the Near East in these cities, except at Caesarea, which was largely abandoned after the city was conquered (Petra seems to have shrunk to a tiny settlement by the Muslim conquest). And, at first, Muslims did not leave a major mark on the urban environment. This began to change in the late seventh century, especially during the reign of Abd al-Malik. This period saw the construction of monumental buildings, such as the Dome of the Rock, to make a statement about the power of the emergent Islamic faith. But, it was not only prestige projects that were built during the time of the Umayyad dynasty. At Palmyra, the Umayyad suq, built in the middle of the Grand Colonnade, is an excellent example of the increasing commercialization of what had previously been public space. New markets appeared in almost every city at this time, including Apamea, Gerasa, and Scythopolis. The mosques in Gerasa and Palmyra, smack dab in the center of the city, made bold statements of the new religious character of the ruling elites.

In Petra and Scythopolis, the 363 earthquake proved devastating, but only the damage at Petra was lasting. Petra's major monuments were leveled (those that were abandoned earlier were now heavily damaged too) and never rebuilt. This is very different from Scythopolis, where earthquake damage was repaired in the late fourth century. By 400 CE, both cities were capitals of imperial provinces (Second and Third Palestine); yet, there appears to have been very little reconstruction at Petra. Other cities suffered natural (and man-made disasters). Caesarea was hit by at least one Tsunami. Both Antioch and Apamea were heavily damaged by earthquakes. Jerusalem, Antioch, Apamea, and Palmyra all suffered major damage in wars. Unlike

Petra, in these cities, damage was eventually repaired, and in most, the recovery was quick. This suggests that Petra did not have the resilience of these cities in the later fourth century.

At Petra, the civic center became a quarry for building materials and marble. The production of lime within the civic center turned marble into plaster for coating walls of new structures, including houses. There were people still living in Petra, as indicated by the construction of three churches on the North Ridge, but the civic center must not have been important to the community. Petra seems to be the first of these cities in which monumentalized buildings were scavenged on a wide scale. Lime kilns are known from other cities including Jerusalem, Antioch, Apamea, Palmyra, and Gerasa, but the ones in these cities tend to be later, with some appearing only in the seventh or eighth centuries.

In late antiquity, industrial facilities became very notable in the archaeological record. Such pursuits are found in the cities in earlier periods as well, but not to the same extant. One exception, perhaps, were the ceramic industries at Gerasa and Petra. But at Palmyra, there is clear evidence of textile production from the Roman period, and at Gerasa, the discovery of a bronze casting facility from the second century shows that the bronze adornments and statues at the Temple of Zeus were made on site. In all these cities, however, in late antiquity, industrial uses are clear and obvious in the archaeological record.

The use of spolia has been documented from every city in both the Roman and late antique periods; however, in late antiquity, the use of spolia dramatically increased. For example, the churches in Gerasa and Palmyra and the Baths of Diocletian at Palmyra were constructed using older material. In late antiquity, especially, monumental buildings were given new purposes. For example, the large open areas of temple temenoi in Palmyra were filled with domestic structures, and in Gerasa, churches surrounded the Temple of Artemis, whereas the processional way was blocked by a church. The hippodrome of Gerasa was used for industrial facilities and houses.

In late antiquity, changes can be seen in the civic plans and the transformation of the streets. In most cities, the main streets were narrowed or filled with new constructions, such as the Umayyad suq in Palmyra. This process was uneven, took centuries to occur, and happened in different places at different times. This seems to support the model suggested by Gideon Avni. Changes to civic plans appear organic and related to historical events. This means that some cities were impacted more than others. Petra, for example, seems to have never recovered from the 363 earthquake, whereas Scythopolis rapidly did. In Petra, while the major buildings of the civic center had been destroyed, shops were rebuilt on top of the rubble and continued into the late sixth century (though many were abandoned much earlier beginning in the late fifth century). In Palmyra, the construction of the Islamic suq represents a very late incursion into the Grand Colonnade, but churches had blocked side streets several hundred years earlier. At Gerasa, the development of shops around the mosque and at Scythopolis the building of an eighth century marketplace further demonstrate the continued importance of the commercial sector of cities during the early Islamic period.

Throughout late antiquity, all evidence suggests that streets were being encroached upon by buildings, sometimes churches, but most often shops. In Gerasa, the Hippodamian city plan seemed to have outlived its usefulness. Most paths through the city slowly became winding or haphazard, without the formal straight lines of the previous plan, but the main cardo and two decumani were respected. A similar occurrence can be seen on the Tell at Scythopolis, where a sprawling domestic neighborhood grew up, ignoring a formal street plan around the fifth and sixth centuries; however, a new formally planned neighborhood appeared in the early Islamic period, countering trends elsewhere.

There seems to be little evidence of demographic collapse in these cities, except at Petra by the seventh century and at Caesarea after the Islamic conquest. On the contrary, where there is evidence at Gerasa, Apamea, Palmyra, and Jerusalem, population within the cities became much denser. Large houses from the Roman period were divided into smaller units to support this increasing population density. As mentioned above, the open spaces were filled with domestic structures. At Gerasa, this might even include the oval plaza, though it is unknown when the structures there may have been built. At Scythopolis, portions of the civic center may have gone out of use for their original purpose, such as the area around Palladius Street, but life on the Tell seems to have continued and prospered. So, there could be variation between cities as well. However, there is no indication that cities were in a rapid decline in the early Islamic period; far from it! Even after the devastating earthquake of 749, Gerasa continued to be a flourishing city.

The beginning of this chapter mentioned the importance of Hadrian in the monumental efforts throughout the Near East; however, other rulers, such as Herod of Judea, Aretas IV of Nabataea, Constantine, and Justinian, played roles greater than the average ruler. The trend of imperial involvement in city development in the Near East began in the Hellenistic period with the founding of Antioch and the other cities of the Tetrapolis and continued right until the end of this book with the actions of Abd al-Malik and Hisham ibn Abd al-Malik. These rulers all promoted their chosen imperial culture. Hadrian pushed for the monumentalization in a Greco-Roman style, whereas Constantine and Justinian constructed massive churches. The Muslim rulers followed with the Dome of the Rock and the al-Aqsa mosque. While individual donors were most important in the early Roman period, it was government or religious figures that were most important for the construction of buildings in late antiquity. In Scythopolis, Caesarea, and Antioch, imperial officials continued to proudly inscribe their building activities in stone. All three of these were capitals of Roman provinces in the Near East. Only in Petra, capital of Third Palestine, are the actions of governors unknown in the building record.

Cities continually adapted to meet the needs of the population and rulers. The earliest Seleucid and Ptolemaic foundations in the Near East were largely non-monumental, but functional. They served, at first, primarily to support the rule of the Greco-Macedonians in the Near East. When that function was no longer important because of the conquest of the region by the Romans, these cities adapted again. Competition within cities between elites and between cities for honor and prestige replaced the military concerns. These were spurred and assisted by local dynasts, like Herod and Aretas IV, whose buildings combined local ideas with Greco-Roman styles. Herod with his development of the colonnaded streets, the building of Caesarea, and the expansion of the Second Temple in Jerusalem represents the complexity of culture in the Near East, which refuses to be delineated into neat categories of "Near Eastern," "Syrian," "indigenous," "Greek," or "Roman." With the growth of Christianity, these cities adapted again, closing or destroying pagan temples, and then building Christian churches, sometimes in what seems to be extreme amounts, as at Gerasa. The Muslim conquest represented another time of change. The focus of the city on industrial and commercial activities is easily seen in the archaeological record, and the building of mosques in the central parts of Gerasa, Palmyra, and especially Jerusalem, should be seen as further adaptation to a new world.

One important conclusion that I have reached is that historical events were extremely important for the development of these cities. I remain a firm believer in the role of long-term processes in the evolution of cities, but I must note the importance of historical factors. The earthquake of 363 seems to have been instrumental in ending the importance of the civic center of Petra. The destruction of Jerusalem and later re-founding of the same city was clearly pivotal there. The legalization and patronage of Christianity irreversibly altered the trajectory of these cities, but most especially Jerusalem. The impact of Hadrian's visit and the invasions by the Persians in the sixth and seventh centuries were also crucial in the development and transformation of these cities. Finally, the conquest of the Near East by Muslims led to the cities changing even more. Had any of these historical events happened in any other way, the evolution and development of these cities would have been markedly different.

## Note

1 Di Segni, L. and B. Arubas. "An old-new inscription from Beth Shean." In Di Segni *et al.* (eds.). *Man near a Roman arch: Studies presented to Prof. Yoram Tsafrir.* (Jerusalem 2009), pp. 115*–116*.

# Glossary

**Agora**   Greek for marketplace. Often equated in the Near East with the Roman concept of the forum. The marketplace functions may have been replaced by the colonnaded streets.
**Apodyterium**   Greek word for the changing room in a bath complex.
**Apostate**   Someone who has turned away from his or her religion. Often used as an epithet for the Emperor Julian [361–363] who was raised as a Christian but revealed that he was a pagan when he became emperor.
**Autonomia**   Greek title meaning "living under their own laws." Granted by Roman emperors as an honorific.
**Bilad al-Sham**   Arabic for "Greater Syria." This roughly corresponds with the modern countries of Syria, Lebanon, Jordan, Israel, and the Palestinian territories.
**Boule**   Greek for town council.
**Bouleutes**   Greek word used for members of the elites in cities who were members of the town councils, equivalent to curiales in the western Mediterranean.
**Caldarium**   Hot room in a bath complex.
**Carceres**   Starting gates in a hippodrome where the chariots would line up before racing.
**Cardo**   The main street in the town or the main north-south road.
**Cavea**   Seating in a Roman or Greek theater.
**Cella**   Latin word for the main building of a temple complex or the inner sanctuary.
**Chora**   Greek for countryside, often used to describe the territory controlled by a city.
**Colonia**   Latin for colony. In the Near East, *colonia* is often used as an honorific title.
**Columns:**
   **Corinthian**   Corinthian capitals are the most ornate of ancient capitals. They are characterized by four sides decorated with acanthus leaves.
   **Ionic**   Ionic capitals look like rolled scrolls.
   **Nabataean**   A relatively simple column design with four points radiating out of the center of the capital.

**Curiales**   Latin equivalent to *bouleutes*.
**Decumanus**   East-west road in a Hippodamian planned city.
**Forum**   In the Near East, the Latin equivalent to agora.
**Frigidarium**   Room with a cold pool in a Roman bath complex.
**Glacis**   A stepped stone structure or a gently sloped hill bank.
**Hippodamian plan**   A city plan in which streets intersect in right angles with often equally spaced city blocks.
**Hippodrome**   Greek word for a chariot racing stadium.
**Horreum (plural, horrea)**   A warehouse.
**Insula (plural, insulae)**   Literally, "an island." In city planning it means a city block.
**Kalybe**   A waterless nymphaeum.
**Limitanei**   A category of Roman troops in late antiquity. Traditionally thought of as frontier (*limes*) guards.
**Liturgies**   Activities performed by Greco-Roman elites in order to satisfy the duties of an office or to curry favor with a city's population.
**Macellum**   An indoor marketplace, normally found in the western Mediterranean. It consists of shops built around a central tholos.
**Metropolis**   Greek for "mother city." It was a title granted by the imperial authorities as an honorific.
**Mihrab**   A niche in the wall of a mosque which points towards Mecca. The congregation faces the *mihrab* during prayer.
**Miqveh (plural, miqva'ot)**   In Judaism, a bath used to become ritually pure.
**Naos**   Greek word for the main building of a temple complex or the inner sanctuary.
**Numerus**   A small unit (a few hundred soldiers) in the late antique Roman army.
**Nymphaeum**   A monumental urban structure which consisted of statues and water.
**Odeum (or odeon)**   A small theater, normally enclosed, used for music performances or the meeting of town councils.
**Opus sectile**   A type of floor decoration created with cut stones.
**Orchestra**   Semi-circular flat, open area in front of the stage in an ancient theater. Often the place where the chorus would dance and sing.
**Phylarch**   Leader of allied peoples (especially along Roman's desert frontier).
**Polis (plural, poleis)**   Greek word for city-state. A polis includes all the territory administered by the city (the *chora*).
**Portico**   In an ancient temple, the portico is the porch in front of a temple's entrance. It is often roofed and could be surrounded by columns.
**Propylaeum, propylaea**   A massive entrance gateway.
**Quadrifons**   Latin for tetrapylon, or a four-sided gate often found at street intersections.
**Samaritans**   An ethnic group from Samaria (now in the West Bank) who follow their own Torah and believe that Mount Gerizim, and not Jerusalem, should be the focal point of the Jewish faith.

**Scaenae frons**   A highly decorated backdrop behind the stage in an ancient theater.
**Shahada**   The Muslim profession of faith: "There is no God but God, and Muhammad is his prophet."
**Siq**   A cleft in the mountains which formed the entrance to the civic center of Petra.
**Spolia**   Reused material in ancient buildings.
**Suq**   A Near Eastern marketplace, often open-aired.
**Tabun**   An oven used outdoors.
**Temenos**   Greek for the sacred space of a temple. In the Near East, this is normally defined by a wall around an open courtyard.
**Tepidarium**   Warm room in a Roman style bath complex.
**Tetrakionion**   Greek for "four columns," it was a type of tetrapylon with columns instead of arched gates.
**Tetrapolis**   The four cities built in Syria in the early Seleucid period.
**Tetrapylon (plural, tetrapyla)**   Greek for "four gates." They were built at intersections in the Near East.
**Tholos**   A round structure with a dome supported by columns.
**Tyche**   Originally the name of the goddess of luck, fortune, and fate. By the Roman period, a Tyche came to be a goddess that was the personification of an individual city.
**Wadi**   Arabic word for a stream, river, or valley that is typically dry but might fill with water during period of rainfall.

# Index

Abbasid xvii, 121, 214
Abd al-Malik 130–1, 137, 165, 229, 231
Abu Karib 223
Aelia Capitolina 145, 149–50; *see also* Jerusalem
agora 28, 34–6, 62–3, 67, 72–3, 75, 78, 103, 105, 109, 112, 124, 128–9, 133, 157, 189, 201, 205, 207, 218, 223, 233
Agrippa, Lucius Julius 71, 73, 90
Agrippa, Marcus 66, 147
Al-Aqsa mosque 137, 15, 165–6, 231
Aleppo 18, 74, 84, 89, 178
Alexander Jannaeus 98, 143
Alexander the Great xvi–xviii, 7, 18, 20–1, 57, 62, 64, 93, 98, 141, 182, 226
Alexandria 5, 55, 62–3, 156, 188, 193
Al-Haram ash-Sharif 136, 138
Ali, Caliph 221
Al-Khazneh 178–9, 183, 193–4
Allat 4, 12, 196, 203, 205, 209, 211, 216–17, 224
Amphitheater 46, 49–51, 66, 76, 122–3, 125, 129, 133, 146–7, 157, 159, 176
Anastasius 80, 122, 124, 133, 170, 174
Andrade, N. 12–13, 21, 200
Antakaya 56–7, 62
Antioch xvi, 5, 13, 15, 16, 18–20, 26, 45, 51–3, 55–92, 95, 98, 132, 134, 141, 154, 165–6, 175–6, 190, 210, 226–31
Antiochus I of Commagene 13
Antiochus I, Seleucid 55
Antiochus III 63–4, 98
Antiochus IV (Epiphanes) 5, 8, 13, 63, 98, 100, 141
Antiochus VII Grypos 64
Antonia fortress 141, 146, 153
Antony, Mark 65–6, 136, 146, 185, 190
Apamea xvi, 7, 9, 13, 16, 18, 20, 25, 28, 48, 53, 55–92, 91, 102, 132, 175, 218, 226, 228–31

Aphrodite 126, 193–4, 196, 199
Apollo 59, 62, 76
Arab 7, 35, 81, 84, 86–7, 164, 178, 191, 223–4
Arabian Desert xvi, 17, 20
Arabia, Roman province 176, 190–1, 224
Arabic xvi, 11, 18, 84, 96, 130, 137, 165, 178, 223–4, 233, 235
Ares 66, 76
Aretas III 190
Aretas IV 176, 178, 190, 193–4, 196–7, 227, 231–2
Aristobulus II 141, 143
Armenia 63, 66, 69, 138, 165, 186
Arsu 189, 201, 205
Artemis 28, 38, 40, 42, 68, 101, 102, 105, 107, 113–14, 116–17, 119–21, 131, 194, 228–30
Athena 12, 68, 73, 205
Augustus 66, 136–7, 140, 147, 154, 156–7, 176, 182, 191, 210, 227
Aurelian 69, 74, 185, 191–2, 211
Aurelius, Marcus 68, 73, 105, 110, 191, 200
autonomia 13, 233
Avigad, N. 152
Avni, G. 8, 16–17, 21, 177, 230

Baalbeck 9, 38–9
Baalshamin 1, 3–4, 99, 191, 203, 209, 218–21, 224
Ball, W. 7, 9–11, 21, 54
Bar Kochba 145, 149, 154
basilica 35, 42–4, 46, 66–7, 71, 75–6, 78, 80, 105, 107–9, 122–6, 145, 152, 159, 163, 166, 173, 205, 207, 219, 228
bath 13, 16, 20, 22, 46, 51–3, 66–71, 75–6, 78, 81–2, 95, 106–7, 109, 114–18, 121–2, 126, 129, 133, 147–8, 151, 158–9, 166, 169–74, 199–200, 209, 216–17, 221, 223, 228, 230, 233–5

Beit Shean *see* Scythopolis
Bel 1–4, 9–12, 28, 38–9, 176, 180–1, 185, 201–4, 207–9, 218, 220–2, 224–5
Beqaa Valley 17–19, 59
Berenike 182
Bilad al-Sham 17, 233
Blues *see* circus factions
boule 13, 132–3, 205, 208, 233
bouleuterion 63, 67, 105, 110, 132, 153, 200
bouleutes 13–15, 233; *see also* curiales
Bronze Age 95, 183
Burns, R. 22, 27, 54, 66–8
Butcher, K. 7, 9–11, 13, 15, 21
Byzantine Empire 7

Caesar, G. Julius 63, 66, 69, 190
Caesarea xvi, xviii, 16, 18–20, 27, 43, 49–51, 53, 95, 91, 112, 121, 132, 136–7, 140–5, 154–60, 165, 167–77, 225–7, 229, 231–2
caliph 1, 7, 20, 130, 137, 164, 165
cella 1, 41, 107, 109–10, 116, 122, 173, 191, 194–5, 203–5, 207, 220–2, 233
Chosroes II 82, 86
Christian xvi–xvii, 1, 4, 6–8, 10, 12, 14–17, 20, 24, 42–3, 45–6, 55–7, 70, 74, 76, 84, 87, 89, 113–18, 125–7, 131, 133–4, 136–8, 140, 145, 151, 152, 159–62, 164–7, 170–1, 174–6, 193, 213, 218–20, 228–9, 233
Christianization 37, 85, 232
circus factions 79–80
Claudius 66, 158
Cleopatra 65–6, 73, 227
colonia 4, 6, 13, 69, 149, 158, 190–1, 233
comes (count) 75, 173, 226
Commodus 68, 76
Constanius 75
Constantine 8, 14, 30, 31, 43, 57, 74, 75, 137, 159, 163, 167, 224, 228, 231
Constantinople 15, 80, 84, 86, 174
Crassus, M. Licinius 65
curiales 13, 233
Cyril, Patriarch of Jerusalem 151
Cyrus, first king of Persia 161

Damascus 16, 19, 84, 93–4, 180, 186, 190, 205
Damascus Gate 36, 150, 152–3, 160, 164–5
Daphne 53, 56–7, 59, 62–3, 67–8, 73, 75, 77–8, 80–1
Dead Cities 74, 89–90

Dead Sea 17, 19–20, 137
Decapolis 20, 61, 65, 91, 93–5, 98–9, 133, 186
Diocletian xvii, 69, 74–5, 107, 167, 185, 201, 205, 207, 209, 211, 216–17, 221–3, 230
Dionysus 102, 114, 126
Dome of the Rock 20, 137–9, 151, 165–6, 229, 231
Dura-Europos 35, 205
Dushares 28, 102, 114, 178, 184, 193–6, 224

earthquake of 363 113, 115, 122, 125, 127, 199, 211–13, 225, 226, 229, 230
earthquake of 749 116, 119, 121, 128, 130, 131–2, 166, 231
Egypt 5, 17, 19, 28, 64, 68, 95, 98, 100, 140–1, 156, 166, 182, 191, 193, 211, 223, 224
Epiphaneia 63, 67, 75
Eudocia 77
Euphrates River xvi, 10, 17–19, 70, 180, 182–3, 185, 191, 205
Eusebius 140, 163
Evagrius 78, 87

Fitna 221
Foerster, G. 110, 122, 126, 131, 133
Forum Boarium 34, 165

Galilee 18–19, 93, 95
Gallienus 69, 191
Gerasa xvi, 1, 7, 12, 15–16, 19–20, 22–3, 27–36, 38, 40–50, 53, 62, 67, 68, 73, 86, 91, 93–135, 152, 175, 194, 205, 207, 223, 226–32
Ghab 18, 59
Golden House 57, 166
Greek xvi–xvii, 1, 4–10, 13–14, 17, 25–6, 35, 39, 46–7, 49, 51, 60–2, 64, 69, 91, 93, 99–100, 136, 138, 141, 145, 154, 156, 167, 174–6, 227, 232, 233–5
Greens *see* circus factions

Hadrian 29–30, 68, 72–3, 78, 101, 106, 112, 114, 145, 148–9, 151–3, 158, 160, 172–3, 190–1, 207–8, 224–6, 228, 231–2
Hasmonean 65, 100, 141, 143, 147, 151, 182
Hauran 19
Helena, mother of Constantine 159, 163
Hellenism 5, 7–8, 10–12

Herod Agrippa I 148
Herod, King of Judea 13, 26, 49, 54, 66–8, 94, 136–7, 140–1, 143–8, 150–9, 164, 166–7, 175–7, 193, 209, 224, 227, 231–2
Heraclius 7, 82
Hippodamian 25–6, 53, 62, 72, 154, 156, 175–6, 192, 227–8, 231, 234
hippodrome 22, 46, 49, 50, 63, 66–8, 78–9, 81–2, 87, 101, 106, 109–10, 113–16, 125, 146–7, 157–9, 171, 176, 228, 230, 233, 234
Hisham ibn Abd al-Malik 130–1, 231
Holum, K 170, 177
Holy Sepulcher 45, 137, 160, 163, 165
Hyrcanus II 141

iconoclasm 131
Idumaean 136
Imru' al-Qays 224
incense 24, 176, 182, 190
indigenous xvi, 5, 7, 8, 10–13, 17, 20, 141, 232
industrial 16, 28, 84, 86, 114–16, 118, 120, 125, 129, 131–2, 164, 172–3, 187, 210, 212, 223, 230, 232
insula (-ae) 25, 72, 85–7, 159, 169–71, 182, 190, 205, 218, 234
Intagliata, E. 218, 225
Iron Gate 59, 83
Isis, goddess 193, 196
ISIS, terrorist organization 1, 2, 4, 22
Islam xvi, xvii, 1, 4, 7–9, 16, 20, 24, 42, 46, 74, 82, 84, 87, 89, 113–14, 119–21, 128–30, 134–7, 162, 165–6, 174–5, 177, 211, 221–3, 225, 229–31
Israel xvi, xviii, 4, 19, 20, 22, 95, 175, 186, 233

Jerash *see* Gerasa
Jerusalem xvi, xviii, 6, 7–8, 12–13, 16, 19–20, 27, 29, 36–7, 45, 55, 63, 75, 77, 95, 101, 121, 128, 134–67, 174–7, 189, 226–32, 234
Jews xvi, 14, 62, 100, 136, 145, 154, 158, 164–5, 167, 227
Jewish 6, 12–13, 20, 24, 55, 79–81, 94–5, 100, 117, 136–8, 140, 143–5, 148–51, 158, 161–2, 167–8, 175–6, 234
Jewish Revolt 4, 51, 94–5, 100–1, 134, 144–5, 149, 154, 175–6, 190, 227–8
Jewish War 66–7, 140, 146, 149, 158–9; *see also* Jewish Revolt

Jesus 93, 131, 134, 136–7, 145, 153, 159, 163, 220
Jezreel Valley 18, 95
John Chrysostom 55–6
John Hyrcanus I 141
Jordan xvi, 1, 4, 19–20, 22, 95, 135, 138, 166, 186, 233
Jordan River 17, 19, 93
Josephus 49, 66, 95, 141, 143, 145–9, 151, 154, 158
Judea 6, 19, 26, 63, 66, 98, 136–7, 140–4, 176, 182, 186, 193, 227, 231
Julian 15, 55–8, 70, 75–7, 233
Jund al-Urdunn 128
Jupiter 9, 12, 39, 63, 151
Justin I 133
Justinian 81–5, 89, 160, 163, 174, 217, 219, 231

Kalybe 32, 35, 234
Kennedy, H. 8, 16–17, 21
kiln 82–4, 101, 160, 115–16, 119–20, 129, 131, 151, 183, 223, 230
Kraeling, C. 15

latrine 73, 85, 118, 164
Lebanon 17–19, 38, 233
Leo, Roman emperor 78
Libanius 55–6, 62, 75, 77, 92
Limestone mastiff 89
Lucian 12

Maccabean Revolt 6, 13, 141
Maccabees 140–1
macellum 34–5, 76, 105, 112, 118–20, 234
McKenzie, J. 198, 225
Madaba Map 150, 152, 160
Magness, J. 152, 177
Maioumas 158
Malalas, John 56, 62, 66–7, 174
Masada 4, 136, 193
Mark, Gospel of 93
Marwan b. Mohammed 221
Matthew, Gospel of 93, 156
Maurice 82
Metropolis 4, 6, 13, 154, 190, 234
Millar, F. 7–9, 21
Mithraeum 159
Mithras 153, 159
Mithridates of Pontus 63, 65
Monophysite 80, 84
monumentalization xvi, 6, 15, 22, 28, 71, 90, 107, 198, 218, 224, 227, 231

mosque 1, 7, 36, 45–6, 84, 87, 113–14, 118–20, 121, 131–2, 135, 137, 151, 165–6, 211, 220, 223, 225, 229, 231–2, 234
Mount Zion 138, 142–3, 147, 160
Muawiya 221
Muhammad xvi, xviii, 1, 7, 137, 165–6, 175, 235
Al-Mundhir 81
Muslim xvi, 1, 8, 10, 15, 17, 46, 82, 84, 89, 91, 113–14, 128, 130–1, 137–8, 151–2, 160, 164–6, 174–7, 211, 218, 221, 225, 229, 231, 232, 235

Nabataean 8–9, 12, 30, 94, 102, 136, 176, 178, 181–8, 190, 193–4, 197, 199–201, 210, 224–5, 227, 233
Nabu 207–9, 218
naos 1, 38–9, 41–2, 99, 101–4, 107, 110, 116, 132, 234
Negev Desert 19
Neolithic 95
New Testament 93, 136
nymphaeum 29, 32–4, 68, 72–3, 78, 85, 104–5, 108–9, 122, 133, 158, 170, 200, 218, 228, 234
Nysa 100, 110

Octavian 65–6, 69, 136, 144, 190
Odenathus 191, 207, 209
odeum (-on) 47, 49, 105, 108, 110, 125, 153, 200, 208, 234
Olympic Games 46, 66, 68–9, 80
Origen 140, 167
Orontes River 18–19, 57–60, 62, 74–5, 77, 81
Orthodoxy 80

paganism 12, 14, 125
Palaestina 140, 154, 177
Palaestina Salutaris (Tertia) 211, 228–9, 231
Palaestina Secunda 122, 133, 229
Palestine 8, 16, 20, 64, 110, 154, 163, 169, 176, 211, 228–9, 231
Palmyra xvi, 1, 2, 4, 6–12, 19–20, 28–9, 32, 38, 47, 53, 176–91, 201, 205–10, 216–32
Palmyrene 1, 69, 182, 185, 191, 200–1, 209, 211–12, 224
Parmenius 63, 66, 76–7, 82
Parthian 13, 57, 63, 65–6, 70, 176, 182, 190–1, 201
Patriarch 57, 80, 84, 151, 164

Paul, Apostle 17, 84, 133, 154, 171
Pax Romana 4, 15, 22, 30, 65, 100, 113, 191, 227
perfume 182, 190, 200, 228
Persia 6–7, 27, 55, 57, 59, 64, 69–70, 73, 81–2, 84, 86–7, 89, 91, 116, 128, 141, 164–5, 174–5, 182, 191, 197, 200, 211, 216, 223–4, 226, 228, 232
Petra xvi, 4, 7, 12, 19–20, 25, 28–31, 38, 40, 44, 47, 48, 53, 126, 176, 178–232, 235
Petra Papyri 213, 223
Pharnaces 66
Philip II, Seleucid 64
Philip the Arab, Roman Emperor 35
Phocas 82
Phoenicia 18–19, 64, 143
Phylarch 15, 223, 234
Pirenne, H. 15
plague 16–17, 57, 74, 82, 89, 116, 133
Pliny the Elder 95, 180, 182
polis 8, 21, 97, 135, 234
Pompey, G. Magnus "the Great" 13, 63, 65, 69, 93, 98, 100, 107, 142–3, 186, 201, 227
Pontius Pilate 154, 158
Praetorian Prefect 38
Ptolemies 5, 63, 98–100, 141
Ptolemy I 5
Ptolemy II Philadelphus 100
Procopius 81, 90, 133, 140, 171, 173
propylaeum (-a) 28, 38, 40, 105, 114, 119, 121, 197, 203, 218, 234

Ramla 16
Red Sea xvi, 182, 211
Richardson, P. 12, 21, 177
Roman Empire 4, 6–7, 20, 30, 37, 42, 69, 128, 137, 140, 153, 174, 176, 191, 223
Romanization 12

St Aaron 178, 181, 214
St Babylas 45, 77
St Symeon the Stylite 57, 78
Samaria 18–19, 234
Samaritan revolt 133, 174
Sartre, M. 7, 9, 11–13, 21
Sassanid 57, 69, 70
scaenae frons 32, 34, 47, 51, 110, 117, 157, 213, 234; *see also* theater
Scythian 99, 227
Scythopolis xvi, xviii, 7, 16, 18–20, 34, 43, 49, 91, 93–135, 140, 154, 165, 175, 225–31

Seleucids 5–6, 8, 13, 59–60, 66, 70, 85, 98, 100, 141, 186, 227
Serjilla 89, 91
Sebaste 136
Seleucia Pieria 18, 58, 60, 62–4
Semitic 9–11
Septimius Odenathus *see* Odenathus
Septimius Severus 69–70, 73, 149
Sergiopolis 46
Severus Alexander, Roman Emperor 191
Shahada 130, 235
Shapur 69, 74, 191
shops 27–9, 35, 38, 42, 63, 68, 71–2, 76–7, 81, 84, 87, 90–1, 103, 105, 107–9, 112–13, 116–21, 123–6, 129–30, 132, 161, 165, 168, 172, 187, 199–200, 208, 212, 214, 221–2, 225, 230–1, 234; *see also* macellum
Siloam, Pool 147, 149, 163, 166
Sinai 12, 186
Siq 178–80, 182–3, 214, 235
Sol Invictus 14
Sophronius, Patriarch of Jerusalem 164
stadium 22, 46, 49, 63, 75, 80, 158, 234
stoa 26, 35, 38, 65, 66, 72, 75, 78, 81, 107, 133, 145
Strabo 182
Strato's Tower 143, 154
suq 9, 16, 87, 91, 130–1, 221–3, 229–30, 235
Synagogue 24, 63, 79–80, 85, 117, 118, 133, 147, 167
Syria xvi–xviii, 1–4, 7, 9–13, 17–21, 22, 34–5, 61–5, 68–9, 72, 74, 76, 81–2, 85, 93, 95, 98, 107, 112, 140–1, 154, 176, 180, 183, 186, 190–1, 200–1, 205, 216, 224, 232, 233
Syriac 8, 10

tabun 121, 129, 235
Tarsus 17
Tchekhanovets, Y 167, 177
temenos 1, 9, 38, 39, 105, 111, 114, 116, 132, 145, 180, 181, 187, 194–5, 197, 199, 203, 205, 207, 211, 216, 218–19, 235
Temple Mount 137–9, 141, 143, 145–6, 149–53, 160, 162, 164–7
Tetrapolis 53, 60–1, 64, 231, 235
tetrapylon 4, 29, 32–3, 55, 67, 78, 80, 102–3, 105, 107, 111, 114, 118–20, 124, 133, 207, 234, 235
Tetrarchy 107

theater 4, 13–14, 16, 20, 22, 32, 36, 46–9, 51, 56, 63, 65–8, 70, 72–4, 76, 80, 86–7, 92, 101, 105, 107, 109–11, 114, 116–19, 122–3, 125, 127, 129, 133, 146, 153, 157, 159, 171, 176, 178, 183, 191, 193, 197–8, 205, 207, 209, 211, 213, 228, 233
Theodoret 73
Theodosius 38, 77, 92
Theodosius II 77–8
Third Century Crisis 66, 69, 73, 101, 228
Tiberias, city in Galilee 16, 95, 128
Tiberius, Roman emperor 66–7, 158, 227
Tigranes 63, 69, 186
Titus 67, 158
Trajan 30, 31, 66–8, 70, 76, 78, 190–1, 200, 205
triclinium (-a) 74, 75, 78, 85–7, 158, 188, 210, 224
"True Cross" 86, 163
Tsafrir, Y. 110, 122, 126, 131, 133, 135, 232
Tyche 62, 72, 172, 193–4, 197, 235

Umar, Caliph 164–5
Umayyad xvii, 84, 109, 119–21, 131, 134, 135, 166–7, 214, 218, 221, 222, 229–30
Umm ar-Rasas 42

Valens 59, 75–6, 78–80, 84
Valerian 69–70, 191
Venus 152, 163
Vespasian 154, 158, 175, 190

wadi 18, 59, 74, 99, 102, 125, 185, 187, 189–90, 192, 196, 199, 200, 203, 205, 211, 224, 235
Wadi al-Qubur 180, 185, 189–90, 192, 201, 203, 205, 208, 211
Wadi Araba 17, 19, 180
Wadi Musa 178–80, 183, 187, 192–4, 196, 198–200
Wadi Parmenius *see* Parmenius
Wadi Sirhan 20

X Fretensis Legion 149, 161–2, 227

Yakto villa 77–80
Yarmuk River 20, 82

Zenobia 69, 185, 191, 201, 209, 211, 225, 228
Zeus 23, 36, 39, 41, 62–3, 68, 70, 73, 85, 95, 99–104, 111, 113–14, 116, 118, 125, 132, 194, 205, 228, 230